In Defense of the Soul

What It Means to Be Human

In Defense of the Soul

What It Means to Be Human

Ric Machuga

Brazos Press

A Division of Baker Book House Co
Grand Rapids, Michigan 49516

© 2002 by Ric Machuga

Published by Brazos Press
a division of Baker Book House Company
P.O. Box 6287, Grand Rapids, MI 49516–6287

Printed in the United States of America

Library of Congress Cataloging-in-Publication Data is on file at the Library of Congress, Washington, D. C.

For current information about all releases from Brazos Press, visit our web site:
http://www.brazospress.com

To
Mom and Dad
whose unwavering support
made a philosophical education
possible

Contents

Preface   9

1. Humans as Rational Animals: 13
   Why Aristotle Still Matters

2. Getting It Right From the Start: 24
   Form, Shape, and the Nature of Things

3. Dividing Nature at Its Joints: 33
   The Difference between Plants, Animals, and Humans

4. Objective Differences in Perspective: 44
   Form Versus Shape

5. The Hows of Science and the Whys of Philosophy: 57
   Why Final Causes Are Still Necessary

6. How Aristotelians Think About What They Know: 64
   Perceiving Versus Conceiving

7. The Challenge of Evolutionary Biology: 80
   Why Aristotelians Don't Fear Darwin

8. The Challenge of Artificial Intelligence: 100
   Calling the Materialist's Bluff

9. The Inadequacy of Materialism: 111
   No Soul, No Words

10. The Bogy of Mechanism: 132
    Why Our Actions Will Always Be Unpredictable

11. Freedom and Rationality: 148
    Can't Have One Without the Other

    Epilogue   159
    Appendix: Assessing "Intelligent Design"   161
    Notes   167
    Glossary   197
    Sources   200

Preface

The choice of pronouns is a sensitive subject. Throughout this essay, I have chosen to write in the first person plural—"we"—for a couple of reasons. While the use of "I" has become standard in many philosophical circles, and while writing in the first person singular implicitly acknowledges individual responsibility for all errors and falsehoods, it also suggests originality. With the possible exception of the emphasis on the distinction between *per se* and *per accidens* efficient causes in the last chapter, nothing in this book is original. My book is much more a *report* of philosophy done by others than it is a piece of original thought, but it is in no way a piece of scholarly research on what others have said and taught. Rather, it is an attempt at a grand synthesis of a huge topic for a nonprofessional audience, so it seemed to me that "we" would nicely straddle the fence between claims of originality and impersonal reporting.

The reader should also be forewarned that "we" will be used with various levels of inclusiveness. Usually "we" refers to all realists, i.e., philosophers and scientists who without equivocation or qualification are committed to the proposition that a knowable reality exists independently of our thoughts and "conceptual schemes." This use of "we" may surprise those not cognizant of the dominance of radical pragmatism verging on subjective idealism and "postmodernism" in academic circles. Simple statements like "rabbits and trees exist" will typically bring smirking smiles to the faces of today's Gnostics. Nonetheless, a few realists have been able to withstand the scorn of their professional colleagues and carry on the tradition of Aristotle and Aquinas. Those who have taught me most are Mortimer Adler, Etienne Gilson, Stanley Jaki, Michael Polanyi, and Karl Popper.

Of course, even realists have their disagreements. In the group listed above, Adler and Gilson are perhaps the most sympathetic to the philosophy of Aristotle. Jaki has much sympathy with Aristotle's realism, but is harshly critical of his physics. Polanyi came to his study of philosophy after a successful career as a chemist and seemed not to be particularly interested in the classical antecedents of his metaphysical conclusions. Finally, Popper wrote as a direct opponent of Aristotle's insistence that the most fundamental questions are always of the form, "What is it?" But these disputes among contemporary realists will find no further mention, even when I use "we" in a more narrow sense to refer to "we Aristotelians."

Perhaps even more troublesome to my contemporary philosophical mentors is the company I am asking them to keep. Besides being a prolific historian of science, Jaki is a Catholic priest who argues that Aristotle was really a pantheist, and hence, hardly a friend of the faith. Gilson, who is perhaps the foremost historian of Medieval philosophy, was a Catholic layman whose rightfully famous Gifford Lectures stressed the metaphysical distance between Aristotle's paganism and Aquinas's Christianity. Adler is the great generalist who scorned the narrowness of professional philosophers, while praising and practicing the dialectical method of Aquinas long before he ever professed faith in Aquinas's God. Polanyi's theological convictions are not evident, at least to me, from his writings. Popper, most would agree, began his philosophical career by praising the method of science vis-à-vis pseudo-methodology of philosophers and theologians. And though his implicit criticism of the latter mellowed considerably in his most recent works, he never came around to Eccles's belief that the human mind is ultimately unintelligible apart from a supernatural creator, even while collaborating with him to write *The Self and Its Brain*. While I personally side with Eccles rather than Popper on this point, the argument of this book is wholly philosophical, and at no point will "we" be used in a way that requires a shared belief in the God of Abraham, Isaac, and Jacob. The kind of realism assumed in this book might thus be labeled "big tent" realism, or to borrow C. S. Lewis's usage, this book could have been subtitled, "Mere Realism."

Philosophical attempts to produce a grand synthesis are not new, but they are certainly out of fashion. Yet, if the Aristotelian/Thomistic theory of human nature is true, we could never know that it is true unless we examined it as a whole. None of its parts are intended to stand by themselves. In this respect, our theory is like the heliocentric theory of the solar system. Copernicus developed a mathematical model of a sun-centered solar system in 1543. Galileo then proposed a plausible theory of the mechanics for such a system, and Kepler discovered that the orbits of the planets were really elliptical (not circular). While each of these individual discoveries have proved to be true, many of their conclusions were dead wrong. Copernicus and Galileo, for example, were both mistaken about the circularity of the planets' orbits, and Kepler's theory of mechanics was, to put it kindly, misguided. It wasn't until 1687, when Newton eliminated these mistakes and formed these scientist's individual discoveries into a single coherent and comprehensive whole, that the truth of a heliocentric theory became evident.

Similarly, a chief virtue of the Aristotelian/Thomistic theory of human nature is its ability to combine ontological, epistemological, and ethical positions into a single balanced, coherent, and comprehensive whole. My hope is to make evident at least some of the beauty of their grand synthesis. I therefore focus on breadth, not depth. I do this for a number of reasons. First, many others have superbly plumbed the individual issues discussed. Second, I have yet to plumb the depth of Aristotle and Aquinas myself on virtually any of the issues discussed here. Third, as Aquinas himself said, many students of philosophy have been "hampered by . . . the multiplication of useless questions, articles, and arguments." As the old but true cliché puts it, they have lost sight of the forest because of all the trees.

To aid in keeping the big picture in view, I have included short summaries at the start of each chapter. Some readers may find it helpful to read these first. Others may find it better to read them after reading each chapter. Still others will find them redundant and best ignored.

The footnotes can all be ignored without disrupting the flow of the argument, and the converse is probably also true—paying too much attention to the notes (at least on the first read) will undoubtedly disrupt the flow of the argument. Nonetheless, for some readers, they will serve a number of purposes. For those who like to run down quotes, references are given. Second, while there are no authorities in philosophy whose expertise, scholarship, or wisdom are sufficient to establish the truth of any particular theory or thesis, many readers will rightfully want some assurance that the ideas developed in this essay are more than the fanciful speculations of the author. Thus, where it was appropriate, I have included quotes from contemporary scientists or philosophers who have come to similar conclusions. Of course, such quotes can also be used as starting points for the reader's own exploration of the topics discussed.

Finally, in many places the notes make explicit the systematic interconnection of ideas. Darwin once described *The Origin of Species* as "one long argument." His point, I take it, was that no single example demonstrated the truth of his conclusion; instead, it was their cumulative weight that proved to be decisive in Darwin's own mind. Similarly, there is no single argument that demonstrates the essential truthfulness of the Aristotelian conception of humans. It is only its ability to unify numerous mundane and fairly obvious facts about humans and the world we inhabit into a single coherent and comprehensive theory of human nature that proved decisive in my own thinking.

1

Humans as Rational Animals

Why Aristotle Still Matters

Humans are neither apes nor angels, but instead, as Aristotle argued a long time ago, we are rational animals, and rationality is "akin to the divine."

Descartes rejected this ancient conception of our essential nature. He said that all reality is composed of two fundamentally distinct substances—mind and matter—and that it is our immaterial mind that makes us who we are. In this view, humans are essentially disembodied spirits, and hence, equal to angels. Though he was himself a Christian, his philosophy unintentionally fathered a brood of crass materialists.

The view defended in this essay is that we don't have a soul, we are a soul. While our conclusions are consistent with the great religions of the West, our argument is wholly philosophical. None of our premises rely on divinely revealed truths. Instead, our argument is grounded in three truths evident to all peoples, times, and cultures—1) plants and animals exist, 2) square circles don't exist, and 3) nothing comes from nothing.

While such truths can't become obsolete as the result of new scientific discoveries, it is necessary to show that the philosophical conclusions derived from these immediately evident truths are consistent with the prodigious discoveries of modern science, especially in evolutionary biology and the emerging field of cognitive science.

The Aristotelian position is distinct from the two most common contemporary conceptions of humanity. Dualists conceive of the body as nei-

13

ther a necessary nor sufficient condition for a person's existence. Material-
ists conceive of the body as both a necessary and a sufficient condition for
human existence. We conceive of the body as a necessary but not sufficient
condition.

According to dualists, immortality is the natural condition of the soul.
According to materialists, immortality is an irrational hope or fear. Aris-
totelians reject both these. In our view, immortality is supernatural possi-
bility but not a natural necessity.

Since our topic touches on our deepest hopes and fears, we must con-
sciously strive to avoid the fallacies associated with both wishful and fear-
ful thinking.

A Short History

About three thousand years ago, the Jewish king David asked, "What is
man that thou art mindful of him?"[1] A thousand years later, the biblical author of Hebrews asked the same question and gave the same
answer—he is a divine creation, a "little lower than the angels . . .
crowned with glory and honor." During the Middle Ages most people
continued to answer this crucial question in the same way. Common
folks gave this answer, at least in part, because this was the age of faith,
but it was also the view advocated by many philosophers during the
Middle Ages. And why was that? In large part, philosophers defended
this already ancient view of humanity because it comported so well with
the answer given by Aristotle, the dominant pagan philosopher of the
Middle Ages in both the Christian West and the Islamic Near East.
According to Aristotle, humans are neither beasts nor angels; instead
they are rational animals, and rationality, Aristotle often added, was
"akin to the divine."[2]

At the start of the sixteenth century, however, this classical understanding of humans' essential nature began to lose its hold. The fact that
King David (a Jew), Aristotle (a pagan philosopher), the author of
Hebrews (a first-century Christian), Averroes and Avicenna (tenth- and
twelfth-century Islamic philosophers and theologians), and Thomas
Aquinas[3] (a thirteenth-century Christian philosopher and theologian)
all gave essentially the same answer no longer held much weight.
Philosophers and an emerging class of scientists began to lose patience
with the vast technical apparatus the scholastics developed to flesh out
and justify the seemingly simple proposition that humans are rational
animals. Soon the technical distinctions became the butt of jokes. Mocking questions like "How many angels can dance on the head of a pin?"

spread to the street. This was the beginning of the end for this ancient conception of humanity. People began looking for answers elsewhere.

Two distinct realms were explored. The first was immaterial substances. Some people began to conceive of humans as essentially disembodied spirits who, during this life on earth, used a physical body the way a sailor captains a ship or a knight rides his horse. In this view, humans are essentially equal to angels. The second was the realm of mere matter. Here the argument was that humans are really nothing more than sophisticated animals or even machines. Humans undoubtedly differ in *degree* from other animals, but there was no real difference in *kind* between apes and humans.

The catalyst and prime mover for both alternatives was a single philosopher—Rene Descartes (1596–1650), often called the father of modern philosophy. According to Descartes, all of reality is divided into two fundamentally distinct substances: minds and bodies. Minds were conceived of as wholly immaterial. Our knowledge of at least one of these—our own—was thought to be uniquely clear and certain. Satan himself, Descartes said, could not deceive us about at least one proposition. This proposition is the famous *cogito ergo sum*: "I think, therefore I am." After all, for deception to work, someone must first *exist* if he or she is going to be deceived.

But when Descartes claimed absolute certainty for his own existence, he was not conceiving of himself as a rational animal. He argued that he could only be certain that he existed as an immaterial mind. The existence of even his own hands and feet were open to doubt. Prior to Descartes, most philosophers would have taken such an absurd implication as sufficient reason for reconsidering their initial assumption—but not Descartes. He retained his conception of humans as essentially disembodied spirits.

Now the belief in disembodied spirits was neither new nor especially controversial. Pagan astronomy required immaterial minds to move the planets, and all three Western religions (Judaism, Christianity, and Islam) included a belief in angels, but the human and angelic realms were always kept distinct. Descartes's innovation and legacy was to conceive of humans as essentially equal to the angels.

He also argued, however, that with the exception of immaterial minds, everything else was mere matter in motion. Sure, the matter in plants and animals took on especially complex arrangements, but according to Descartes, both plants and animals could be explained in wholly mechanistic terms. Furthermore, if we were to have a truly scientific understanding of the universe, then we must not be satisfied until everything except the human mind was explained in wholly material terms.

This had some bizarre implications. Dogs and cats, for example, could no longer be thought of as conscious beings. Given Descartes's starting point, they were as incapable of consciousness as a clock. His division of reality into two distinct and unrelated substances—conscious, immaterial minds and extended, material bodies—left him no other possibility. Once again, such implications did not cause Descartes to reconsider his initial assumptions.

There is much irony here. Descartes was not an irreligious man. He sincerely believed that his elevation of humanity to angelic status would be of great service to his Christian faith. The effect of his philosophy, however, was almost the exact opposite. Most of his followers happily discarded his notion of immaterial substances and latched on to his mechanistic explanation of everything else. The great immaterialist thus fathered a brood of materialists who had nothing but disdain for Descartes's religion.

The Central Thesis

The central thesis of this essay is that both Descartes and his materialist successors are fundamentally mistaken about the essential nature of humans. We are neither angels nor apes. Rather, we are rational animals. Our nature is an essential *unity* of both the material and the immaterial. As it is sometimes said: we don't *have* a soul, we *are* a soul. As a motto and battle cry, this formula captures well the ancient conception of humans as rational animals. For this formula to be more than a bludgeon with which to beat one's opponents, however, it needs to be understood. This in turn requires an understanding of its metaphysical underpinnings.

There is good news and bad news here. The good news is that the Aristotelian metaphysics that supports this ancient conception of humanity is fundamentally an articulation and defense of common sense. Aristotle, unlike Descartes, was not out to prove that one's certainty concerning one's own arms and legs or the consciousness of dogs and cats really was philosophically naive. Instead, Aristotle's metaphysics is largely a defense of our ordinary beliefs about the world against the attacks by his fellow philosophers.

The bad news is that even the ordinary, when looked at philosophically, becomes quite extraordinary. Though Aristotle lived long before telescopes would reveal the wonders of the heavens and microscopes would demonstrates the complexities of even a single cell, he fully respected the richness and complexity of our universe. If this complexity is real, how can our theoretical understandings of it be simple? The distinctions and arguments employed by Aristotelians in systematically articulating and defending common sense must be at least as complex and complicated as the real world. While we will strive to be simple, we try not to be simplistic.

Furthermore, our method must remain wholly philosophical. True, Jews, Christians, and Muslims have historically been drawn to the conception of humans as rational animals at least in part because it comported well with their faith, but the argument of this book is not theological. None of its premises are drawn from divine revelation. Instead, they are all the product of reflecting, analyzing, and synthesizing the observations that people living in all ages, places, and cultures make every day.

What sort of premises can claim such universal acceptance? First, that plants and animals exist. Second, that square circles do not exist. And third, nothing comes from nothing. It takes neither philosophical training nor sophisticated scientific apparatus to know these statements are true. It is on such foundations that the Aristotelian understanding of humans as rational animals either stands or falls.

There are some noteworthy implications in Aristotle's decision to ground his philosophy in such simple and obvious premises. First, Aristotle's fundamental principles are timeless. Belief in the existence of plants and animals is not the sort of thing that further scientific study will one day demonstrate to be nothing more than a primitive superstition.

But even if the conception of humans as rational animals can be shown to follow rationally from such obviously true premises, many moderns are likely to remain unconvinced. Modern science may not have disproved the very existence of trees and rabbits, but it has made countless discoveries since the time of Aristotle that have changed our understanding of the essential nature of such things. Unless it can also be demonstrated that Aristotle's definition of humanity as rational animals is also consistent with the truths of modern science, it will have little relevance today.[4] Thus, a second implication of Aristotle's simple and obvious premises is that a good portion of our discussion will be demonstrating that his philosophical understanding of humanity is consistent with the findings of modern science, especially evolutionary biology and the emerging field of cognitive science (including "artificial intelligence").

In short, our *positive* argument in favor of Aristotle's conception of humanity will be based on observations and truths known to all people at all times. However, we will also argue *negatively* that the many new observations and truths of modern science do not demonstrate or even imply that the ancient view is false.

Perhaps we should say that Aristotle's conception of man is consistent with the findings of modern science *stripped of its philosophical prejudices*. There is no doubt that many people will disagree strongly with the conclusions of this essay. While we have no pretensions of changing their minds, we hope to show that their objections are in fact grounded in certain philosophical dogmas, not in the discoveries of modern science.

A Prospectus

Long journeys are begun for a couple of reasons. Some people simply enjoy the adventure of heading off to far away places—the stranger and more exotic the better. Other people enjoy the comfort and convenience of their local surroundings and only travel under duress. Still others travel for mixed motives.

The ground covered here is certainly extensive. Much of it will be quite foreign, so readers looking for adventure will not be disappointed. But even the most adventurous can lose heart when the goal of the journey is unclear. Therefore, before attempting to nuance premises with important distinctions, we will state with bold simplicity the position defended and the two opposing positions rejected.

Our definition of humanity contains both a genus and a difference. Humans are members of the animal kingdom. That is our genus. And while our animal nature can be understood in wholly material terms, we are different from all other animals in that we use concepts as tools to reason about that which cannot be observed. All other animals lack this ability. Furthermore, this difference requires a nonmaterial element traditionally referred to as the intellect. The intellect is not, however, *in* us as a captain is in a ship or as sap is in a tree. Rather, the nonmaterial is *in* us the way meaning is in words. Humans are essentially a unity of body and soul. If we think of the body as the material condition and the intellectual soul as the nonmaterial condition, then we can define the relation between body and soul like this: Immaterial souls are a necessary but not sufficient condition for our existence.

In other words, without an immaterial soul our rational abilities would be inconceivable—that is what it means to say that immaterial souls are a necessary condition. But the mere existence of an immaterial soul is not what makes a human being. Souls without bodies might exist, but they would not be human beings—that is what it means to say that immaterial souls are not a sufficient condition for our existence.

There are two alternative definitions of humans. The first, and undoubtedly the most prevalent today, is commonly called dualism. It has a long and venerable history. Aristotle's own teacher, Plato, was a dualist. Augustine, who referred to Plato's philosophy as "Egyptian gold," certainly had dualistic sympathies. Avicenna, the great Islamic philosopher, also took considerable inspiration from Plato,[5] but it is Descartes whose name is now inevitably associated with dualism, and with good reason.

Descartes conceived of humans as an essential duality of body and soul. According to Descartes, souls *are* in bodies the way a captain is in a ship or sap is in a tree. Just as captains exist when they are not in their ship or as sap can exist outside of a tree, so too, in this view, souls are conceived of as being immaterial substances that do not require bodies to exist. In fact, some dualists follow Plato and look upon the body as an impediment to the flourishing of the soul. In other words, dualists believe that immaterial souls are not only a required condition for human existence, but souls are *all* that is required. Unlike Aristotelians, dualists do not believe that our body is an essential element of human existence.

The opposite of dualism is monistic materialism, which we will often shorten to simply materialism. Recently this view has been called metaphysical naturalism or simply naturalism. While materialists/naturalists may be in a minority in the population at large, among today's philosophers and scientists they are probably in the majority.

According to this view, "souls" are in bodies the way the ability to hold water is in a cup or the way great acceleration and handling is in a fine sports car. To say that a cup *has* the ability to hold water or that a sport car *has* excellent performance is not to say that there is some mysterious immaterial substance "inside" the cup or car. It is only to say that the material properties or features of cups and cars enable them to do certain things. Cups and car are wholly material. Their ability to hold water or perform well is "in" them only in a metaphorical sense. While we commonly talk about our "soul," "mind," and/or "spirit" as something that we have in us, according to materialists, this is a loose and metaphorical way of speaking. According to materialists, immaterial souls don't exist. But since humans obviously exist, that means that "souls" are not *required* for existence as a human being. Thus, we are nothing more than our bodies and brains.

We can summarize the three traditional conceptions of human nature as follows:

Aristotle: Material bodies and brains are a necessary but not sufficient condition for our conceptual abilities. Immaterial intellects are also required.

Dualism: Material bodies and brains are neither a necessary nor a sufficient condition for our conceptual abilities. Immaterial minds are all that is required.

Materialism: Material bodies and brains are both a necessary and sufficient condition for our conceptual abilities. Immaterial substances[6] don't exist.

These three conceptions of humans have implications for both how we live here on earth and what we can rationally hope for when we die. According to dualists, since the body is not an essential part of our nature, the death of the body is fairly insignificant. When the body dies *we* simply discard it the way a snake sheds its skin. In fact, the metaphor of a snake shedding its skin may be too weak. Some dualists, like Plato, teach that the death of the body is more like the liberation of inmates from a prison. For Plato, the metaphor of a caterpillar and a butterfly is better. The caterpillar enters the cocoon with many legs and leaves with two wings, but here, having fewer material appendages means the freedom to fly. With either metaphor, according to dualism, the immortality of the soul is the *natural* state of humans after the death of their bodies.[7]

According to materialists, the death of the body is neither to be hoped for nor feared—it is simply the end of life. Of course, trying to contemplate our nonexistence is both difficult and painful. Nonetheless, since there is nothing we can do to change the facts of the matter, human hopes and fears surrounding death are simply irrational.

According to the ancient view of humans as rational animals, when the body dies, the person also dies. In this regard, the death of a human's body is just like death of a flea's body: in both cases, the person and flea are dead. Yet, in the ancient view, humans are not *just* an animal. They have rational abilities that transcend the properties of their physical bodies and brains, so all is not lost at death. The death of the body, in this view, is like the end of a song.

Beethoven's "Ode to Joy" exists in two ways. First and fully, it exists as a song when it is performed. Second, and not nearly so fully, almost as a shadow, it exists as a mathematical pattern of notes. If a supernova destroys the earth completely, then the "Ode to Joy," in its full and flourishing existence as a song, will also be destroyed. Yet, the destruction of the earth and all that is therein will not destroy the existence of the "Ode to Joy" as a mathematical relation among notes. If we continue the analogy and imagine billions of years from now the recreation of another earth and a second Beethoven who writes a song that is note-for-note identical with the original "Ode to Joy," when that song is performed it will not be a new song. Rather, it will be the same song with a long hiatus between performances.[8]

Fully unpacking this analogy will have to wait, but for a sentence in a prospectus we will say this: If humans are rational animals, then the "resurrection" of a person is a real possibility, though it would require a *supernatural* intervention reversing the natural course of events.

Thus, for the dualist, immortality is a *natural* fact, and for the materialist it is an *irrational* hope or fear. Our view splits the difference. If humans really are rational animals, then immortality is neither a natural fact nor an irrational hope. Instead, it is a possibility that would require a *miraculous* resurrection of the body to actualize.

Two Fallacies

Both philosophers and rhetoricians study arguments, but they study arguments with a different end in sight. The goal of rhetoric is persuasion; the goal of philosophy (as we understand it) is the pursuit of truth. Rhetoricians study logic because good arguments are sometimes persuasive. However, bad arguments can also be persuasive. In fact, during the heat of a battle, bad arguments are often times more convincing than good arguments. Logicians call such arguments fallacies. From the philosophical point of view, fallacious arguments are useless because they can be used to support either side of an argument. Of course, if a person's goal is to "win" an argument, the judicious use of fallacies can be quite beneficial. However, if the goal is to discover the truth, fallacies must be avoided at all cost. Any "argument" that can support opposite conclusions is like a square circle—it is not really an argument, but only a rhetorical trick.

Knowing the past history of an automobile is certainly important to the purchaser of a used car, and knowing the psychological motivation behind a person's crime is certainly essential to a judge making a sentence, but from a wholly logical point of view, knowing the history of an argument or the psychological states of the argument's defenders is almost always irrelevant. Attempts to discredit arguments by casting aspersion on their historical or psychological origin are sometimes referred to as a genetic fallacy. Since arguments about humans' essential nature touch upon our deepest hopes and fears, it is extremely tempting to analyze the psychological motivation of one's opponents rather than analyzing their arguments.

Materialists have often argued that belief in the immortality of the soul is a myth constructed by political and religious leaders as a means for seizing and maintaining power. For example, according to Karl Marx, religion is nothing more than an opiate for the masses. It is a tool of the politically powerful for first oppressing the people and then numbing them to their own pain. Crudely put, their trick goes like this: though your present life may be miserable, don't revolt, because if you do, you will lose your reward in the hereafter.

While Marxists are certainly correct when they say that religion is often put to hypocritical uses, logically speaking, this is irrelevant. The fact that something is learned from teachers and others in a position of social authority doesn't mean it is false. Nor is the moral character of the teacher especially relevant. The multiplication tables and the chemist's periodic table must both be learned. But whether hypocritical humans teach these tables or the tables "miraculously fall from the sky" is irrelevant to the question of whether or not they are true.

A second version of the same fallacy comes from Freud. It goes like this: Belief in a Heavenly Father who will save one's soul is nothing more than the wishful thinking of the faint hearted. When we hurt ourselves as children, we turned to our parents for comfort. But as we get older, we realize that even the best parents could not remove all our pains. Therefore, we "invent" a belief in a supernatural father who can give us the comfort that we so desperately desire as we experience the pangs and trials of life, then we "conveniently" forget (repress) the fact that we are not God's creation. Rather, God is our creation.

Though such Freudian arguments are common, they are no better from a logical point of view than the Marxist argument. Of course, if the idea of God really was our own creation, then that would be an argument for materialism. But the fact that many people desperately hope for a God who will insure their immortality tells us nothing about whether this wish will be fulfilled. While we don't always get what we hope for, sometimes we do. When we do receive our hearts desires, the gift is no less real just because it was something we had previously desired.

If it is fallacious to criticize an argument by pointing to the "wishful thinking" of its defenders, then it is also fallacious to criticize the "fearful thinking" of arguers. This is the flip side of the Freudian argument and supports the opposite conclusion. If some people believe because of their wishes and hopes, other people don't believe because of their pride and fear. Two recently published books, both written by nonbelieving professional philosophers, testify to the place of pride and fear among professional philosophers.

The first example comes from John Searle's latest book. Though religion is not specifically the issue, Searle's admission that his profession is not immune to defending philosophical positions for less than philosophical reasons is pertinent to our point. Today, there is a persistent belief that all categories—from rabbits to black holes—are nothing more than "social constructions." Of course, we all understand that the existence of black holes is still open to doubt, but why would anyone have doubts about the reality of things like rabbits? Searle says, and we concur, that such doubts are largely motivated by the fact that "it satisfies a basic urge to power. It just seems too disgusting, somehow, that we should have to be at the mercy of the 'real world.'" And again, "As I suggested earlier, many people find it repugnant that we . . . should be subject to and answerable to a dumb, stupid, inert material world. Why should we be answerable to the world? Why shouldn't we think of the 'real world' as something we create, and therefore something that is answerable to us? If all of reality is a 'social construct,' then it is we who are in power, not the world."[9]

The second example is from Thomas Nagel. Its pertinence is clear. He writes that the "fear of religion [has had] large and often pernicious consequences for modern intellectual life . . . I speak from experience, being strongly subject to this fear myself . . . and am made uneasy by the fact that some of the most intelligent and well-informed people I know are religious believers."[10]

In short, truth must be our master. When it corresponds to our hopes, we should be thankful. When it heightens our fears, we must be courageous. In neither case should we allow our pride to fool us into believing that *we* are the arbiters of reality.

2

Getting It Right From the Start

Form, Shape, and the Nature of Things

Ontology is the study of mere existence. It asks, What sorts of things exist? None of the physical or life sciences can properly address such a question because they do not take a sufficiently general point of view. Any answer that they give will beg the question in favor of a wholly material account of reality.

Form is not shape, and everything that exists in nature is composed of both form and shape. This is the distinguishing characteristic of Aristotelian philosophy. Historians call it hylomorphism.

"Form" refers to the essential nature of things. Essential natures answer the question, What is it? "Shape," as we are using the term, refers to the most complete possible quantifiable description of a thing. It is what the sciences study.

Starting with Descartes, hylomorphism has been scorned and ridiculed. Among contemporary philosophers it is simply ignored. We believe, however, that it is impossible to provide a philosophically adequate account of words (and many other things) without adopting some sort of distinction between form and shape.

Finally, we suggest that the way meaning is in words provides an analogy for the way souls are in bodies.

Socrates is a central figure in Aristophanes's play *The Clouds*. He spends most of his time speaking from a pit because he was too busy discussing

24

philosophical matters to watch where he was walking. A millennium and a half later, Moliere satirizes philosophers through a character who mindlessly repeats the scholastic formula, "Form is not shape." He is continually harassing people who say "shape" when they should be saying "form." For the audience, of course, there is not a dime's worth of difference between form and shape—a thing's shape is its form and vice versa. Philosophy is mocked for insisting on distinctions when there is no real difference.

We beg to differ. There is a real difference between form and shape. Though some may think the difference minor or pedantic, we believe that modern philosophy's disdain for the distinction between form and shape ultimately demonstrates the truth of Aristotle's remark that a little mistake at the beginning of a philosophy can have disastrous consequences at the end.

The Ontological Perspective

In philosophical jargon, this is a chapter on ontology. Ontology is the study of existence itself. It is the most general and most abstract of all disciplines.

Moving from the particular to the more general, we can say that politics and ethics study human beings in their role as rational members in a larger community. Psychology studies humans as individual rational animals. Biology studies humans as animals. Chemistry studies humans as complex organic compounds. Physics could, if it wanted to, study humans as simply a mass of atoms. For example, it could calculate how much kinetic energy an average human being would generate in a fall from a ten-story building.

Ontology takes an even more general, and hence, more abstract point of view. It studies humans simply as *beings,* i.e., things that exist. Since ontology is more general than even physics, it begs fewer questions. Physics is self-limiting. It only concerns itself with "stuff" that is capable of motion. If it moves, then it is a suitable item for physical analysis.

But what about "stuff" that is not capable of motion because it isn't physical? There are physical instances of the numeral seven, but is the *concept* seven itself physical? Emotions like anger and thoughts about complex problems in physics certainly have *effects* in the physical world, but are the emotions and thoughts themselves physical?

These are real, not rhetorical, questions. A simple yes or no to these questions should satisfy no one. Yet, if we approach the question from anything less than the ontological point of view, that is precisely what we will get. By their own choice, everything biologists, chemists, and physicists study is physical. If we are assuming the perspectives of any of these disciplines, thoughts and emotions must *by definition* be either unreal or physical.

It is simply silly to suggest that biology, chemistry, or physics has now *proved* that the human soul is really nothing more than electro-chemical actions of the brain or that it is merely an ephiphenominal (and hence not fully real) aspect of the brain. This may be true, but it cannot be discovered by these disciplines because these disciplines limit their subject matter to physical stuff from the outset. *If* it is true that feelings and thoughts are identical to certain brain processes or that they are not fully real, then this is a truth that could only be discovered—as opposed to merely assumed—by taking an ontological point of view.

Unfortunately, most people have little patience for ontology. In fact, even many contemporary philosophers think of ontology as a relic of the past. Many philosophers say that while Aristotle's ontological discussions may be of interest to historians, he can have nothing to teach us because his ontology is scientifically obsolete.

There is a partial truth in this claim. Science has changed our understanding of the physical universe, and this will undoubtedly have implications for ontology. In Aristotle's universe, for example, there was one set of physical laws that described what happened here on earth and a different set of laws to describe what happened in the heavens. Today, not even the most fervent defender of Aristotle would hold such a view, but it is not at all obvious that such scientific changes have any effect one way or the other on the distinction between form and shape.

Even if it does have implications here, to change an accepted ontology is not the same as eliminating ontological questions. Ontological questions remain, such as, What is the soul? Is consciousness merely a physical property of the brain? Is a person's will free? Can mere matter think? It is only the commonly given answers that change. Ontology is part of metaphysics and metaphysics inevitably buries its undertakers.

Furthermore, not all change is progress. When you start down a wrong path, the best thing to do is to turn around and start over. A major theme of this book is that a wrong turn was made around the sixteenth century. It was then that Descartes tried to treat humans as if they were really angels (immaterial substances) and science as if it were wholly a matter of observing, recording, and predicting the behavior of purely physical stuff. We believe that Descartes's starting points were fundamentally misguided. Therefore, we are going to begin by turning back and taking another look at the Aristotelian notion of "substantial forms."

Descartes's loathing of substantial forms, however, had some justification. Aristotle and Aquinas only employed the notion of substantial form to answer questions about *what* things were, but many of Aquinas's scholastic followers mistakenly extended this notion to answer questions about *how* things work by reference to substantial forms. This misemployment of the idea of substantial forms really did impede the progress of science, but the fact that some people misuse hammers does not mean that hammers are useless.

The fact that intellectuals like Voltaire had great success mocking an idea he never understood is not a good reason for us to laugh. Should we mock Voltaire for tolerating the slave trade and subjugating women? What about Voltaire's belief that the entire universe was permeated by a wholly unobservable element called "ether" that explained gravity's mysterious ability to affect things without touching them? Does the fact that Einstein's theory of relativity makes the "ether" unnecessary mean that we can now dismiss all of Voltaire's ideas with a witty one-liner?

Be forewarned: this book is not for the chronocentrically inclined. Those who are incapable of taking old ideas seriously should probably read no further. There are very few new ideas in this book. Most of it is an elementary exposition and updating of a very old idea. The idea goes back to Aristotle and is called hylomorphism. "Hyle" was the Greek word for wood. It became a metaphor for the fundamental stuff out of which all things were made. "Morph" simply meant form. However, as Aristotle used the term, it did not mean "shape." In fact, "form" and "shape" are antithetical, not synonymous, terms in Aristotle's philosophy.

Forms Are Not Shapes

All things are composed of both form and shape. "Form" is that which makes something *what* it is. "Shape," as we are using the term, refers to the totality of a thing's physically quantifiable properties, i.e., its physical shape and size, height, weight, chemical composition, etc., *in its most complete description.*

In the case of a box, its shape simply is its length, breadth, and height. In other cases—like a hammer—matters are more complex. If a person's sole intent is to find the smallest possible box for shipping a hammer, then knowing its length, breadth, and height would be sufficient. But if a person's intent is to *make* a hammer, then merely knowing the dimensions of the smallest box into which it would fit is insufficient. Here, our knowledge of a hammer would require a more complete description of its physical shape and the chemical composition of its parts.

The shape of a box and the shape of a hammer are not different in kind; they are only different in complexity. For example, three views of a hammer on a blueprint fully describe its shape. By combining an understanding of each of these views, a person is a long way toward knowing how a hammer is made.

The essence of shape, as we are using the term, is that it is *quantifiable*. We see this in the designer's reduction of the crucial aspects of a hammer to a series of numerical dimensions. Of course, in addition to numerical dimensions, the designer will use words to describe the materials out of which different parts of the hammer are made—fiberglass for the handle and high carbon steel for the head. But even these, with sophisticated chemical analysis, could be reduced to a set of quantifiable relations among the atoms in the steel and fiberglass.

Carried to the limit, a thing's shape includes even esoteric properties like electrical conductivity and gravitational fields. In short, and again, as we are using the term *shape* it refers to all the quantifiable physical properties of an object.

There is another way to describe a hammer that is different in *kind* from descriptions of its shape, even when the idea of quantifiable shape is taken to its limit.[1] When a child makes a trip to his father's garage, points to the hammer on the workbench, and says, "What's that?" no description in terms of shape will answer the child's question. The only good answer is, "That's a hammer." Often times when a child, or even an adult, is given the name of an unfamiliar object, a second question follows, "And what's a hammer?"

At this second stage of inquiry, the child is asking for a definition, not merely a name. Modern philosophers often misunderstand this second question. Parents realize that the child is asking for the definition of the hammer; modern philosophers typically interpret the child's question as a request for the definition of the *word* "hammer."

What is the difference between defining hammers and the word "hammer"? Everything![2] This is a prime example where a little mistake in the beginning causes huge problems latter on. Quotation marks around a word can indicate that the reference is the word itself, not the things or events to which the word refers. For example, it makes perfect sense to say both that red is a color and to say that "red" has three letters, but the sense of the sentences is quite different. The distinction between red and "red" captures this difference. In the first instance, we are referring to an actual color, but in the second instance, we are only referring to a word.

Back to the original question. When a child asks "What's a hammer?" is the child asking: (1) "What's a hammer?" or (2) "What's a 'hammer'?" Aristotelians follow their common sense: the child is asking about the nature of hammers. The child wants to know about the *thing* that dad has in his hand. The majority of modern philosophers, however, are committed to saying that the child is asking for the definition of the word "hammer." They say this because it has become a dogma of modern philosophy that only *words* have definitions.

We are not intending anything derogatory by describing this belief of modern philosophers as a dogma. There is nothing wrong with dogmas. All philosophers have their dogmas, including Aristotle and Aquinas. Dogmas only become pernicious when they are unexamined and/or false.

On the surface it seems obvious that there is something wrong with the modern dogma. After all, anyone who sees a child looking at his father's hammer and trying to grab it automatically assumes the child wants to know about the actual hammer. The child is certainly not looking at and reaching for the abstraction "hammer." Appearances, however, can deceive, so it is worth trying to understand *why* modern philosophers are so insistent when they assert that only words have definitions.

The answer goes back to Descartes's loathing of substantial forms. Notice that a parent's answer to the child's second question about the hammer typically goes like this: "A hammer is a tool used for pounding nails." By so answering, the parent is telling the child *what* a hammer is. The problem, from the modern point of view, is that such an answer is only a hair's breadth from Aristotle's "loathsome" idea of substantial forms. Defining what a thing *is* presupposes that it has an essential nature. By tolerating the obvious sense of the child's question and the parent's answer, one is implicitly adopting an Aristotelian ontology. Answers to questions about what a *thing* is and statements about substantial forms are equivalent.

In other words, it is one and the same thing to say that only words have definitions and to claim that substantial forms are obsolete and prescientific. If we believe that we can meaningfully say what something is, then we must also disbelieve the modern dogma that only words have definitions, and vice versa. If we believe that it is impossible to determine what a thing's essence (substantial form) is, then we must accept the modern dogma that only words have definitions. Since talk about essences and the modern dogma about words go hand in hand, it would be begging the question for either the Aristotelian or the modern philosopher to employ one in support of the other. It seems we have reached a stalemate.

Fortunately, things are not so bleak. There is no need for either side to resort to rhetorical tricks because there is still room for rational arguments. If either side in a dispute about fundamental principles can demonstrate that the opposing position is *internally* inconsistent (i.e., self-contradictory), then that is a strong argument in favor of the other. Aristotelians believe that this is possible.

Let us, for the sake of the argument, assume that only words have definitions. Moderns who make this assumption are forced to make two other assumptions. They must assume first that words exist and second that words have meanings. If our opponents are not willing to say that certain ink marks (or acoustical disturbances) really *are* words and that it is their meaning that *makes* them words, then their thesis is literally nonsense (i.e., without meaning). At the bare minimum, they must be willing to say, "'Red' refers to things that are red."

So, suppose we ask a modern philosopher about the meaning of two instances of the same words printed with a different shape. How should a modern philosopher respond if she is asked whether "red" and "RED" both have the same meaning? If she says that these two sets of ink marks mean something different (because they have different physical shapes), then she undercuts her assumption that words exists. She is implicitly asserting that "red" and "RED" are nothing more than ink marks without verbal significance. On the other hand, if she says that "red" and "RED" are two instances of words with the same meaning, then it cannot be the shape that gives ink marks their meaning.[3] Meaning or in-*form*-ation must be something quite different from shape. Though "red" and "RED" are physically different, *what* they are—their substantial form—is the same. They are two instances of the same word because they have the same meaning.

Again, form is not shape. Form determines *what* something is; shape (including *all* other physical properties) determines *how* something acts and reacts in a material world. The meaning (or information) that is contained in a word or symbol is *not* the result of its shape. If form were shape, then "red" and "RED" would differ in meaning. Instead, they differ only in shape.

The Soul Is the Form of a Body

With this ontological background, we are in a position to define the nature of souls. Simply put, the soul is the form of the body. Souls, however, are not in bodies the way dirt is *in* a rug. Rather, souls are in bodies the way meaning is *in* words.[4]

Small words often cause much philosophical trouble. When parents or teachers try to explain words like "in," "on," and "beside" to children, they typically use a visual aid like a box and a block. They put the block in various locations with respect to the box and have the child respond with the words "in," "on," and "beside." This is a good way to *begin* instruction in language, but it can't *end* there. If it did, no one would understand the previous sentence. If "in" always meant what it does when we say that the block is *in* a box, then what could it possibly mean to speak of "instruction *in* language"?

Aristotelian philosophers have a name for the different ways words are used. Two words used in the same way are said to be univocal—that is, they speak with one voice. For example, in the sentences "There are many blocks in the box" and "There is a lot of dirt in our rug," the word "in" is being used in the same way. But in the sentences "There is a lot of dirt in our rug" and "There is a lot of meaning in what you say," the word "in" is being used analogically. While there is a clear connection in the use of "in" in all these sentences, there is also a clear difference. Words are analogical when they refer to things that are *related* but different.

Failure to fully appreciate the analogical use of words is at least partially responsible for many common misunderstandings concerning the nature of souls. Descartes, for example, asked the seemingly innocuous question, "*Where* does the mind connect with the body?" When he discovered that the pineal gland in the brain didn't appear to have any other function, he speculated that *it* was the location of the interaction between the mind and the body.

Descartes's mistake was not biological; it was philosophical. Even if it turned out that the pineal gland had no function, that would not be an argument in favor of Descartes's speculation. Descartes's real mistake was that he believed that souls were *in* bodies the way the dirt is *in* rugs. If he had read Aristotle more carefully, he would have understood that souls are *in* bodies the way meaning is *in* words. Descartes's misunderstanding of "in" and his definition of souls as "immaterial *substances*" are closely connected. Each reinforces the other and both are mistaken.

But Descartes wasn't all wrong. Many contemporary Darwinists and cognitive scientists make a similar, but opposite, mistake. They too assume that "in" has only one meaning. When they dissect brains or study their evolution and find no evidence of "gaps" where souls might reside, they conclude that either souls don't really exist or that they are nothing but brains. Descartes, of course, would disagree, and in this he is not mistaken. Souls really do exist, but they do not exist in the "gaps" of *material* substances.

The rest of the book defends the Aristotelian alternative to Descartes's dualism and many Darwinists' materialism, but Aristotle's alternative should not be thought of as a compromise. A compromise splits the difference between two extremes. For example, if a seller is asking $7,000 for a car and a buyer is offering $6,000 for the car, a compromise would be to sell the car for $6,500. Materialists say that there is only one kind of thing that really exists; dualists say that there are two kinds of things that really exist. The Aristotelian alternative is *not* to say that there are really one and a half *kinds* of things. After all, what's *half* a kind? Instead, Aristotle argues that the only philosophically acceptable way to make sense of any physical object is in terms of both forms and shapes, but neither forms nor shapes are *kinds* of substances. Rather, they are that which *together* makes any substance what it is. The next chapter describes the different kinds of substances that have "ontological standing" (i.e., really exist) according to Aristotelians.

3

Dividing Nature at Its Joints

The Difference between Plants, Animals, and Humans

The universe is one thing composed of many parts, but how can this be? How can one thing also be many things? How can many things be one thing?

Both Heraclitus and Parmenides argued that it couldn't, and that our common sense view of the universe is mistaken. Heraclitus denied the essential unity of the universe. He said that everything was in a permanent state of flux. Parmenides argued for exactly the opposite conclusion. He said that nothing ever changed and that all motion was an illusion. Aristotle argued that both were mistaken. He said that both change and permanence were real.

Darwin's claim that biological species are really nothing more than relatively fixed varieties has philosophical affinities with Heraclitus. Parmenides's "logical monism" has fallen out of fashion, but modern materialists agree with half of his thesis, namely, that real change in kind is impossible. Mechanically inclined materialists tend to emphasize the wonders of modern technology. They claim that it is only a matter of time before computers can be programmed to do everything humans can do and then some. Biologically inclined materialists emphasize the incredible powers of natural selection and the "phylogenetic continuity" of nature. They conclude that humans are

33

nothing more than the product of million of years of differential reproductive rates coupled with the laws of natural selection.

The rest of the chapter describes Aristotle's alternative. In his conception, there are at least three essential divisions or categories in nature—plants, animals, and humans. Plants are organic wholes that are alive and able to reproduce. The common distinction between the living and nonliving in terms of material complexity is inadequate. Living things are heterogeneously ordered; nonliving things are not.

Animals are organic wholes that are both alive and capable of feeling. Humans are animals that are capable of using language to reason about things that cannot be seen, heard, tasted, felt, or smelled.

The chapter concludes with an initial statement of the essential compatibility of the Aristotelian and scientific understandings of the universe.

What's a Universe?

We live in a universe. In one sense, there is nothing profound or puzzling about living in a universe. What could be more simple or obvious? Nonetheless, reflecting on the *meaning* of this seemingly simple claim gives rise to one of the oldest philosophical problems. It is often called the problem of the one and the many. Etymologically, "universe" contains two roots—*unus* which means "one" or "whole" and *versus* which is the past participle of "to turn." Now "to turn" implies some sort of change, movement, or multiplicity, so the philosophical puzzle becomes, How can that which is *one* also be *many*?

It seems like a simple logical truth that if the universe is essentially one thing, then it is not also many things, and vice versa. If the universe is essentially many things, then it is not also one thing. It appears that we must chose between either (1) the essential "oneness" or unity of the universe or (2) the essential "manyness" or variability of the universe, but in no case does it seem possible to have *both*. It is logically inconsistent to emphasize the fact that the universe is a single coherent whole *and* the fact that it is composed of many distinct individuals. At least that is how it seemed to two philosophers whom Aristotle had read—Heraclitus and Parmenides.

Heraclitus emphasized the multiplicity and flux in the universe. He argued that divisions that we perceive in the universe are not real. We seem, he said, to perceive a world composed of mountains and rivers, tables and chairs. But, in fact, if we limit ourselves wholly to what we really perceive and refrain from jumping to conclusions, then we see that the universe (and everything in it) is really in a constant state of flux. Mountains are continually worn down and rivers are continually being filled with silt. Tables and chairs have even a shorter duration.

They are often here today and gone tomorrow. The old saw that the only thing that doesn't change is change itself captures well Heraclitus's understanding. Applied to biology, this understanding of the universe has affinities with a Darwinian account in which species are themselves in a continual state of flux.

The other extreme among the ancients was Parmenides. He emphasized the unity and singularity of the universe. It was *change* that he said was unreal. In fact, the very idea of change, he said, is not just unscientific, it is flat out illogical. His argument was simple.

First premise: For something to change means that it becomes what it is not. For example, if on Monday Aristotle is a living human being and on Tuesday Aristotle is dead, then Aristotle no longer is a real human being, but is instead nothing more than a corpse. Second premise: What *is not* is unreal. In other words, what *is* exists and what *is not* does not exist, and obviously, if something does not exist, it is not real. The conclusion follows straight away—change must be unreal. Reduced to a syllogism, it looks like this:

1. For something to change means that it becomes what it is not.
2. What "is not" is unreal.
3. Therefore, change is unreal.

If forced to choose between these two extreme understandings of the universe, it is hard to say which is crazier. Among twentieth-century philosophers, the extreme "logical monism" of Parmenides is totally out of fashion. Since the opinions of the masses are often shaped by current (or recently past) intellectual fashions, it is not surprising that very few nonphilosophers find Parmenides's arguments even intelligible, much less plausible.

But many philosophers and scientists today accept at least half of Parmenides's position. Change comes in two varieties—change in place (local motion) and change in kind (a human becoming a corpse). Parmenides denied the reality of both kinds of change; modern materialists only deny the reality of change in kind. If materialism is true, the whole of reality reduces to a single thing—matter and the scientific laws that describe its motion. But if only a single kind of thing (matter in motion) is truly real, then obviously any real change in kind is logically impossible.

Two different sorts of arguments support materialism, though they lead to a single conclusion, namely, all apparent differences between things (e.g., between humans and apes) are really nothing more than differences in the way matter is arranged.

The favorite argument of the mechanically inclined materialists emphasizes the wonders of modern technology. This argument concludes that it is only a matter of time before computers can be programmed to do everything humans can do and then some. Materialists of this persuasion say that what the uneducated call "souls" are really nothing but brains, i.e., complex machines.

The favorite argument of biologically inclined materialists emphasizes the incredible powers of natural selection and the "phylogenetic continuity" of nature. This argument concludes that humans are nothing more than the product of million of years of differential reproductive rates coupled with the survival of the fittest. These materialists say that what the uneducated call "souls" refers to nothing more than a piece of folk psychology that reflects human desire for hegemony vis-à-vis the rest of the animal kingdom.

Either way, the conclusion is the same: The differences that common folks think they perceive in nature—for example, between the living and the nonliving, between plants and animals, or between animals and humans—have no significant underlying foundation in reality. According to all materialists, everything is composed of a single set of material elements, and all perceived differences are mere differences in the arrangement of material elements out of which they are composed.

As we said at the end of chapter 1, Aristotelians eschew both extremes. Change and permanence are both real, but neither is ubiquitous. While there is much continuity in nature, there are also discontinuities. Now standing in the middle has its advantages and disadvantages. Common sense tends to pull people to the middle of issues, so those standing in the middle usually have peer support. Those in the middle, however, don't have the luxury of having to defend only a single flank—they get shot at from both sides.

The rest of this chapter is primarily descriptive. We will describe and define the five different kinds of things that Aristotelians say constitute real "joints" in nature without spending much effort defending Aristotle against his critics on both the left and the right. That will come later.

Three Kinds of Souls

The first common-sense division in nature is between things that are alive and things that are not alive. One of Aristotle's books on things that are alive was titled *De Anima*. The title is often translated into English as "On the Soul." "Anima" is simply Greek for "animated." When the Greeks thought of souls, they were thinking about that which made things alive, as opposed to dead or inanimate. Souls were thus conceived of as *ability*, not as an immaterial *thing*. (Aristotle argued, however, that at least one kind of ability, namely, the ability to reason conceptually, implies the existence of an immaterial intellect that was conceived as a substance.[1]) In short, "soul" functions more like a verb than a noun.

A conception of souls as essentially abilities naturally leads to a distinction among three different kinds of souls—(1) those that make bodies alive; (2) those that make bodies sentient; and (3) those that make bodies able to reason conceptually. Furthermore, it is natural to think of these three abilities as hierarchically nested. Plants are alive; many animals are both alive and sentient. Humans are both alive and conscious *and* are able to think conceptually about abstractions.[2]

Saying that animals are both alive and sentient doesn't mean that they have two souls—one that makes them alive and one that makes them sentient. Instead, they have one soul—an animal soul—that is able to do both. Animal souls are therefore one notch above plant souls. Similarly, humans don't have two souls—an animal soul that enables life and consciousness plus a human soul that enables rational thought. Instead, they have one soul that does all three—live, feel, and think.

So what does it mean to say that something is alive? One obvious characteristic of things that are alive is growth. Acorns are quite small. Yet, when planted in good soil and the proper conditions prevail, they grow into a tree that is quite large. Nonetheless, growth itself cannot be the defining characteristic of life. Thunderclouds, mountains, and factories often start quite small but "grow" into something quite large.

One clue that the way an acorn grows into oak trees and way small wisps of steam "grow" into a giant thundercloud are very different is the fact that we feel an urge to put quotation marks around that second use of "grow." This feeling that there is something slightly funny about this second use of "grow" is not trivial. Ignoring this minor difference leads to major mistakes. It indicates an implicit understanding that the second use of "grow" is metaphorical. It is true that clouds grow, but they do not grow in the same way that acorns grow.

What is the difference between these two senses of "grow"? They are the same in that both acorns and wisps of steam begin small and, without ever losing their spatial and temporal continuity, become quite large. They are different in that trees and clouds are not *divisible* in the same way. If you divide a cloud, you end up with two smaller clouds, but if you divide an oak tree in two, you do not end up with two smaller oak trees.

The differences between the way things divide is the result of differences in the way things are composed. Trees and clouds are both composed of parts. The parts of a tree, however, are heterogeneously arranged, whereas the parts of a cloud are homogeneously arranged. Parts are heterogeneously arranged when they have different individual functions or purposes, yet they exist as a single whole in such a way that each part contributes to the continued existence of all the other parts. A tree without roots is not half of a tree; it is dead wood. Heterogeneous parts, in short, are always systematically arranged into an organic whole. On the other hand, parts are homogeneously arranged when each part is able to maintain its own existence apart from the other parts. A cloud with half its mass removed is still half a cloud. The individual water molecules that coalesce into a single cloud constitute only an accidental whole whose parts serve no larger purpose.

We are now in a position to define "life." Something is alive if and only if it is composed of functionally interrelated parts that are heterogeneously ordered such that the existence of individual parts is not sustainable apart from the whole.[3]

At this point we may have tried the patience of more than one reader. Why go to all this rigmarole to define life? After all, everyone already knows when something is alive and when it is dead. What's the point?

Though a complete answer will have to wait, we beg the reader to stay with us a little longer. We are still in the process of constructing a foundational ontology. As with the building of all foundations, progress can be slow. But we will tempt the reader with a carrot.

Though the definition of life just produced may appear to be a little boring, its implications are large. Both the Christian critics and the naturalistic defenders of Darwinism typically presuppose a quite different definition of life. In this other definition, life is a matter of mathematical complexity. Given enough complexity, say the naturalists, life will simply arise by pure chance. The critics reply that the naturalists do not fully appreciate just *how* complex life really is. Even if we grant billions of years for atoms to bounce around, say the critics, the odds against life arising by pure chance are still astronomically small. But note: both sides assume that life is simply a matter of complexity. Their only disagreement is whether such complexity can come about wholly as the result of natural forces.

If Aristotle's ontology is correct, both sides in this dispute have missed the point. Mathematical complexity is neither a necessary nor sufficient condition for life.[4] Mathematical complexity is a function of the *number* of parts. The more parts something has, the greater the odds against that thing being taken apart and then put back together in the same order by chance.

For example, suppose one comes upon a table with two pennies, each of which has the heads side up. If these pennies are disturbed, the odds against random forces rearranging them on the table so that both pennies are heads up is one in four. However, if one comes upon a table with one hundred pennies, each of which is heads up, then the odds against random forces rearranging them in the same way after an earthquake is two with a hundred zeros after it. It would be silly to say that the table with one hundred heads up pennies is more *alive* than the table with just two heads up pennies.

For the same reasons, it is simply not possible to define life in terms of mathematical complexity. Though we do not gainsay any of the mathematical complexity of even a single-cell organism, we daresay that the mathematical complexity of Mount Everest is greater than the mathematical complexity of a single-cell organism. The justification for this claim is simple: there are *many* more parts (molecules, atoms, electrons, or whatever science discovers to be the fundamental building blocks of this universe) in Mount Everest than there are in a single-cell organism. Yet, single-cell organisms are alive and Mount Everest is not. No degree of mathematical complexity is either a necessary[5] or sufficient condition for life. Therefore, no definition of life in terms of mathematical complexity will ever capture the *essence* of what it is to be alive.[6] For now we must stick with our original *qualitative* understanding of life: Something is alive if and only if it is composed of functionally interrelated parts such that the existence of individual parts is not sustainable apart from the whole.

The second kind of soul is that which makes animals both alive and sentient. By "sentient" we first mean that something is able to feel. Even many relatively simple animals may have some feelings, whereas the most mathematically complex (i.e., biggest) plant has no feelings. Again, we must beware of reductionist ontology. Often times materialists will attempt to account for the difference between plants and animals in terms of their parts. Animals have nerve cells and a central nervous system, whereas plants don't. Though this is true, it doesn't capture the ontological difference between things that are able to feel and things that aren't able to feel. There is absolutely no good reason why nerve cells attached to a central nervous system should be able to feel, whereas cambium layers attaching roots and leaves should not be able to feel. It is no use saying that nerve cells are necessary conditions for the ability to feel and since trees lack nerve cells they can't feel. The problem is that "nervous system" *means* "a system which is able to feel." Or as a mocking Moliere might say, the reason animals are able to feel is because of their sentient powers!

Contemporary philosophers have a name for the *felt* quality of sensations. They call it "qualia." The term is a useful one because it calls our attention to a very common, yet truly extraordinary, fact about existence—some things hurt, and some things feel good! That there should exist such things as feelings is a second fact that should cause ontological wonder.

One indication that qualia is ontologically wonderful is the fact that so many contemporary philosophers and scientists have attempted to explain away its existence.[7] In this regard, Darwin was a more honest researcher. True, Darwin thought he could provide a naturalistic account of how a complex organ like an eye could evolve, but in doing so he never pretended to have explained the existence of qualia. Darwin's only claim was that if he were *granted* a single, simple, photo-sensitive group of cells that was able to turn light into even the faintest of feelings, *then* he could explain how something so complex as a human eye might develop. In fact, the sophistication might become so great as to permit color distinctions so fine that a Michelangelo could create the images on the Sistine Chapel.

A lack of ontological self-awareness has blurred the vision of both the critics and defenders of Darwinism. The wonder is *not* that from the faintest of feelings natural selection is able to make eyes. The wonder is that a nervous system would produce the faintest of feelings. In terms of complexity, there may not be much difference between the cells in a Venus flytrap and those first cells that produced feelings. In fact, it is probable that the difference of mathematical complexity between a Venus flytrap and the first cells to produce feelings is not as great as the difference between the complexity of the first cells to produce feelings and the human eye. Yet the transition from plants that grow to animals with feelings crosses a threshold, whereas there is no threshold between cells capable of producing faint feelings and cells capable of the discrimination necessary to paint great works of art.

To illustrate this point, consider two pairs of individuals: Mike & Mary and Sally & Sam. None of them is capable of jumping over thirty feet, though all of them are excellent walkers. Mike and Mary are separated by a forty-foot chasm that extends for one hundred miles in both directions. Sally and Sam are separated by five miles of gently rolling hills with a nicely paved walking path. Which pair of individuals is further apart? The question is ambiguous. For purposes of talking, Mike and Mary are nearer to each other. But for purposes of kissing, Sally and Sam are nearer to each other.

Similarly, there is an ambiguity in the question of which pair is more similar—a Venus flytrap and the first animal with a nervous system or the first animal with a nervous system and humans with sophisticated eyes. In terms of genetic similarity (or mathematical complexity), there may be greater similarity between sophisticated plants and simple animals than between simple animals and highly developed animals. In ontological terms, however, there is greater similarity between the most highly developed animals and very simple animals than there is between complex plants and simple animals. That difference, in a word, is qualia.

Finally, there are human souls. In addition to being alive and conscious, humans are capable of self-knowledge. Most animals know many things about their environment, but they are only able to use experience to reason about things that can be observed. Chapters 6 through 10 focus on the nature and varieties of knowledge. Here we will only mention the outward indication of our uniqueness—humans are able to use and understand words that make reference to things that can never be experienced.

Flying purple people eaters don't exist. But people, and only people, can write songs about flying purple people eaters. Since flying purple people eaters don't exist, they have no shape. Nonetheless, they have a form, i.e., a definition. The nonexistence of flying purple people eaters doesn't stop people from understanding what it would *mean* to be a flying purple people eater. Humans' ability to use language as a tool for abstracting forms from shapes is a third ontological wonder.

Now the claim that humans have unique abilities is not intended to downplay the abilities of animals. Many animals have abilities that no humans possess. Tigers can run faster and jump higher than any human. Bats can use echolocation to find bugs in dark, and dogs can sniff out drugs sealed in plastic. Bees can even use dance to communicate to other bees the location of rich nectar sources! All of these abilities, while quite impressive and even amazing, are ontologically on the same level. All of them are examples of sophisticated reasoning about the physical properties of things. While we should never minimize the glories of the animal kingdom, we shouldn't allow ourselves to be fooled into believing that even the most highly trained animal is capable of the *kind* of abstract reasoning that comes quite naturally to even uneducated children.

We will defend these currently provocative claims in chapter 6, but for now we will only note one more implication in Aristotle's ontological distinction between humans and all other animals. Because they are able to experience qualia, animals can do things that no plant can do, but abilities are both a blessing and a curse. A Golden Retriever's eyes will light up and her tail will wag as fast as a fan when she is being taken to swim and fetch sticks in a lake; a flower's eyes only light up metaphorically on a sunny day when the bees are out pollinating in force. But then, no daisy fears pruning shears the way dogs fear veterinarians.

Similarly, being able to reason about things unseen and unexperienced is both our glory and our curse. It took anthropologists a hundred years to disabuse Europeans of their silly pride in Western ways. We have all heard the stories of nineteenth-century missionaries who seemed to worry more about putting blouses on Polynesian women than preaching the gospel, but today, missionaries from Irian Jaya show slides to evangelical congregations of topless women worshipping in jungle clearings.

Yet a hundred years of anthropological research has not disabused us of two facts about humans well known by the ancient Greeks. No matter where humans live and no matter how varied their cultural practices, all humans (1) fear what none have ever experienced—death—and (2) desire what they can never see—God or gods. The fear of death and the hope provided by religion are two universals that have survived anthropological scrutiny. Humanity's curse and blessing would both be inconceivable were it not for our ability to use language to reason about abstractions.

Two Kinds of Things That Lack Souls

At least two kinds of things lack souls. Aristotle called these elements and compounds. Aristotle lived long before the discoveries of modern chemistry, and we will not pretend that his discussion of elements and compounds anticipated modern chemistry. Nor, conversely, should we snicker at the scientific mistakes that crept into his philosophical discussions of these matters.

As we will be using the term, "element" simply refers to the fundamental unit of material existence whose only characteristic is shape (though we will have to qualify this momentarily). All that can be said about elements is that they either exist or they don't. In other words, elements, as we are using the term, have a single ability—to exist.

"Compounds" are material things composed of elements. But in addition to shape, compounds have various *qualities* like color, smell, electrical conductivity, and gravitational fields. Thus, compounds have at least two abilities—first to exist and second to exist in a particular sort of way. To exist in a particular sort of way is simply to be a particular sort of thing, and as we said in the first chapter, all things are composed of both "stuff" and "form." The only thing we can meaningfully say about elements is that they exist, but with compounds, we can meaningfully say two things—*that* they exist and *what* kind of existence they possess. That is, we can say that they are green or blue, heavy or light, good or bad conductors of electricity, and so on.

Again, these are *ontological—not scientific*—definitions of elements and compounds. We are not attempting to do armchair physics and chemistry. *That* there are elements and compounds is a truth of common sense refined by philosophical analysis. *What* these compounds are and the exact nature of their physical properties is something only scientific research will reveal.

Notice too that we did not include ontological elements in the last sentence. This was intentional. First, it is conceivable that the fundamental building blocks of the universe will turn out to be metaphorical onions—all layers and no core! Whether there is or is not a single kind of indivisible unit out of which everything else is made is a great unknown, and like any universal negative, it would be tough to prove that some alleged fundamental unit is really fundamental, i.e., not able to be broken down further. The history of modern physics is strewn with the names of fundamental particles that turned out to be less than indivisible.

Second, in an important sense, ontological elements do not exist as things. *Pure* shape is as inconceivable as a smile without a face. In the ontology we are outlining, elements have the same use and function that the asymptote has in analytic geometry. Rather than thinking of elements as things, it is better to think of them as a *limit* toward which the scientific analysis of compounds can approach but never reach.[8]

Of course, limits are abstractions that cannot be seen or touched with even the most sophisticated instruments. The five ontological kinds that we have distinguished constitute a classification scheme, but it does not pretend to tell us what scientific experiments and careful observation will discover about the individual within these classifications.[9] Contrary to popular impressions, Aristotle did not pontificate on scientific issues without first putting nature to the test by gathering all the observations possible. A fundamental dictum of all Aristotelians is that philosophy and science complement each other; they do not compete. We will say more about this in the next chapter.

4

Objective Differences in Perspective

Form Versus Shape

Does the natural world contain real differences in kind or are all perceived differences really reducible to differences in degree? Many people believe that such questions are really nothing more than a matter of opinion or perspective. While it is true that different perspectives produce different answers, nonetheless there are objectively correct answers that are not reducible to the tastes, preferences, or opinions of the observer. How this is possible is illustrated by considering a simple graph and the differing results that are obtained when it is viewed from different perspectives.

Illustrative analogies or models must not be taken literally. To picture a world composed of both shapes (material attributes) and forms (natural kinds, essences, and/or substantial forms) is impossible. Shapes can be pictured; forms can only be conceived.

With this proviso in place, the vertical dimension of a graph then roughly models the ontological ordering of the natural kinds discussed in the previous chapter. This dimension represents the formal component of things. The horizontal dimension of the graph roughly models the material components of things. This is the dimension science studies.

The gaps that divide nature ontologically are wholly formal and can only be seen from the side—they are necessarily invisible to the scientist. Since ontological gaps constitute differences in kind, not degree, they are irreducible.

Philosophical realism is the theory that nature is composed of distinct ontological categories that are distinguished by real "joints." How many ontological categories exist in the natural realm is a matter of dispute among realists. Some say that there are as many ontological categories as there are biological species. Others say that there may be as few as five—elements, compounds, plants, animals, and humans. We favor the latter position.

Our graph also illustrates the complementary nature of philosophy and science. In the Aristotelian tradition, philosophy's data is limited to the first principles mentioned in the previous chapter—plants and animals exist, square circles do not, and nothing comes from nothing. These are not the sorts of truths that can either compete with or be refuted by the ongoing discoveries of modern science.

Objective Differences in Perspectives

Does the natural world contain real differences in kind, or are all perceived differences in nature really reducible to differences in degree? That question is addressed in this chapter. The question manifests itself in different ways. Ancient atomists like Democritus and Lucretius argued that all of reality was composed of impenetrable atoms and the empty space in which they continually moved. As the atoms assumed different groupings and relations with other atoms, all the different kinds of things we observe—from rocks to trees to people—were formed. Yet, the underlying reality of all things is really the same. It was only the number, shape, and arrangement of the atoms that was different. True, living beings were composed of super fine and spherical atoms that interpenetrate the whole body. Nonetheless, these "soul atoms," like everything else, were wholly material. Needless to say, such a philosophy contrasted strongly with the common sense point of view that rocks are in some fundamental sense different from trees and trees are likewise different from dogs.

Though materialism is an ancient doctrine, Aristotle's common-sense refutations seem, historically speaking, to require continual repetition. Since the publication of Darwin's *Origin of the Species* in the nineteenth century, this is especially true, if for no other reason than to make it obvious that the "war between science and religion"[1] is really a war between misunderstood science and misunderstood philosophical realism. More on that later in this chapter.

The incredible multitude of biological species that appear different and distinct, Darwin argued, in fact have all had their origin in no more than a few primitive living germs. Many contemporary biologists have taken this thesis one step further to argue that even these primitive living organisms were not different in kind from what preceded. They frequently note that it is now possible to take nonliving molecules and, under the proper conditions, produce the precursors of live cells in the laboratory. The conclusion, they add, is obvious— it is only a matter of time before we will be able to create life itself. Then only the religious obscurants will deny that there is an unbroken line of development from inorganic molecules all the way through to the most complex living organism. This is the thesis of phylogenetic continuity, and it will be discussed in greater detail in chapter 7. Here we will only address the purely conceptual relation between phylogenetic continuity understood as a scientific claim and the common sense belief that there are real differences of kind in the natural realm.

Many of the most vocal opponents of phylogenetic continuity believe that it is a threat to religion because it contradicts the biblical claim that God created all creatures "after their own kind." Not surprisingly, these believers marshal theological objections to evolutionary biology. Recently, however, opponents of phylogenetic continuity have argued that there are *empirically* observable gaps in nature that contradict evolutionary theory, hence they conclude that the evolutionists' claim that nature is one continuous whole with no room for divine action doesn't even hold up to purely scientific scrutiny.

By and large, both sides of this dispute view the struggle as a "zero-sum" conflict—what one side wins, the other side must lose. Is this true? Logicians have long distinguished between the "weak" and "strong" use of the word "or." When a waitress offers a diner either soup or salad with his meal, she is probably using "or" in its strong sense to mean that dinner comes with one or the other *but not both*. But in many cases, "or" only means that at least one of the alternates must be true. For example, if Fred says that it will either rain or snow tomorrow we would not typically think that he was mistaken if tomorrow morning it rained and in the afternoon the rain turned to snow. This is an example of the weak "or" where three possible conditions would make the statement true: (1) it rains tomorrow, but doesn't snow; (2) it snows tomorrow, but doesn't rain; and (3) it *both* rains and snows tomorrow.

Aristotelians argue that the alternatives of phylogenetic continuity and real differences in kind are in fact jointed by the "weak or" and this dispute should not be viewed as a zero-sum game. Our argument will be that rocks, trees, and dogs are really different in kind *and* that contemporary scientists are absolutely correct to assume the phylogenetic continuity of all species. How is this possible?

Consider the following graph with only two dimensions.

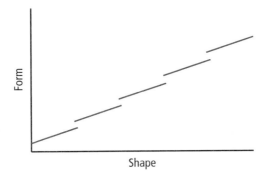

Someone viewing the graph from below will observe only a single continuous line. Someone viewing the graph from the side, however, will observe five distinct line segments. Who is correct? In a wholly two-dimensional world, such a dispute would be impossible to peacefully adjudicate. It is impossible for any person with only a side perspective to understand the person arguing that there is only a single continuous line. The converse is equally true. But in a three-dimensional world, a person viewing the graph from the top can see that both sides to the dispute are correct. Viewed from below, there really is only one continuous line, but viewed from the side, there really are five distinct lines. These two different perspectives make all the difference in the world. If both sides would acknowledge the legitimate difference of perspectives, an honorable peace could be won.

The peace would be truly honorable. No trace of "cheap relativism" is required to gloss over real disagreements about how the world is constituted with talk of "everyone having a right to their own opinions and perspectives." It is true that all observations are made from a particular point of view, but it is false to conclude that all observations are equally subjective. In our example, "perspective" has a wholly *objective* meaning. This objective sense of perspective is absolutely necessary for making sense of the Aristotelian understanding of human nature. We must continually struggle against the contemporary reduction that equates "perspectives" with personal preference or tastes. For example, it is commonly said that from the perspective of the rich, a cut in the capital gains tax would be welcomed, but from the perspective of the poor and middle class, a capital gains tax cut looks like a bad idea. The implication here is that there is no *real* difference in the object of perception, but instead, the difference is in the perceiver. Rich people would like such a tax cut; the middle class and the poor would not. The contemporary assumption is that there can be no rational argument because

the dispute is assumed to be no more than a matter of personal preference, or perhaps simply self-interest.

The Aristotelian use of the word "perspective" is quite different. When
figure one is viewed from the side, there are *real* gaps; when it is viewed
from below, there are not. Any person viewing figure one from the side
who denied that there were four real gaps would be wrong. Of course,
these four *vertical* gaps would be totally invisible to someone viewing
from below. This too is the objective truth about a bottom-up perspective!

Natural Kinds Are Ontologically Ordered

There is a sense in which the view from the side corresponds to the
philosophical or ontological perspective, and the view from below corresponds to the scientific perspective. In other words, the vertical dimension represents form, and the horizontal dimension represents shape.
Before fleshing this out, we must again repeat that to *picture* a world
composed of both shapes (material attributes) and forms (natural kinds,
essences, and/or substantial forms) is impossible. Shapes can be pictured; forms can only be conceived. The distinction between picturing
and conceiving corresponds to the two different senses of "in" we discussed in the first chapter. Meaning is not *in* words the way dirt is *in* a
rug. The dirt that is in rugs can be sucked up by a vacuum cleaner and
then observed by our eyes. We could even take a picture of the dirt pulled
from a rug with a camcorder, but the most powerful vacuum cleaner in
the world is not able to "suck" meaning out of words, nor is it possible
for a camcorder to take its picture. Only our intellect is able to pull meanings out of words. When it does, that meaning can be *conceived* or understood, but it cannot be pictured.

Another way to illustrate this all-important distinction between what
can be perceived and what can only be conceived is to think about circles and chiliagons. (Chiliagons are thousand-sided objects.) All people
are able to form a distinct mental image of a circle. People are also able
to form a distinct mental image of a square. Saying that these two mental images are distinct simply means that to our "mind's eye" or imagination they appear to be different. Some people are even able to form
distinct mental images of circles and octagons, but no one is able to
form a distinct mental image of a chiliagon and a circle. Nonetheless,
conceptually the two are absolutely distinct. If a carpenter was hired to
make a very large thousand-sided house, he would have no difficulty
figuring out the angles at which to cut the sides of the wood outlining
its parameter.

Theoretical physicists frequently remind us to never confuse a scientific model with the reality that it attempts to picture. The same is true in philosophy. Conceptual distinctions can never be adequately pictured or modeled; they must ultimately be understood. But with this proviso firmly in mind, it is nonetheless suggestive to view the difference between the X axis and the Y axis as picturing the difference between the ontological perspective that reveals form and the scientific perspective that reveals shape. So viewed, the horizontal dimension represents all material properties (shape). This is the dimension of science.[2] Only extensive observations and carefully constructed experiments give us factual knowledge about a thing's material characteristics, and in many cases the best way to obtain such knowledge is through measurement and quantification. Since a thing's shape, as we are using the term, includes *all* its quantifiable attributes—from how much it weighs to the frequency of the light waves it reflects—there is also a sense in which movement from left to right on the horizontal axis represents increasing *mathematical* complexity.

The vertical dimension represents formal properties. Movement along the vertical axis represents increasing *ontological* complexity. It also pictures the Aristotelian claim that natural kinds are ontologically ordered.[3] Each line segment represents one of the five natural kinds—elements, compounds, plants, animals, and humans—discussed in the previous chapter. The fact that there are gaps on the vertical axis, whereas there are no gaps on the horizontal axis, also illustrates how ontological differences in *kind* can coexist with biological continuity. Thus, it is quite possible that the biological difference between chimpanzees and humans is only one of degree, even though the ontological difference is absolute.

Biological differences of degree are often put in mathematical terms. Humans and chimpanzees, we are told, share 98 percent of their genes. So again, we need to discuss the difference between mathematical complexity and ontological complexity. Consider the following two words:

1) **Red**
2) *Red*

Suppose we took a separate picture of each of these words with a digital camera. The file size of the first would be bigger than the second for the simple reason that the first is bigger than the second. A wholly observational perspective—like that of the digital camera—creates the possibility of quantifying mathematical complexity. In the exact same way, the physical shape of all words is wholly determined by the location of the molecules out of which they are composed. Since the first word is bigger than the second, it is composed of a greater number of molecules than the smaller. Therefore, to specify the precise location of each molecule in the first word is mathematically more complex than to do the same with the second (smaller) word, but obviously the greater mathematical complexity of the first word does not carry with it greater *meaning*. Speaking formally or ontologically, the complexity of both words is the same.

Similarly, from a wholly observational perspective, Mount Everest is *materially* more complex than President Bush for the simple reason that it is bigger. However, ontologically speaking, Mount Everest is only able to do two things—exist and be the subject of accidental characteristics (i.e., qualities). President Bush, on the other hand, is able to do five things—exist, be the subject of accidental characteristics, be alive, be sentient, and be rational. Therefore, President Bush is *ontologically* more complex than Mount Everest.

Generalizing from this example, we can say that the ontological order is determined by what things are able to do, i.e., their powers and abilities. Natural kinds with more powers or abilities are ontologically higher than natural kinds with fewer powers or abilities.

Here is another illustration. Carbon is able to reflect light, and if it is rubbed on paper it makes a dark mark. A plant can do both of these too. But in addition to these sorts of powers and abilities, a plant is able to grow and reproduce. Animals exist at the next ontological level. An animal, in addition to being able to do all the sorts of things that compounds and plants can do, is able to experience its environment. This conscious awareness of the environment exhibits itself in all sorts of ways. Dogs yelp when they are hurt, raise their hackles when they are fearful, and wag their tails when content. Humans constitute the final level in the realm of nature. We can do everything other animals can do—grow, reproduce, and perceive the world around us. But we can do one more thing—we can conceive of chiliagons without ever having seen one.

Ontological Orders Are Irreducible

The ends of a continuum differ in *degree;* differences of *kind* require discrete objects. For example, young and old constitute opposite ends on the continuum of age. Continuums, by definition, are gapless. The implication of gaplessness is two-fold. First, it is impossible for there to be two points on a continuum, no matter how close they are to each other, such that it is impossible to place a third point in between. Second, all distinctions between ranges on a continuum—young and old, hot and cold, near and far—will be "infected" by some degree of arbitrariness. That is, where nature exhibits a continuous development, distinctions on that continuum will reflect (at least partially) human *decisions*, not scientific or philosophical *discoveries*.

For example, the educational system in the United States distinguishes between infants, toddlers, preschoolers, children, adults, and seniors. But since age constitutes a continuum, these distinctions, while useful for developers of curriculum and designers of classrooms, do not reflect real differences in nature.

Two facts strongly suggest that these categories are human creations (as opposed to natural or divine creations). First, the categories into which we divide people for educational purposes are continually changing. Second, the categories used in the United States are not the same as those used elsewhere in the world. Here, as is true of most continuums, the divisions vary with both the temporal and geographical location of those who are making the distinctions.

Of course, the diversity of categories does not strictly *prove* a lack of natural or divine distinctions. It is possible that all places and periods have been mistaken because they have failed to observe some real difference, so it would be wrong to argue that where there is diversity of opinion there *must* be nothing more than arbitrary distinctions. Nonetheless, it is still the case that when lines are being drawn on continuums, it is *likely* that there will be diversity of distinctions. It would be pure coincidence that all people in all places and all historical periods, with their vast differences in preferences and problems, drew the same distinctions on a natural continuum.

But nature is not solely composed of continuums. Aristotelians argue that common sense correctly recognizes the existence distinct and discrete *kinds*, i.e., classes of things whose members really are different from members of other classes. Those who maintain that nature is composed of both continuums and discrete kinds are called realists.[4] Now as we have already mentioned, there is some disagreement among realists about how many distinct classes exist in nature. Some say there are only five or some other small number of distinct classes, for example, elements, compounds, plants, animals, and humans. Others say that the number of distinct classes is as large as the number of biologically distinct species.[5]

Whatever the number of real categories, Plato's vivid metaphor of "dividing nature at its joints" captures well the realist claim that reality is composed of *both* natural continuums and discrete classes. Our graph thus includes both continuous segments to represent the existence of natural continuums and gaps between the segments to represent the existence of discrete classes. Each line segment corresponds to a natural kind and each gap to a natural joint.

Concrete examples of the distinction between differences in kind and differences in degree are not hard to find. Consider, for example, the rough and ready distinction between biological species and varieties. Dogs and cats are biologically distinct species that cannot interbreed. Irish Setters and Golden Retrievers, however, are only distinct varieties. That is, while there are obvious differences between the looks and behaviors of Setters and Retrieves, the difference is only one of degree. If Irish Setters and Golden Retrievers are interbred over a number of generations, the differences between the two will become finer and finer until at some point they become indistinguishable.

But this will never happen (on a similar time scale) with dogs and cats for the simple reason that they can't interbreed. Hence, there is nothing "halfway" between a dog and a cat analogous to a dog that is half Irish Setter and half Golden Retriever.

The parenthetical phrase in the previous paragraph is important. According to Darwin, biological species are not really distinct (different in kind) from biological varieties. He argued that species are nothing more than well-marked varieties. If Darwin were right about this,[6] then this would be a powerful argument against realist philosophers who identify ontological species with biological species.

But Darwinism does not have the same implication for realists who only maintain the existence of five or some other small number of distinct ontological species. Remember, the central thesis of this book— namely, that humans are neither apes nor angels—only requires the existence of a small number of ontological species. It is possible to defend our central thesis even if the scientific evidence eventually points to the existence of no more than two distinct ontological species—rational animals and everything else.[7] For now, let's stick to the claim that there are five naturally occurring and ontologically distinct kinds of things that are hierarchically ordered. As we said earlier, that means that there must be five distinct line segments on our graph arranged in such a way that there is a *vertical* gap between them. The *gap* represents a distinction in kind, not just degree.[8] The fact that one line is *above* the other represents an ontological ordering that is necessarily invisible to a wholly scientific perspective.

We have already argued for the hierarchical ordering of ontological species in terms of their abilities and powers. Each increase in rank represents an additional ability or power. Plants grow in a way that compounds cannot, animals have powers of sense that plants lack, and humans have the ability to conceive what no animal has ever sensed. Of course, the *ontological* ranking of plants, animals, and humans does little to solve difficult problems in the *biological* classification of species. One obvious problem is that there are many biological organisms that do not easily fit in either the plant or animal or human classification. Bacteria hardly make it to the lowest ontological classification, and insects, which clearly move like animals, may well be totally incapable of feeling anything, and hence must fall somewhere between the plant and animal classification.

Furthermore, as medieval philosophers of nature were wont to say, on the "ladder of being" the lower always touches the higher. Thus, even in our ontological classifications there is going to be some fuzziness. Aristotle himself said that we could have very little confidence in a line drawn between functionally complex and sophisticated plants vis-à-vis simple and primitive animals.[9] For example, there is a great range of abilities in the plant kingdom when it comes to nutrition. Most plants rely primarily on their roots, but the Venus flytrap has sophisticated mechanisms in its flowers to capture insects and then turn them directly into food. While the degree of complexity represented here greatly exceeds that of a fern or pansy, a competent botanist could trace in a step-by-step fashion how the nutritional cycle of a fern develops over time into the much more complex nutritional cycle of a Venus flytrap.

Again, when we compare sophisticated plants with primitive animals, it is not at all clear which, from a purely material or quantifiable point of view, is more complex. The mathematical complexity of a large Venus flytrap is undoubtedly greater than a small oyster just because it contains many more protons, neutrons, and electrons. It is even possible that a Venus flytrap has a greater number of functionally distinct parts than an oyster. That is, there may be a greater number of function units (cells arranged into organs) in a flytrap than in an oyster, but no amount of even functional complexity by itself explains qualia.[10]

Now it may be extremely difficult to determine exactly where on the scale of phylogenetic development organic compounds first experience qualia, but the fact that at some point an animal acquires the ability to experience the faintest of feelings means that they are ontologically different in kind from the most complex plant. While there is much room for scientific guidance in locating the point at which animals become sentient, no amount of scientific investigation will ever eliminate the common sense distinction between those things that have feelings and things that do not. From the ontological point of view, qualia is not like horseshoes—close doesn't count. An organism either is or isn't able to experience pleasure and pain, but such common-sense ontological truths are of little help to biologists classifying questionable species.

The only claim being made here is that qualia is a brute fact of common experience. Science may one day be able to say some useful things about how it emerged on earth, but to explain it away is not useful.[11] Nor is it useful to pretend that the scientific assumption of "phylogenetic continuity" somehow blurs the distinction between sentient and nonsentient organisms. We will have much more to say about the distinction between ontological and epistemological questions in chapter 6 and in chapter 7, where we will demonstrate that ontological sharpness can readily coexist with epistemological fuzziness.

Science versus Philosophy

Suppose that there is a phylogenetic continuity among all species and that at the molecular level there is even an observable continuity between complex inorganic compounds and the most simple living organism. How would that affect the distinction between ontological kinds and biological species? In a single word, the effect is zero.

Again, we must remember all that we've already said: science's realm is the horizontal axis; philosophy's realm is the vertical axis. Here we will only add two crucial points. First, an understanding of reality's richness requires at least two points of view. From below, science seeks to understand the incredible complexity of nature's "shapes" (material properties) and their causal interactions. From the side, philosophy seeks to describe the formal differences among things. This is necessary if we are to maintain the diversity of the universe. Without this analytic effort, we are left with Parmenides's block universe in which there is no real change or diversity.

Once these formal differences are defined, however, the analytic task of philosophy becomes synthetic. Now philosophy attempts to understand the analogies that connect the distinct kinds defined during its analytic phase into a single coherent whole. Without this synthetic phase, there would be no unity in the diversity. Only Heraclitus's world of undifferentiated flux would remain. During this admittedly metaphysical phase, philosophers seek to understand to the best of their ability the wonder of the fact that we live in a cosmos, not a chaos, and that this unity-with-diversity is, at least in part, intelligible.

The scientist and the philosopher not only view nature from different perspectives, they are also produce different results. By understanding nature's material properties and causal interactions, scientists increase human control over nature and thereby increase our creature comforts. By contemplating nature's formal beauty, philosophers increase human enjoyment of life and thereby increase our rational pleasures.[12] When pure science and speculative philosophy reach the limit of their explorations, though, they tend to intermingle.[13]

By defining objectively distinct perspectives, Aristotelians seek to eliminate needless and fruitless competition between science and philosophy. The fundamental point of this chapter is that *ontologically real distinctions do not require gaps in the horizontal dimension*. Viewed from below, nature is a seamless web.[14] Materially complex molecules at some point turn into proteins that then turn into organisms able to replicate, which finally turn into incredibly complex animals that are able to think rationally—us. The movement from left to right on the horizontal axis is wholly a matter of degree. There need not be any gaps, however small, along this entire progression. Nothing we have said requires a unique metaphysical substance—a "life force" or a "free will"—to interrupt or break the phylogenetic continuum.[15]

Furthermore, philosophers in search of breaks in the horizontal axis are not really philosophers; instead, they are amateur scientists. By not continually keeping in mind the distinction between shape and form, they are trespassing on the scientist's turf. Philosophers, who work with nothing more than common experience and careful thought, have no business making a priori pronouncements about what scientists will or will not discover about a thing's shape (material properties).[16] Of course, that has not stopped prior generations of philosophers from filling the gaps in scientific knowledge with mysterious metaphysical substances, but looking back, we can all see that their project was misguided. There is little reason to believe this pattern will not continue into the future.

The converse, however, is equally true. No matter how complete the scientific description of the horizontal plane, any statement about the vertical plane is simply a non sequitur. There is no reason to believe that *ontological* differences in kind must show up as gaps in the horizontal plane. Viewed from the side, there may be vertical jumps that would be completely invisible to someone viewing the same situation from below. A vertical line a mile long is only a point on the horizontal scale, and a vertical gap five stories high will appear as nothing more than an unbroken line when viewed from below.

The fact that the ontological ladder is invisible to the scientist (whose job is to describe the horizontal dimension) hardly constitutes an argument against its reality. If materialism is true and reality is a single, gapless line moving from left to right, we could only *know* that this was the case by adopting the philosophical perspective, i.e., by viewing it from the side. In an Aristotelian understanding, science and philosophy are complementary disciplines. A complete description of reality requires both. Any competition between them is the result of one or the other trespassing in forbidden territory.[17]

One final point about the philosophical and scientific dimension. Movement from left to right on the horizontal dimension, as we have said, represents increasing mathematical complexity. It also appears to correspond to the flow of time. While it is possible that ontological kinds and biological species are both historically constant (unchanged over time), the facts strongly suggest otherwise. True, Aristotle and his prenineteenth-century followers assumed that species did not change over time, but it now appears virtually certain that they were wrong. Plants evolved prior to animals and animals evolved prior to humans. In short, increasing mathematical complexity parallels the flow of history.

So too, the flow of history has increased scientific knowledge. Only a fool would assert that Aristotle knew as much about biology as did Darwin. Science is dependent upon specialized observations and experiments. By *specialized* observation and experiments we simply mean those situations in which people set out to deliberately look for new facts about nature. The contrast here is to ordinary observations and experience—that is, the things we know from experience without deliberate effort. For example, night follows day, the sky is blue, snow is cold, animals feel pain, plants grow, tigers can run faster than people, sexual intercourse produces babies, etc. Such knowledge is historically constant. People living in the twentieth century have no more common experience than did people living in Aristotle's time, though we obviously have access to much more specialized knowledge.

Some modern philosophers have attempted to ground their philosophy on the latest findings of science.[18] Such a philosophy cannot be a timeless philosophy. Instead, it will have to change with every advance made by science. Aristotelian philosophers, however, take a quite different approach. They ground their philosophy in nothing other than logic and common experience. If the fundamental distinction of Aristotelians between shape and form was good in Aristotle's day, then it will be good today. That is not to say that the application of this distinction to newly discovered situations will not have to be continually updated, but it is to say that the cavalier charge that Aristotelian metaphysics is "outdated" in light of the advances modern science is as silly as a charge that Greek drama, poetry, and art is "outdated" in light of the Hollywood film industry, the word processor, and expensive air brushes.[19]

5

The Hows of Science and the Whys of Philosophy

Why Final Causes Are Still Necessary

This chapter focuses on the difference between final and efficient causes. It makes three points. Final causes complement efficient causes. Final causes work through efficient causes. Final causes do not replace efficient causes.

There is much facile theology that attempts to replace efficient causes with final causes. Such attempts will always flounder on the problem of evil. Darwin was right. While there is much beauty in nature that points toward a divine designer, there is also much pain and ugliness that points in the opposite direction. The Ichneumonidae *was especially troublesome for Darwin.*

The difference between final and efficient causes is illustrated by two "collections" of driftwood in the shape of an arrow. People intentionally made one; the other was the result of the random action of the wind and waves. Though Aristotle never denied that intentional actions work through efficient causes, only the first collection is an arrow because only the intentional actions of humans can inform driftwood with meaning.

Hilary Putnam's "pressure cooker" example illustrates the complementary nature of final and efficient causes.

Finally, we argue that a person's ontology ought to be more than a series of arbitrary choices. True, ontological "commitments" have philosophical implications, but it is intellectual cowardice to allow the "fear of religion" to

*so strongly dictate one's ontology commitments that the arguments for imma-
terial intellects are not even considered.*

Efficient and Final Causes

Thus far we have been considering things and their abilities; now it is
time to consider causal *relations* among things.

Perhaps the least understood and most maligned aspect of Aristotle's
metaphysics is his insistence that there are two kinds of causes—efficient and final.[1] Final causes have been mocked in jokes. Question: Why
do people have noses? Answer: So that they have a place to hang their
glasses! They have been the material for innumerable strawmen. Question: What is a final cause? Answer: A final cause is one where the future
affects the past! They have also been the subject of firm resolutions.
Here, for example, is Descartes's: "The entire class of causes which people customarily derive from a thing's 'end,' I judge to be utterly useless
in physics."[2]

So what are final causes and how do they differ from efficient causes?
Simply stated, efficient causes determine a thing's shape. Final causes
determine a thing's form. In other words, efficient causes explain *how*
things are made. Final causes explain *why* things are what they are. In
terms of our graph in the previous chapter, efficient causes are operative on the horizontal axis and final causes are operative on the vertical axis. In this chapter, we will flesh out three characteristics of final
causes.

- Final causes *complement* efficient causes.
- Final causes *work through* efficient causes.
- Final causes *should not replace* efficient causes.

We will consider these in reverse order.

Final Causes Do *Not* Replace Efficient Causes

A slightly more caustic mocking of final causes than we mentioned
in the opening paragraph goes like this—Question: Why do bunny rabbits have white tails? Answer: So that hunters have something to aim
at! Here the butt of the joke not simply final causation, but the *facile
theological* employment of final causes. But this time the joke works
because it refutes facile theology on its own terms. We will explain.

If all questions of the form, "Why are things the way they are?" are answered with the response, "Because God designed and made them that way," then the existence of evil constitutes an insoluble problem for the religious believer. Obviously there is much that is beautiful and amazing about nature. Much of nature is worthy of creation by a supernatural artist or designer. But to jump from here to the implicit rejection of more mundane explanations of nature's wonders in terms of material causes and effects ignores an equally obvious point about nature, namely, much of nature looks terribly chaotic and even evil. If all things are to be explained by their supernatural origin, then earthquakes, famines, and the fact that nature is "red in tooth and claw" point more to a demonic than a divine origin.

It is common knowledge that Charles Darwin lost the Christian faith of his youth. Oftentimes, his loss of faith is explained in terms of his discovery of evolution. His own letters and autobiography, however, refute this explanation. It was more the problem of evil than the fact of evolution that caused him to lose his faith. In response to his contemporary and friend at Harvard University, Asa Gray, Darwin asked whether God ordained "that the crop and tail-feathers of the pigeon should vary in order that the fancier might make his grotesque pouter and fantail breeds? Did He cause the frame and mental qualities of the dog to vary in order that a breed might be formed of indomitable ferocity, with jaws fitted to pin down the bull for man's brutal sport?"[3] More than once Darwin worried about the *Ichneumonidae.* This member of the wasp family paralyzes a particular kind of caterpillar with its sting. It does this so that it can then lay her eggs inside of the still living caterpillar and thus its larva can have fresh meat to eat on their way out![4]

Once Darwin came right out and said that he would not *want* to believe in a God who would condemn all unbelievers to eternal punishment because "this would include my Father, Brother, and almost all my best friends." As one of Darwin's biographers notes, "There may be more sophisticated reasons for disbelief, but there could hardly have been a more persuasive emotional one."[5]

The point here is simply that those who would *replace* efficient causes with supernatural final causes deserved to be mocked, or at least they deserved to be reminded that nature is *both* beautiful and ugly, amazing and chaotic, divine and demonic. It is just a little ironic that it sometimes takes nonbelievers to remind Christians of their own doctrine—we are now living in a sin-cursed world, not the new heavens and new earth!

Yet, the Enlightenment mockers of final causes also deserve criticism if they thought their jokes refuted Aristotle. Long before final causes became a topic for jokes, Aristotle already realized that there is a philosophical problem with a facile theological understanding of final causes. In book two, chapter eight of his *Physics*, Aristotle argues that it is better to say that it rains because "the vapor that has been drawn up is bound to cool, and having cooled, to turn into water and come down" than it is to say that Zeus sends "the rain in order to make the corn grow." His reason is simple: sometimes the rain causes the corn left on the threshing-floor to rot! Aristotle understood very well that, theologically speaking, final causes are a two-edged sword. Not only do final causes point to divine beneficence, they also point to demonic munificence.

Final Causes Work *Through* Efficient Causes

In the same chapter of the *Physics*, Aristotle anticipates another "modern" sounding objection to final causes. "Where all the parts [of animals] turned out just as if they had come to be something [designed], these things survived, suitably put together by chance; otherwise they died, and do die." A passage like this, written by an ancient Greek, strongly suggests that facile theology is not just a modern phenomenon. Evidently, back in Aristotle's time, people were arguing that the incredible order and complexity of animals and their parts could *only* be explained in terms of divine creation. What this passage shows is that an alternative proto-evolutionary account was part of the skeptic's arsenal long before Darwin wrote.[6] Here the skeptic grants that the mathematical complexity of animals and their organs looks *as if* they were designed, but in fact they are a product of random variations. When these random variations are beneficial to the animal, it lives; when they are not, it dies.

Since Aristotle never intended final causes to *replace* efficient causes, there is no reason to believe that he would not have welcomed with open arms the detailed data Darwin provided in his many works arguing for the evolution of species by natural selection.

How, then, did Aristotle conceive of final causes working *through* efficient causes? In evolutionary terms, the movement from left to right on the horizontal axis in the graph in chapter four represents the forward flow of time. Things near the left side are not only less complex than things near the right side, they are also older.[7] Now biologists are quite correct to argue that simple organisms (things to the left) did not develop into more complex organisms (things to the right) because the more complex organisms exuded some kind of mysterious "influence" backwards in time. From a purely Aristotelian standpoint, such influence would violate one of Aristotle's most fundamental principles—nothing comes from nothing. Since the future is "not yet," it is nothing. Thus, it would be absurd to speak of the future causing events in the present. In evolutionary terms, the movement from left to right is the movement from the past through the present and into the future. Since things in the future do not exist, they can have no causal influence on that which does exist.

The crucial difference between final and efficient causes is that they answer different questions. Efficient causes answer questions about *how* the physical properties of things interact among themselves. Final causes answer questions about *why* something is what it is.

For example, given enough time, the action of the wind and waves (efficient causes) might arrange three pieces of driftwood into the *shape* of an arrow pointing to the north. But the wind and the waves never arrange driftwood into the *form* of an arrow, i.e., three pieces of wood that, in a proper context, mean "go north." Only the intentional action (final causation) of a person can put meaning (in-*form*-ation) into driftwood.

Two things identically shaped are not always the same kinds of things. The three pieces of driftwood arranged by the wind and waves in the shape of an arrow are not in fact an arrow. They can look *as if* they were an arrow. In fact, the two sets of driftwood as viewed through the lens of a camcorder might be absolutely indistinguishable. The one produced wholly by efficient causes (the wind and waves) *is* a meaningless arrangement of sticks. But, on the other hand, the one produced with the help of final causes (a person's intention) *is* an arrow, i.e., an intentional symbol with meaning. If all one possessed was a photograph (or any other sophisticated "scientific" image), it would be impossible to answer the question *What* is pictured? The reason is simple. Scientific instruments record the effects of efficient causes. But the essential nature of things (what they *are*) is the result of *both* efficient causes and final causes. Without considering final causes, we could never know *what* something was.

Yet in the natural realm, final causes obviously work *through* efficient causes. When friends wish to leave a message for late arrivals to a beach party, they might look for some driftwood to form an arrow pointing in the direction of the party. Now only a fool (or one with a large philosophical ax to grind) would deny that these friends use their hands and arms to shape the arrow pointing north. Furthermore, it does not take much training in biology to be able to explain the electro-chemical processes that cause the hands and arms to move as they do when shaping an arrow out of driftwood. Again, while Aristotle was himself ignorant of these specific efficient causes, he would have devoured the wealth of information contained in a modern biology textbook.

Final Causes *Complement* Efficient Causes

Our confident prediction of what Aristotle's reaction would be if he read a modern biology textbook is based on his explicit statements in several places that final causes and efficient causes function in a complementary fashion. "There are two modes of causation [efficient and final], and . . . both of these must, so far as possible, be taken into account in explaining the works of nature, or . . . at any rate an attempt must be made to include them both; and . . . those who fail in this tell us in reality nothing about nature."[8]

Though he has no announced allegiance to Aristotle, Harvard philosopher Hilary Putnam makes this same point with simple elegance. We all understand perfectly well what it means to say, "The cause of the pressure cooker exploding was the stuck valve." However, from a purely observational standpoint, we can just as easily say that the reason the pressure cooker exploded was the absence of randomly placed holes in its lid. The only reason for preferring the "stuck valve" explanation is that pressure cookers by design are made with a single hole in the lid controlled by a valve. Had pressure-cooker makers not intended there to be a single hole in the lid, we would not identify a stuck valve as the cause of the explosion. A purely "scientific" or observational explanation begs the question because, as Putnam concludes, the "notion of things 'causing' other things is not a notion which is simply handed to us by physics."[9]

The same problem arises when one tries to give a purely "scientific" explanation of any biological organism without including final causes.[10] It is impossible to say what a heart *is,* much less *does,* without specifying what a heart is *for.* Organisms by definition must be intentionally ordered such that the whole is greater than the sum of its parts. A heart that serves no function is no heart!

The ultimate failure of biological reductionism is that it assumes the whole is nothing more than the sum of its parts. (We will say much more about this in the next two chapters.) But as Aristotle noted a long time ago, this is a fallacy of composition. Music *is* composed of acoustical disturbances, but it is not *merely* acoustical disturbances; written words *are* composed of ink lines on paper, but they are not *merely* ink lines on paper; computer software *is* a collection of electrons, but it is not *merely* a collection of electrons. In all of these cases the whole is more than the sum of its parts, and thus any reductionist explanation of music, written words, or computer software is always conceptually incoherent.

When doing biology, Aristotle made this point absolutely clear. Aristotle asked whether an explanation of animal behavior in terms of efficient causes or an explanation in terms of final causes was to be preferred. His reply: "Is it not rather the one who combines both in a single formula?"[11]

Metaphysics Is Not Esoteric

This brings to a close our description of Aristotle's ontological distinctions between forms versus shapes, essential natures versus accidental characteristics, and efficient versus final causes. These ontological distinctions are, as the contemporary metaphor puts it, the ultimate furniture of Aristotle's world.

Implicit in the metaphor of "ontological furniture," however, is the claim that a philosopher's ontology is really a matter of taste, not truth. Victorians liked their parlors cluttered and gaudy; moderns prefer simpler and more modest interior design. But certainly the Victorians were not wrong to decorate their houses the way they did. So too, many contemporary philosophers say that ontological commitments are simply a matter of taste.[12]

To Aristotelians, such an approach to philosophy begs the most crucial question: Can humans *understand* the universe in which they live? Perhaps we can; perhaps we can't. One thing is clear—we will never know until we try. To suggest that the foundation of all philosophy—ontology—is nothing more than a matter of taste gives up the natural desire of humans to understand their world before even trying.

We believe that Aristotle's ontology makes sense out of common experience in a way that no other set of "ontological commitments" has been able to do. Again, we stress the notion of *common experience*. Philosophy in the Aristotelian mode is not esoteric. The beauty of music, the meaning of words, and the informational content of computer software are not to be discovered by searching for a "magical" element in the gaps between efficient causes. All we need to do is to step back and look at the whole instead of the parts. Beauty, meaning, and information all have to do with the *form* of things, not their *shape*.

Forms require no special equipment or secret talent to observe, but they do require courage and a willingness to struggle against current sensibilities. As Alasdair MacIntyre says, realism is inherently theistic,[13] and as Aristotle acknowledged, rationality is "akin to the divine." Could it be that a "fear of religion" is largely responsible for current philosophical fashions? However we answer this essentially psychological question, we can still be disappointed that so many philosophers write as if a mere preference for an "austere" ontology constituted an argument against Aristotle's more "robust" ontology.

6

How Aristotelians Think About What They Know

Perceiving Versus Conceiving

The first five chapters dealt with ontology. We now turn our attention to epistemology.

According to Descartes, it is impossible to have direct (and hence, certain) knowledge about anything other than one's own mental states. This is the famous cogito ergo sum—"*I think, therefore I am.*" *Aristotelians unequivocally reject the* cogito *as the proper starting point in philosophy. The first principles of philosophy—plants and animals exist, square circles don't, and nothing comes from nothing—are directly evident and do not require, nor are they susceptible to, philosophical proof.*

Knowledge is the product of both reason and experience. We know that plants and animals exist because we see them with our eyes. We know that square circles don't exist because we "see" with our intellect that two sides of a contradiction can't both be true—if something is a square, then it can't also be a circle, and vice versa.

The distinction between seeing with our eyes and seeing with our intellect requires a further distinction between the occasion and justification of knowledge. Second, we must be clear that our intellect, while it will never make us armchair scientists, does provide us with more than trivial tau-

tologies. Finally, we must understand that in the Aristotelian tradition our senses provide more than can be captured on a camcorder.

The justification for this last claim is simple—humans know that nothing comes from nothing and hence are able to reason inductively; induction requires more than the sounds and images of camcorders, therefore humans must be able to "see" things that camcorders cannot.

In addition to making empirical generalization, humans reason inductively when they understand through a process of abstraction what a thing is. This too is something camcorders cannot do. The phrases "rational animal" and "featherless bipeds" have the same logical extension—they both refer to the same set of individuals, but only the former describes what a human is. "Featherless biped" only describes accidental properties of humans.

Modern logic is a wholly extensional or relational logic. It rejects the possibility that two predicates—like "rational animal" and "featherless biped"—could have the same extension and yet be logically distinct. It also begs the question to argue that Aristotelian logic is out of date, old fashioned, or unable to truly reflect reality because it is nonextensional.

In the classical tradition, nonhuman animals were referred to as brutes. There was no disrespect intended here. Brutes have always been known to be extremely able and intelligent, but their intelligence is limited to the perceptual realm. While brutes are able to make sophisticated inferences based on observed regularities, there is no evidence that they are able to reason conceptually—i.e., that they understand the difference between cause and coincidence or that they ever know what something is. There is no limit to a brute's knowledge of a thing's shape and the way a thing's shape interacts with the shape of other things, but there is an absolute limit to a brute's understanding of form. It is zero.

Finally, the gauntlet is thrown down for those who would contest this last claim. If anyone can teach a nonhuman animal to behaviorally demonstrate an understanding of the word "tomorrow," everything Aristotle taught about the distinction between brutes and humans will have been proved wrong.

Cartesian Doubt

The first five chapters of this essay dealt with metaphysics. There we asked, Are there real wholes made up of parts or is the whole nothing more than the sum of its parts?[1] Are some categories real or are they nothing more than "social constructs"? Do some classifications correctly divide nature at its joints, or are all distinctions merely in the eye of the beholder? Realists defend the first alternative in each case. This raises a question: What real categories or division exist? That is, what *kinds* of things exist? Where are the joints in nature? Our tentative answer was that there are at least five real divisions in nature—elements, mixtures, plants, nonrational animals, and humans. The next three chapters deal with epistemology. Here we will ask, How is this known? But first we need to consider a generic objection to our procedure thus far.

Beginning with Descartes, modern philosophers have claimed that doing metaphysics prior to epistemology is a mistake. They say that asking, How do we know what we know? begs the question because it presupposes that humans actually know things about the world. Those who make epistemology their starting point typically employ a version of Descartes's argument. He argued like this: Illusions are common phenomena. So how do we know that the entire universe isn't an illusion? Dreams are also common. We have all had dreams we *believed* to be true until we woke up. How then can we be sure that *all* of our beliefs aren't dreams? Even worse, how can we be sure they aren't the products of some Evil Genius's deception?

There are two short responses to Descartes's skepticism. First, Descartes is guilty of the fallacy of composition. What is true of parts is not always true of wholes. All the parts of a Volkswagen Rabbit may be light enough to enable a person of average strength to pick up without the need of a winch, but it does not follow that a person of average strength can pick up the whole car without a winch.

Thus, it may be true that without special training no one can be absolutely sure that any *particular* twenty-dollar bill isn't counterfeit. But with training in nothing more than simple logic, anyone can be absolutely sure that *all* twenty-dollar bills aren't counterfeit. "Counterfeit" *means* not real. If no *real* twenty-dollar bills exist, then it would be logically impossible for anyone to produce a counterfeit twenty. Similarly, unless people's normal experience of seeing cats and dogs were truthful, it would be impossible for us to have illusions or dreams about cats and dogs.

The second response is to simply ignore Descartes. Life is short. All the time and effort we spend attempting to prove the obvious takes away time and effort working to discover truths that aren't obvious. Aristotelians don't waste much time trying to *prove* that cats and dogs exist, square circles don't exist, and that nothing comes from nothing,[2] nor do they have much patience with those who do. The reason is simple: the premises of all arguments must be better known, more obvious, and less dubious than their conclusions. Therefore to *prove* that cats and dogs exist, that square circles don't, and that nothing comes from nothing, we must necessarily find some proposition that is more obvious to common experience than the three mentioned above. But in fact, no more obvious proposition has been produced.[3] Therefore, attempts to prove that cats and dogs exist, that square circles don't, or that nothing comes from nothing are logically absurd.

Aristotelians believe that this "epistemological turn" of modern philosophy leads to a dead end. Epistemology is important, but the most important question is not, Do we know anything? Rather it is, How do we know what we know?

Two Kinds of Knowledge

Knowledge is the product of both reason (conception) and experience (perception). We know that trees and dogs exist because we experience them. We know that square circles don't exist because reason tells us that two sides of a contradiction can't both be true—if something is a square, then it can't also be a circle, and vice versa.

Though saying that reason and experience are both sources of knowledge seems to be fairly obvious, several common misunderstandings must be avoided. First, truths of reason are not innate. We must distinguish between the *occasion* of coming to know a proposition is true and the *justification* of that proposition. The occasion or circumstances of our coming to know is a psychological category. There are many interesting questions here. Learning theory, for example, is especially relevant for teachers. Is "hands on" experience combined with group projects the best way to teach geometry, or does a more traditional and "theoretical" approach work best? These are important questions for psychologists and teachers, but they are not especially relevant to the philosophical question of whether or not the Euclidean geometry correctly represents reality. This is a question about the *justification* (or lack of justification) of the axioms and theorems of Euclidean geometry.

Historically speaking, psychology as an independent discipline is fairly young. Prior to the nineteenth century, psychological questions were handled by dramatists, poets, and philosophers, so it is not surprising that philosophers like Plato and Descartes addressed both questions about the rational justification of knowledge and the psychological occasions that produced knowledge. While Aristotle agreed with both Plato and Descartes that pure reason was an important source of knowledge, Aristotle disagreed with their psychology of innate knowledge.

The most plausible example of innate knowledge is the law of contradiction, but even here Plato's claim that such knowledge is innate strikes Aristotelians as highly implausible. After all, human babies are not born reciting the law of contradiction. If, heaven forbid, a child was deprived of all sensory input from birth, that child would know nothing, including that square circles don't exist. All knowledge begins with an observation by one or more of the senses. As Aristotelians continually repeat, "Nothing is in the understanding unless it has first been in the senses."

This denial of innate knowledge fits well with our definition of humans as rational *animals*. Angels may have innate faculties that produce knowledge without the aid of bodily organs, but humans are not angels. Because Aristotelians believe that humans are a unity of body and soul, it naturally follows that psychologically speaking all human knowledge would involve both reason (conception) and experience (perception).

David Hume, an eighteenth-century British philosopher, initiated a second error surrounding truths of reason. He said that all truths of reason were *wholly* formal.[4] A formal truth is a proposition that we known to be true solely by an examination of its structure. The three traditional laws of logic are again the most plausible examples of formal truths:

- Any statement of the form—"S is P and non-P"—is always false.
- Any statement of the form—"S is S"—is always true.
- Any statement of the form—"S or non-S"—is always true.

Now, Hume and Aristotle did not disagree about the truth of the above propositions. Where they differed concerned their significance. Aristotle argued that the above propositions give us a fundamental insight into the nature of *reality*. Hume argued that they only tell us about the nature of *words*. And words, said Hume, are nothing but conventional symbols created by humans.

Hume's goal was to trivialize logic by reducing it to nothing more than a set of humanly constructed tautologies. (It this regard, we are once again up against that dogma of modern philosophy that *only* words have definitions.) As one contemporary philosopher said, knowing that it either will or will not rain tomorrow does not make us meteorologists.

Aristotelians, on the other hand, do not believe that the truths of logic are trivial tautologies without real content. Instead, they argue that the three laws of logic provide a fundamental insight into the nature of existence. We will discuss this point further in the next section. There we will argue that the Aristotelian point of view is preferable because Hume's alternative theory of logic makes science impossible.

A final error to be avoided concerns the nature of experience and how it is understood. This error treats human experience as if it were equivalent to that of a camcorder. Camcorders do not literally see trees and dogs; rather, they record *images* of trees and dogs. It is only when these images are viewed by people (or in rare cases by other animals) that pictures of trees and dogs are observed.

Once again, the source of this error was Descartes. In fact, his skepticism concerning the existence of things like trees and dogs and a camcorder understanding of experience go hand in hand. Descartes assumed that there was a metaphysical "gap" between the act of observing and what was observed. According to him, what we really *see* when we look at a tree or dog is ideas, images, or sense-data of a tree or dog. The actual trees and dogs that produced these ideas, images, and/or sense-data had to be *inferred*. No one ever directly observed trees and dogs. Instead, Descartes argued that the justification of all statements about dogs and trees can only be based on *reasoning* from effect to cause.

It is as if the human soul were a little man inside Descartes's head who was viewing images taken by a camcorder. That little man is faced with the following question: Are these images of dogs and trees the causal effect of real dogs and trees or are they the effect of the evil machinations of demons whose only joy in life is to deceive us poor humans?

We have already mentioned two fairly obvious reasons for rejecting such Cartesian doubts. In the next section, we will consider a couple more subtle problems that result from a camcorder understanding of experience (perception).

Two Kinds of Induction

Roughly speaking, inductive reasoning is the ability to draw conclusions based on observations and experiments. For example, people who live in northern California know that a strong south wind and dark clouds in the morning means that it is likely to rain before evening. Such knowledge doesn't depend upon taking college courses in meteorology; simple observation of the weather patterns over a couple of winters is sufficient.

As we said in chapter 5, however, not all inductive reasoning is the result of ordinary observations. Sometimes the pattern of events is not open for all to observe. In these cases, we construct an experiment to help us answer our questions. These can range from the simple and mundane to the incredibly complex and sophisticated. Here's an example of the former. Most days when we turn the key of our car's engine, it starts. If one day we turn the key and nothing happens, we will want to know why the usual sequence of events was broken. Since simple observation doesn't reveal the answer, we try changing the usual circumstances by hooking up jumper cables to the battery. When the car then starts, we reason on the basis of a simple inductive experiment that a dead battery caused our car not to start in the first instance.

Of course, the complexity and sophistication of experiments conducted by nuclear physicists is much greater than in our simple experiment with a car that failed to start, but the difference is only one of degree. Reflection also reveals that the difference between simply observing a causal relation between clouds and rain, as in our first case, and constructing an experiment using jumper cables, as in our second case, is also one of degree. We will thus call all varieties of reasoning that rely on an observed connection between events *empirical induction,* and at least for now we will not worry about whether these observations are open to all or the result of specially constructed experiments.

The first problem with Descartes's camcorder understanding of experience is that it undercuts the foundation of empirical induction. Several times we have mentioned the three assumptions of common sense— plants and animals exist, square circles don't, and nothing comes from nothing. We have already discussed the first two, now we must discuss the third—nothing comes from nothing, or in more modern terms, every cause has an effect. Though the old formulation of the first principle of empirical reasoning is a little more general (it covers both the occurrence of events and the existence of things), here we will treat the old and new formulation as equivalent.

The assumption that every event has a cause is the first principle of empirical reasoning because without it all empirical inductions are either unjustified or utterly mysterious. If things can either "pop" in or out of existence for no reason at all, then it is impossible to justify the claim that strong south winds *cause* rain or that dead batteries *cause* cars not to start. In Hume's phrase, the best that experience will give us (without assuming the first principle of empirical reasoning) is that these events are constantly conjoined. Mere correlations, however, are insufficient for doing real science because many events are "constantly conjoined" without being related as cause and effect. A story is told about one economist who noted that during the twentieth century, peak sunspot activity has been perfectly correlated (constantly conjoined) with the peaks of the business cycle. Whether there really is such a correlation is irrelevant—even if there were, it would be absurd to conclude that sunspot activity is either the cause or the effect of the business cycle.

The point here is that if a camcorder understanding of experience is being assumed, then experience will never provide anything but constant conjunction because camcorders don't and can't know the crucial first principle of inductive reasoning—nothing comes from nothing. They don't have this sort of knowledge for the simple reason that the principle is *universal,* whereas camcorders only exist in particular places and times. Since camcorders only exist in particular locations, they can only record what takes place in and around those places, but the principle that nothing comes from nothing applies to all places in the universe, including places where no camcorders have been.

Even if we somehow imagine putting a camcorder in every corner of the universe, the problem is not solved. "Nothing comes from nothing" is tenseless. It applies not only to the present but also to the past and future. For the truth of this principle to be captured on a camcorder, camcorders would have had to exist from the beginning of time to the end of time. Since this obviously isn't the case, conceiving of all empirical knowledge as mere images, ideas, and/or sense-data undercuts the *justification* of all empirical inductions. Something more is needed. For now, we will simply name this added ingredient without yet attempting to understand it—let us call it "rational insight."[5]

Conceptual Induction

A second kind of induction we will call "conceptual." Empirical induction concerns causal relations between events. Conceptual induction concerns things and their forms, i.e., their essential natures. Put differently, empirical induction tells us what makes something happen; conceptual induction enables humans to know *what it is*. A camcorder understanding of experience fails here as well. A couple of examples will make this clear.

In the second chapter we distinguished between defining hammers and defining the word "hammer." Keeping this distinction in mind, consider these two definitions of humans (not the *word* "human").

- Humans are rational animals.
- Humans are featherless bipeds.

Both definitions refer to the same group of individuals. There are no featherless bipeds that are not human and, conversely, there are no humans who are not featherless bipeds. In logical terms, these two definitions have the same extension. The extension of a term is simply everything to which it refers. Metaphorically, the extension of a term is everything that could be captured on a camcorder. These two definitions have the same extension because if one camcorder was programmed to capture images of all rational animals and a different camcorder was programmed to capture images of all featherless bipeds, both camcorders would record the same group of images.

But who would think that being a rational animal or a featherless biped were equally good definitions of humanity? Being a rational animal names our essential nature, whereas being a featherless biped does not. The facts that humans lack feathers and walk on two legs are trivial characteristics when compared to our ability to reason conceptually. If, all around the world, parents, for some bizarre reason, started giving birth to children with feathers, we would be puzzled, but we would not worry that the human race was in danger of becoming extinct. If parents all around the world started giving birth to children, however, who were incapable of rational thought, then we would correctly begin to worry whether the human species will endure. The reason we treat these two "what-if" scenarios differently is that lacking feathers is not part of our essential nature, whereas being able to think rationally is.

The point of this example is similar to (if not the same as) the point being made in the first five chapters. Again, in Plato's vivid metaphor, defining humans as rational animals "divides nature at its joints," whereas defining humans as featherless bipeds is nothing more than an arbitrary label that accidentally refers to the same group of individuals as the word "human." [6] It is the ability to perform conceptual inductions like this that accounts for the distinction between good and bad definitions of humans, and this ability, in turn, is nothing other than the epistemological side of the previously sketched metaphysics.

Here is another example of human rational insight that enables humans to perform conceptual inductions to abstract essential natures from their experience. A single animal can serve as an example for three different concepts, e.g., Golden Retriever, dog, and mammal. When a camcorder "pictures" the same animal, however, it cannot *conceive* of it first as a Golden Retriever, then as a dog, and finally as a mammal. In other words, in the experience of a camcorder, there can be no distinction between the reference of a word (its extension) and the meaning or sense of a word (or what logicians call its intension). The meaning or sense is the product of conceptual induction. Human rational insight allows humans to understand the difference between a dog and a mammal even when their experience presents only a single animal.

A final example of rational insight is our understanding of what something *is* even when the thing in question lacks extension. For example, humans understand the meaning of "the present king of France" even though it would be impossible to "picture" such a person for the simple reason that no such person exists. Or consider the concept of "tomorrow." All normal human children beyond the age of four or five understand the meaning of this word, yet there is nothing in the child's physical experience to which the word refers. No camcorder can take a picture of tomorrow. How, then, can children understand the term? For now, we can only say that they do, and that however they do it, they do not do it by associating the word with a set of sense-data.

Nor do humans understanding the meaning of "the present king of France" or "tomorrow" the way some materialistically-minded philosophers have thought. Such philosophers have said that words with no extension—like unicorn—gain their meaning when people take different sets of sense-data and then cut them up and recombine them in a different fashion. For example, they take an image of the head of a rhinoceros and place it on their image of the body of a horse. The problem with this suggestion is that there is nothing that even *partially pictures* either the present king of France or tomorrow.

Again, our conclusion at this point is only negative and quite modest. We are assuming that humans do reason inductively and that in many cases inductive reasoning is justifiable. We then distinguished two different types of inductive reasoning. The first concerned the relating of events as cause and effect, as opposed to events that were merely constantly conjoined. The second concerned our ability to know *what* something is, as opposed to merely knowing the extension of a word. Our negative conclusion was that however humans are able to obtain these two kinds of inductive knowledge, they do not do it like a camcorder. We then attached a name to this ability and called it "rational insight" without any pretensions of thereby understanding what this ability amounts to.

Old and New Logic

Logic is not philosophically neutral.[7] There is an important difference between the new logic that is often called "predicate calculus" and classical or Aristotelian logic. One superficial difference between the two is that modern logic looks a little like "chicken tracks" to beginning students, but the philosophically important difference concerns their diverse subject matter. Predicate calculus is a logic of relations or events, whereas Aristotelian logic is a logic of things and their essential natures.[8]

Having said this, it is clear why most moderns prefer predicate calculus to classical logic. If you start with the dogma that only words can be defined, then there are no essential natures, and hence, there is nothing for Aristotelian logic to reason about!

Kinder and gentler modern logicians are not quite so blunt. They would say that while their logic focuses on relations between and among things (as opposed to the things themselves), it does not *forbid* one from making statements about things. For example, if we let "H" abbreviate "human" and "M" abbreviate "musical," then we can say that "some humans are musical" like this: "there exists an x such that x is human and x is musical" or in symbols

$$(\exists x)\,[Hx \bullet Mx]$$

If we wanted to say *all* humans die, then, letting "D" represent all things that die, we would write:

$$(x) [Hx \supset Dx]$$

This reads: "For every x, if x is human, then x is something which dies."

Perhaps this is a little wordy, but many modern logic teachers tell their students that these are simply more precise and powerful ways of understanding ordinary propositions. In some contexts this may be true. If the two alternative expressions are being considered merely as text-book examples in the wholly logical analysis of deductive argument, then there is probably no significant difference between the new and old logic. Furthermore, modern logicians typically argue that the work it takes students to learn the "new" logic is time well spent because only modern logic is able to understand the logic of statements like: "Fred is the father of Sam and the grandfather of Luke." Try translating that into a categorical proposition! Here, modern logicians are correct—statements like this aren't handled well by Aristotelian logic.

On the other hand, what modern logic books don't make clear is that traditional logic was considered to be more than just a formal matter. In the old textbooks, the standard categorical proposition—"All humans are mortal"—is first considered in a chapter on *definition,* and only then as a premise in a deductive argument. The reason is simple: traditional logicians are concerned *both* with truth and formal validity, whereas modern logicians are only concerned with formal validity. To beat a horse that we hope is just about dead, consider these two arguments:

> All humans are mortal.
> Socrates is a human
> Therefore, Socrates is mortal.
and
> All humans are featherless.
> Socrates is a human.
> Therefore, Socrates is featherless.

Both arguments are formally valid. Considered *merely* as exercises in a textbook chapter teaching formal inferences, both will do equally well. In fact, in some ways, the second is better because it is sillier, and silly examples help students focus on the structure of the inference instead of its content. However, if we are considering these as *more* than mere examples of formal validity and instead as tools for uncovering truths about reality, then the former is clearly *better* because mortality is an essential aspect of our human nature, whereas being featherless is not.

Thus, we will admit that Aristotelian logic is *incomplete* (since it does-n't handle relational propositions well), but it can't be *replaced* by the new logic (since modern logic can't handle propositions asserting what something *is*).

If the "kinder and gentler" modern logician is willing to let this last sentence stand, then well and good. Unfortunately, many modern logi-cians feel compelled to add something like: "Logicians have no busi-ness nor basis for making a distinction between significant and trivial predicates. If two arguments are formally identical, then there is noth-ing more to be said from the logical point of view." To this we will protest one final time that a crucial question is being begged—Are there, or are there not, essential natures about which humans can reason inductively?

As we discussed in chapter 2, the real difference is between those who are willing to answer a child's straightforward question—What is a ham-mer?—and those who are not, without qualification, willing to tell the child what she wants to know. This same disagreement has appeared in a slightly different guise in the dispute between the old and new logi-cians. Further *direct* discussion of this issue is probably futile. From here on out, we will simply assume that at least *some* things—com-pounds, plants, animals, and humans—are really distinct because of their distinct natures. Furthermore, we will assume that questions of the form—What *is* that?—are legitimate questions that, when answered truly, "divide nature at its joints."

Brutes and Humans[9]

I love dogs. Such an autobiographical comment is an attempt to insure readers that I intend no offense with the subheading of this section. "Brute" is simply a traditional way to refer to nonrational animals. Instead of continually repeating the phrase, "nonrational animal," we will some-times use the single word "brute" without thereby demeaning the ani-mals so many of us love, cherish, and spoil rotten.

Another disclaimer: No right-minded person claims that brutes can-not think.[10] Anyone who spends a single day with my dog Samantha would be convinced that she is quite smart. If we say, "Let's go for a walk," her eyes instantly light up and her tail begins to wag. Whenever we need to use the word "walk" in her presence without intending to take her for a walk, we spell it so as not to disappoint her. Now, after six years, we can't even do that because she knows W-A-L-K spells walk!

Sometimes it is said than nonhuman animals are incapable of rea-soning with abstractions that they have never directly experienced. This too is false. Our previous dog, Sundance, was born and raised in Oregon. Like most dogs, he quickly developed a strong dislike for veterinarians. When we moved down to California, a place that he had never before been, I was sure that our first trip to the vet's office would, so to speak, be a "freebie," and that I would not have to wrestle Sundance through the door. Silly me! As soon as I opened the car door at the vet's office, the wrestling match began. Clearly, Sundance knew inductively that he was about to be poked with needles.

Of course, these are only two instances of the amazing abilities of brutes. Other pet owners and animal behaviorists could certainly add many more. Nonetheless, the Aristotelian tradition maintains that brutes are nonrational. We can flesh out this claim in terms of the previous distinction between conceptual induction and empirical induction. Brutes match, and in some cases even surpass, humans in their ability to perform empirical inductions. There is no evidence, however, that brutes know *what* anything *is,* i.e., there is no evidence that they can perform conceptual inductions.

Many animals that live in close proximity to people become quite proficient at reading people's "body language." Dogs know that a smiling face is likely to be followed by a dog bone or some other treat, whereas a frowning face is likely to be followed by a (metaphorical!) "Boot out the door." In so doing, dogs are reading natural signs and making empirical inductions in the same way that northern Californians know that strong south winds and darks clouds means rain.

Furthermore, they are able to "displace" such knowledge and apply it to a context quiet different from the original experience, as my example with Sundance demonstrates. When Sundance knew that he was about to be poked by a vet's needle for the first time in California, there was nothing similar about the road we followed, the place we stopped, or the color of the building to suggest he was being taken to the vet's office. So how did he know? Simple empirical induction—the strong smell of rubbing alcohol was constantly conjoined in his experience with vet's needles. In short, Sundance was able to ignore all the irrelevant data in his experience and focus in on the one piece of crucial data— the smell of alcohol is constantly conjoined with needles. This enabled him to use his experience to form empirical inductions about widely varying situations. (Forgive me for bragging about my own dogs' abilities, but these examples illustrate nicely how philosophical reasoning, at least as understood by those working in the Aristotelian tradition, is based primarily on *common* experience, not the highly specific experience of animal behaviorists.)

The question thus becomes, If the ability to make sophisticated empirical inductions does not constitute evidence of rationality, then what does? We can answer this question by becoming clearer about the distinction between empirical and conceptual induction.

Dogs are pragmatists.[11] They don't care whether or not their empirical inductions are grounded upon *real* divisions in nature or *mere* correlations. All dogs (and other brutes) care about is whether their empirical inductions *work*—do they, or do they not, enable them to get what they want and avoid what they don't want. (In saying this, we are assuming for the moment that no brute desires to know the truth *just because it is true*.) The distinction between an empirical *correlation* and natural *causation* is unknown to brutes because it is unnecessary to a wholly pragmatic knowledge of the world.

Though we have already considered a similar sort of distinction between an accidental property of humans (being featherless bipeds) and the essential nature of humans (being rational animals), one more example will not hurt.[12]

One of the oldest buildings in the United States is Emerson Hall at Harvard University. It has existed for well over three hundred years. During those many years, no person who has walked through its doors has been able to speak Inuit, a language of Native Americans in Alaska. Suppose Sam, a Native American whose first language is Inuit, wins a scholarship to Harvard University. When he walks though the doors of Emerson Hall for the first time, will he lose his ability to speak Inuit? Obviously not. Just because it has *always* been true in the past that people who walk through the doors of Emerson Hall are unable to speak Inuit, we all understand that there is nothing about walking through these doors that *makes* a person unable to speak Inuit.

Furthermore, suppose that Sam (or anyone else who spoke Inuit) never walks through the doors of Emerson Hall. In other words, suppose that people have *always* been unable to speak Inuit after entering Emerson Hall. It would still be false that walking through the doors of Emerson Hall *makes* one unable to speak Inuit. Even if there is perfect correlation between walking through the doors of Emerson Hall and not being able to speak Inuit, humans understand that there is no real connection between these two events. Here there is a sharp distinction between what humans know and what brutes know.

As long as a pragmatic correlation serves the brute's purposes well, the brute would be absolutely uninterested in being told he was being deceived about the truth of the matter. The reason for this complete lack of interest is simple: no brute understands the difference between a perfect correlation and a causal connection.

A somewhat crude summary goes like this: brutes know a whole lot about *how* things work in nature. With respect to knowing how nature works, brutes and humans only differ in degree. In knowing *why* nature works as it does, however, the difference between brutes and humans is a difference of *kind*. No brute has the slightest understanding of nature's *whys*, whereas human understanding of why nature does what it does (i.e., of natural causes based on a true understanding of nature's joints) continues to increase with each generation.

The fact that our understanding of natural causes increases with each new generation is not at all surprising given our ability to communicate with language, but it is probably misleading to simply say that brutes and humans differ because humans can use a language but brutes cannot. If we remain content with such a vague phrase as "use a language," pet owners and animals behaviorists are sure to object. They will correctly point out that there is much evidence that many brutes have a language of their own or are capable of learning the meaning of a large portion of a human language. Therefore, it is absolutely crucial to distinguish between the *conceptual* use of language and the use of language as "natural signs" referring to correlations between perceptible things or events. No matter how sophisticated brutes become in their ability to learn and understand words functioning as "natural signs," nothing of philosophical interest will have been established. (We will discuss this crucial distinction between natural signs and conventional symbols further in chapter 9.)

Lest this sound like mere sour grapes from one trained in philosophy and not animal behaviorism, let me end this chapter with a straightforward challenge for Aristotle's critics. If animal behaviorists ever succeed in meeting this challenge, then Aristotelians will be forced to admit that there is no real difference in kind between brutes and humans.

The challenge is to construct an experiment in which a brute demonstrates that it understands the phrase "the day after tomorrow." The concept referred to here is not difficult. All normal five-year-olds understand the phrase in their heads, even if they often have a hard time controlling the *desire* for immediate gratification.

How can we be so sure that children really understand the meaning of "tomorrow"? Here is one way. Create a situation in which the difference between present gratification and delayed gratification is so great that all test subjects (human or brute) who really understand the meaning of the offer and are convinced that the offer of future gratification is genuine will choose to delay the gratification of their present desires. Conversely, if that point is reached and if the test subject (child or brute) is convinced of the genuineness of the offer *while nonetheless choosing present gratification*, then we would be forced to conclude that the subject lacks an understanding the concept of "the day after tomorrow."

If animal behaviorists succeed in meeting this challenge, they will have demonstrated that not only can brutes reason about natural signs but they are also able to understand concepts that are impossible to perceive with their senses. Or in terms of the first chapter, they will have demonstrated that brutes understand not only shapes but forms as well.[13]

7

The Challenge
of Evolutionary Biology

Why Aristotelians Don't Fear Darwin

William Paley popularized the "Watchmaker" argument for a supernatural designer. He argued that the only way to adequately explain the observed complexity in nature is to posit a divine designer. Aristotelians totally reject this use of final causes. They never use final causes to fill gaps in scientific understanding or to explain mere complexity.

Final causes are properly applied in biology when they describe what an event or thing is. There is nothing factious in biologists describing the first pair of claws on a lobster as pincers or saying that the turtle came ashore to lay her eggs, yet both of these descriptions presuppose final causes.

Not only is such a use of final causes permitted in biology, it is also required. Nothing that Darwin and his successors have learned about evolution eliminates biologists' need of final causation.

Of course, many modern biologists think that Darwin's discovery makes final causes unnecessary. But it is only Paley that is refuted by Darwin; Aristotle's arguments are untouched. The reason is simple—without an appeal to genetic codes, natural selection is unintelligible. But like words, no code can be understood in wholly material terms. Without forms, there is no in-form-ation.

80

Some philosophers of biology have tried to find a middle way between positing real codes (which require forms) and conceiving of genes as meaningless collections of matter. They claim that DNA acts as if it were a code without really being a code. A story with three scenarios demonstrates why there is no such "middle way."

Other biologists attempt to escape the dilemma by appealing to "differential rates of reproduction." In this regard, Cairns-Smith's theory that life began with the information transfer among clay crystals is discussed. Though he implicitly recognizes the Aristotelian underpinnings of his theory, many of his admirers, like Richard Dawkins, do not.

Dawkin's confusion is caused by his failure to understand the difference between ontology and epistemology. Ontologically speaking, the information contained in clay crystals must be an all-or-nothing affair, though epistemologically speaking it may very well be fuzzy.

The original dilemma remains. For evolution to be intelligible, there must be some sort of code or information transfer between generations. But if something really is a code or information, there is no purely material way to understand this fact about nature. Thus, any scientifically adequate account of nature must include both shapes and forms.

The Use and Misuse of Final Causes

As we have already mentioned, Descartes thought that "the entire class of causes which people customarily derive from a thing's 'end' . . . [are] . . . utterly useless in physics"[1] (and by "physics" Descartes was referring to anything with spatial dimensions, which all animals clearly have). Most modern philosophers and scientists would agree with Descartes, but they have reached their conclusion about final causes for quite different reasons than Descartes. Descartes believed not only that he had *proved* God existed, but also that the existence of God was a foundational premise for sound philosophy and science. Remember, according to Descartes, without a God who is both good and omnipotent, there could be no guarantee that all our images are not the product of some evil genius's demonic deception. Without a good and omnipotent God providing such a guarantee, we would be forced to utter skepticism.

The problem of skepticism is only a single instance of the larger problem of evil that sooner or later confronts all theists. In addition to people's errors of judgment, there is much physical pain and suffering, and it is not only humans who suffer. Remember the *Ichneumonidae* wasp that troubled Darwin so much. Why would a good God intentionally design a wasp that paralyzed caterpillars so that when it laid her eggs in the gut of the caterpillar, her offspring would have fresh meat to eat on the way out? Darwin could not find a good answer to this question, so he ended up denying the premise. That is, he concluded that God does not design *Ichneumonidae* wasps; rather, they are the result of the blind forces of natural selection.[2]

Darwin's response to the problem of evil was ontological. We can't know why God would intentionally create the *Ichneumonidae* wasp, Darwin reasoned, because in *reality* God didn't create it.

Descartes's response to the problem of evil was epistemological. God's ways are so far above what humans can understand that it is utter presumption for humans to pretend to understand the "whys" of creation. Descartes was sure that God had a good reason for creating such things as *Ichneumonidae* wasps, it is just that humans are incapable of knowing or understand what that reason is.

This humble skepticism about understanding the ways of God was also the foundation for Descartes's rejection of final causes. Final causes may exist, but if they do, humans are not capable of understanding what they are. "It is not without rashness," said Descartes, "that I think myself capable of inquiring into the ends of God."[3]

Where do Aristotelians stand on this issue? To answer this question, we will first flesh out two distinct roles that final causes have played in biology. One role final causes have played is as premises in the "design" argument for the existence of God. William Paley, a nineteenth-century theologian, is the usual name associated with this argument. If a person stumbles upon a watch in the desert, Paley argued, it would be obvious that something with this degree of complexity must have a designer, even if the person has never before actually seen a watch or a watchmaker. Watches are not the sort of mechanism that can be created by blind chance. So too, the incredible complexity of all species of life, even something so elementary as a single cell bacterium, could not come about by blind chance. Though we have never actually seen the supernatural creator of nature's wonders, according to Paley, the inference to such a Designer is just as certain here as it would be with a watch found in the desert.

Aristotelians totally reject this use of final causes.[4] Aristotle's employment of final causes is absolutely distinct from Paley's. Paley appealed to final causes because he thought there could be no efficient cause of prodigious mathematical complexity. The logic of the design argument requires that natural causes (efficient causes) and supernatural causes (final causes) be conceived of as *competing* explanations. When natural causes are incapable of explaining phenomena, then and only then is it rational to introduce supernatural or final causes. Aristotle, on the other hand, employs final causes as a *complement* to efficient causes, not as an alternative. We can better understand the *proper* use of final causes if we first consider their misuse.

Final causes are misused when they function as fillers. For example, in the design argument, the crucial premise is that brute and blind efficient causes are incapable of explaining the existence of mathematically complex organs. A contemporary admirer of Paley, for example, writes that, using the standard neo-Darwinian models of evolution and probability theory, we now know that "the complexity of the biochemical world could not have originated by chance even within a time span of ten billion years."[5] Thus, there must be some *other* kind of explanation. Since there is obviously no human designer, the designer of complex organs must be superhuman.

Aristotelians have two objections to the use of final causes as fillers. The first is logical and historical. Assuming that scientists do not currently *know* the efficient causes that account for the mathematical or material complexity (as opposed to the formal or functional ordering) of biological organs does not mean that no efficient cause exists. Once again, we see the Aristotelian insistence on a robust realism that clearly distinguishes between what we *know* (epistemology) from what is *real* (ontology). Furthermore, Aristotelians insist that the priority given by modernity to epistemology is pernicious. What we can know or understand does not determine what is or exists. As we saw in the previous chapter, the "epistemological turn" leads to a philosophical dead end.

The misuse of final causes also leads to a scientific dead end. By attempting to close gaps in knowledge with supernatural fillers, the progress of science is obstructed. Fortunately, working scientists implicitly understand that the appeal to supernatural fillers is bogus, and hence they continue to search for efficient causes of effects that are currently mysterious. Part of their perseverance is motivated by the simple fact that scientists' efforts in similar past situations have been rewarded with success. History provides numerous examples of gaps in scientific understanding that were once filled supernaturally but are now filled with mundane material (efficient) causes.[6]

The second reason Aristotelians reject the invocation of final causes to explain mathematical/material complexity is that such appeals inevitably confuse form and shape. Shapes can be simple or complex, but there is no particular relation between complexity and form. Some material things are extremely complex, for example, the precise location of each atom that makes up Mount Lassen. But mountains have no form (i.e., final cause or meaning). Rather, they have only shape. Conversely, many things whose shape is relatively simple have an obvious form—three pieces of driftwood placed on the beach by friends that means "go north."

In other words, final causes are not required to answer questions about material complexity; rather, they are required to answer questions about meaning or form. Final causes explain *what* something is not *how* it is made. The reason we need to introduce final causes to explain something like RED is *not* that this formation of ink molecules is especially complex. The only reason one must introduce final causes is that without mention of the final cause, one cannot understand what these ink molecules *are*—namely, a word.

No more needs to be said about the misuse of final causes in biology. What can be said about their proper use? Final causes are properly applied in biology when they are describing *what* an event or thing *is*. Furthermore, when final causation is properly introduced it does *not* replace explanations in terms of efficient causation; rather, it complements them. For example, it is proper, necessary, and not factious for biologists to describe the first pair of claws on a lobster as *pincers*. It is also proper to say that a turtle came ashore *to* lay her eggs. Now both of these accounts are explanations in terms of final causes. A camcorder can take a picture of the *shape* of the first pair of claws on a lobster, but (for all the reasons we have already discussed) it cannot take a picture of their *form*—i.e., what they are, namely, pincers.[7] So too, a camcorder can take a picture of a turtle coming ashore *and* laying its eggs, but it can't take a picture of a turtle coming ashore *to* lay its eggs for the simple reason that *goals* are not something that can be pictured.[8]

Of course, talk of turtles' goals is sure to make biologists nervous for a couple of reasons. First, biologists may be justifiably dubious about the suggestion that an animal with a relatively primitive central nervous system like a turtle would be able to form any kind of conscious intention. Aristotelian philosophers do not disagree. But having a goal and being conscious of that goal are two distinct matters.[9]

In fact, rather than being in disagreement with biologists who refuse to attribute consciousness to biologically simple organisms, Aristotelians would add another argument to support the biologists' doubts about turtles acting for goals of which they are conscious. Since goals are not something that can be perceived, but instead must be *conceived*, it is impossible for any animal incapable of using conceptual language to form conscious intentions or goals. Here the empirical evidence of comparative autonomy and the conceptual arguments of philosophy provide distinct routes to the same conclusion.

The second reason biologists are chary of introducing final causes into scientific descriptions is a fear that it may stifle the search for efficient causes. Given the misuse of final causes that we previously discussed, there is some justification for this fear. But as we explained above and in chapter 5, the Aristotelian use of final causation is wholly complementary and in no way competitive with respect to efficient causes. Here again are Aristotle's own words, "there are two modes of causation [efficient and final], and . . . both of these must, so far as possible, be taken into account in explaining the works of nature, or . . . at any rate an attempt must be made to include them both."

Aristotle fleshes out his point with an example. Consider a wolf that has raised his hackles upon seeing another animal entering its territory. Should we explain this behavior in terms of final causation—e.g., the wolf is raising its hackles to scare off the invader? Or should this behavior be explained in terms of efficient causes—e.g., the sight of another animal caused the wolf's blood temperature to increase, which in turn cause the muscles on his back to tense up, thereby making its hair stand up?[10] Of course, Aristotle's own understanding of the efficient causes at work in raising hackles is somewhat dated, but there is nothing dated about his insistence that *both* accounts are necessary.

We can further illustrate this point by again referring to the graph from chapter 4. The dimension of *shape* (the horizontal axis) can represent the efficient causes that explain how the mechanisms of the body work in the production of particular behaviors. The dimension of *form* (vertical axis) will then represent the final causes that explain why the animal is behaving as it is. Since the vertical and horizontal axes are separate and independent dimensions, nothing that can be truly said of one can contradict or compete with what can be truly said of the other.

We've shown that final causes are proper and not factitious, but can we also show that they are necessary in biology? Aristotle thought we could. After explaining that biologists should strive to include both efficient and final causes, he said, "Those who fail in this tell us in reality nothing about nature."[11] To see why he would say this, consider side-by-side these two descriptions of a turtle's behavior:

- The turtle came ashore *to* lay her eggs.
- The turtle came ashore *and* laid her eggs.

The first description employs final causes; the second does not. Or to employ the camcorder metaphor, the first cannot be perceived because it can only be conceived, whereas the second can be both perceived and conceived. Since biology, at least prima facie, is a science based on observation, it might seem that the second description is preferable because it mentions nothing that is not perceivable. But here appearances are deceptive. In fact, the second description, far from being scientifically superior, is really scientifically useless. The reason the second description tells us nothing of biological interest is that *perceptually* it is indistinguishable from countless other descriptions. For example,

- The turtle came ashore *and* kicked some sand.
- The turtle came ashore *and* stepped on a piece of driftwood.
- The turtle came ashore *and* reflected a photon into the eyes of an owl.

All of these, from a wholly perceptual perspective, are equally good descriptions of what a turtle did, yet none of them are of any interest to biologists. Why? In Aristotelian terms, the answer is obvious—these latter three descriptions only describe *accidental* characteristics of a turtle's life, whereas the first defines part of what it means to *be* a turtle because it is part of the essential nature of all animals to reproduce their own kind.

Nonetheless, most working biologists are convinced that there is a better, non-Aristotelian explanation of why they should only be interested in the turtle's egg-laying behavior and not its sand-kicking, driftwood-stepping, and photon-reflecting behavior.

The Struggle for Existence

One common alternative account focuses on the notion of a "struggle for existence." That account goes like this: Turtles that don't come ashore and lay their eggs will not reproduce. This in turn means that the part of the genetic code that constitutes the efficient cause of egg-laying behavior will not be passed on to the next generation. Therefore, there is no need to introduce final causes. Rather, it is simply the case that those turtles that *by chance* have survival-producing behavior encoded in their DNA live on as a species; those that don't, die out.[12]

There are a couple of things to note concerning this argument. First, it is hardly new. Compare it with Aristotle's remarks that we already quoted from chapter 2 of the *Physics*. "Where all the parts [of animals] turned out just as if they had come to be something [designed], these things survived, suitably put together by chance; otherwise they died, and do die." Of course, Aristotle (like Darwin) had very little detailed understanding of the precise causal mechanism at work in the passing on of characteristics to the next generation, but the fact that only the most fit will survive is hardly a modern discovery. In saying this, though, we are by no means minimizing the significance of our new understanding of DNA and the genetic code.

Does this new understanding make the appeal to final causes unnecessary? Not at all. In fact, it makes final causation even more explicit! Remember our paradigm of final causation—the word. Nothing can become a word if it is *wholly* the product of efficient causes. Since "word" and "code" are simply alternative names for the same thing, it is conceptually incoherent to speak of genetic codes being *wholly* the product of blind chance (efficient causes). Wind and waves (efficient causes) can no more create a code by themselves than they can arrange driftwood into the *form* of an arrow.

Again, the wind and the waves might by chance arrange driftwood into the *shape* of an arrow. But then this arrow-shaped arrangement of driftwood would not *be* an arrow, and hence, it would have no meaning. Likewise, over eons of time, chance events might arrange complex molecules into something that *looks* identical to DNA. However, *looking* exactly like DNA (i.e., existing in the shape of DNA) and *being* DNA are two distinct matters. The difference is conceptual, not scientific—only *real* codes can have a meaningful role in an explanation.

Materialistically inclined biologists cannot have it both ways. If DNA really is a *code*, then it can explain inherited characteristics, though final causation has not been eliminated. On the other hand, if DNA is not really a code, then final causation has been eliminated. In this case, however, the scientific *explanation* of inherited characteristics is also eliminated. Without real codes, the fact that dogs give birth to dogs and not elephants is simply one incredibly mysterious fact about how events in nature are constantly conjoined.[13]

"As If" Scenarios[14]

One way out of this dilemma would be to find a "middle way" between being a code and not being a code. The preferred language for the materialist who adopts this strategy is to speak of DNA *as if* it were a code. (Notice that materialists in Aristotle's day also employed this argument— "where all the parts turned out just *as if* they had come to be something" designed.) The "as if" strategy goes like this: DNA can't really be a code (that would introduce final causation), but it can be *physically* identical to a code. Since efficient causes are oblivious to anything except the physical characteristics of causes and effects, that which is physically identical to a code will function causally precisely *as if* it really were a code without having to be a code.

The strategy is clear and simple, so let's put it to the test. Imagine two groups of people planning a beach party. All agree on which beach the party will be held, but whether it will be at the north or south end is left for the people who arrive first to determine. To save late arrivals from having to guess which way their friends went, a simple code is agreed upon—an arrow made out of driftwood will be constructed to point the way.

The first scenario goes like this: Mike and Mary arrive first, decide to party at the north end and then construct a driftwood arrow pointing in that direction. Sally and Sam arrive second. They see the arrow, turn to the north, and find Mike and Mary who have the barbecue ready to begin cooking the hamburgers. In this first scenario a *real code* exists and everything goes precisely as planned.

The second scenario is similar, though slightly more complex and assumes some mathematically improbable, but not impossible, events. Once again, Mike and Mary arrive first, decide to party at the north end and make a driftwood arrow pointing north. So far, there is no difference between the two scenarios. But on the second scenario, people arriving after Mike and Mary but before Sally and Sam are gathering firewood for a bonfire at the south end of the beach. In the process, they remove the arrow pointing north. In this scenario, it is *as if* the gods were smiling down on Sally and Sam. By brute, blind chance the wind and the waves deposit three other pieces of driftwood at the entrance to the beach that are *physically* identical to the ones previously removed! Sally and Sam now arrive, see what looks to *them* like an arrow, turn to the north, and once again arrive just in time to have dinner with Mike and Mary.

The moral that materialists want to draw from these two scenarios is that brute, blind chance is able to create things that physically function *as if* they were codes without actually *being* codes. Are they correct? There are two distinct criticisms of the materialist's argument—Paley's and Aristotle's. Paley's admirers would quibble with the materialist's premise. It is just minimally possible for brute, blind chance to create something like an arrow, they will say, but it strains credulity to its breaking point to apply such reasoning to DNA and the genetic code. The odds against brute, blind chance creating something so mathematically complex as a single DNA molecule are simply too great.

Though we have referred to this as Paley's criticism, it has its roots in the Cartesian confusion of form and shape. The assumption here is that it is the complexity of a molecule's *shape* that determines whether something is or isn't a real DNA molecule with an embedded genetic code. While Paley's admirers will grant that wind and wave might make something with a physical shape identical to an arrow, they claim that it is not possible for brute, blind chance to make something with a physical shape that is many orders of magnitude more complex.[15]

Aristotle's admirers criticize the materialist's conclusions on completely different grounds. They will not quibble with the materialist's premises. Instead, Aristotelians criticize the validity of the *inference*.

They are quite willing to grant the materialist's premise that with enough time brute, blind chance could create something with a *shape* that is identical to a DNA molecule and its embedded code, but since form is not shape, such empirical possibilities are logically irrelevant.

The wholly philosophical problem with the materialist's argument is that the second scenario is *conceptually* dependent upon scenario one. If we do not *presuppose* events like those recounted in the first scenario, then events like those of the second scenario events could not be coherently conceived. To speak of something *as if* it were an X presupposes that elsewhere X's *really* exist. By denying that there really are codes embedded in plants and animals and that DNA only acts as if it were a code, the materialistically inclined biologist has sawed off the limb on which her explanations rest. To explain why this is the case, we will sketch a third scenario.

The third scenario is identical to the second, only this time there is a scientist sitting on the bluff overlooking the beach. She observes all that transpires—she *sees* Mike and Mary make an arrow, the other people remove the pieces of wood forming an arrow, and then watches as the wind and waves deposit three other pieces of wood in the shape of an arrow. When Sally and Sam arrive, see the fortuitous "arrow," and walk north, the scientist says to herself, "How lucky these folks are! They see something that looks exactly *like* an arrow, when in fact what they really saw was three meaningless pieces of driftwood that brute, blind chance deposited on the beach." This account makes perfectly good sense, but only because we live in a universe in which the shape

$$\rightarrow$$

typically embodies the form of an intentional symbol. In a universe in which some other shape embodied the form for the intentional symbol meaning "move in this direction" the scientist's explanation would be incoherent. We will explain.

The first thing to note about this third scenario is that the scientist's own understanding of these events is necessarily different from Sally and Sam's understanding. Sally and Sam only walk north when they see the "arrow" because they *believe* it to be a real arrow with an embedded code. If they knew what the scientist knew, they would not confidently have turned and walked north expecting to find Mike and Mary.

The second thing to note is that the scientist's account only makes sense to her because it *assumes* that shapes like

$$\rightarrow$$

are a *form* of an arrow. But as we have said several times before, there is no intrinsic relation between shapes and forms. There is absolutely nothing about the *shape* of an arrow that gives it its meaning.

The significance of this point becomes clear if we imagine the third scenario occurring in some other universe atom-for-atom identical to ours. There is only a single difference—namely, that in this alternative universe, people make their arrows in the shape of an

$$\Sigma$$

In this scenario—let us call it three-prime—things shaped like mean nothing, while things shaped like Σ mean "move in the direction of the opening."

Now imagine a scientist in scenario three-prime, who is atom-for-atom identical to the scientist in scenario three, observing what is also atom-for-atom identical to what is observed in scenario three. Finally, imagine scientist three-prime saying to herself, "How lucky these folks are! They see something that looks exactly *like* an arrow, when in fact what they *really* saw was three meaningless pieces of driftwood that brute, blind chance deposited on the beach."

Here the scientist is talking gibberish. Remember, in scenario three-prime, what Sally and Sam see is an arrangement of driftwood in the shape that looks like , but on planet three-prime this is a totally meaningless shape. When Sally-prime and Sam-prime see three pieces of driftwood that look like , they see nothing but a meaningless arrangement of wood and they do *not* see something that looks even vaguely *as if* it were a code with meaning. Thus, while the scientist in scenario three and the scientist in scenario three-prime see physically identical pieces of driftwood and speak to themselves identical words, only the words spoken in scenario three make any sense. And the only reason the scientist's words make any sense in scenario three is that they implicitly assume that shapes like are the form of a *real* arrow, i.e., something that has a real and agreed-upon meaning.

In short, physical objects can only function *as if* they were a code when they are situated in a world where other things with the same or similar physical shapes *really are* a code.[16]

The attempt by the materialist to find a "middle way" out of the dilemma posed at the end of the previous section therefore fails. Unless we live in a world in which DNA or something similar *really* does embody a code, that is, unless we live in a world in which final causation is present, inheritance cannot be explained in terms of DNA functioning *as if* it embodied a code. In a world in which there are *no* real genetic codes, the fact that dogs give birth to dogs and not elephants must conceptually remain one incredibly mysterious fact about how events are constantly conjoined. In other words, trying to conceive of a world in which there are *only* "as if" genetic codes is as impossible as trying to conceive of a world in which there are *only* counterfeit twenty-dollar bills.

In summary, the notion of "the survival of the fittest" or "as if" scenarios based upon this notion can never be a *replacement* for final causation. This should have been obvious from a moment's reflection on the meaning of "fittest." This notion is itself explicitly normative. Something can only be more or less fit if there is a goal toward which it is striving—in this case, the goal is the continued existence of both the individual and the species. Nonetheless, it bears repeating that contemporary Aristotelians welcome the progress modern biology has made in understanding the efficient causes that explain exactly *how* traits of one generation get passed on (with occasional minor modifications) to the next generation.

Differential Rates of Reproduction

A peaceful coexistence between science and philosophy with an agreed upon division of labor, however, will not satisfy the materialistically minded. Their most recent attempts to achieve dominance appeal to the notion of "differential rates of reproduction." The benefit of such language, from their point of view, is that it replaces terms that are explicitly normative ("survival" and "fittest") with terms that are wholly *quantifiable.* For an exposition of this argument, we will consider Richard Dawkins's *The Blind Watchmaker.*

Dawkins acknowledges an apparent circularity in the evolutionist's argument. Natural selection might be able to explain the *improvement* of species, but how can it explain their *origin?* Before life can evolve, it must first exist, so how can "nature" select the preferred life forms before any life forms exist? In other words, before natural selection can do its job, "replicators" must exist, but these replicators cannot be living species because the origin of life is now the point at issue. The problem is that the only kind of replicators we have any knowledge of are all living! To break this circle, Dawkins appeals to the research of A. G. Cairns-Smith.

Cairns-Smith argues that the original *replicators* were not alive. In fact, they were not even *organic* in the chemical sense of the term. (In chemistry, an organic compound is one that contains carbon atoms.) Organic chemistry is a distinct discipline because of the almost unique chemical properties of carbon atoms that make them capable of forming extremely complex molecules. Silicon has similar properties, but since all life on earth (not to mention oil and plastic) is carbon based, it is the carbon atom that has pride of place among chemists.

Thus, when Cairns-Smith argues that the original replicators were made out of clays without a single carbon atom, it is clear that if he succeeds, the circularity mentioned at the beginning of this section will have been overcome. In others words, we will have discovered replicators upon which natural selection could work its wonders without presupposing the existence of living species.

Furthermore, clay replicators are *much* less complex chemically than even the most simple single-cell organism. Thus, the existence of replicating crystals of clay would also blunt Paley's design argument by making the slope of increasing complexity much more gradual. Of course, from an Aristotelian point of view, material complexity is not the real issue. Nonetheless, these points are worth mentioning since they help us understand the strong appeal of such arguments to the materialists.

Now Dawkins and Cairns-Smith would be the first to remind us of the highly speculative nature of the hypothesis we are going to consider. But while the scientific devil is often found in the details, philosophers have the luxury of pondering the bigger picture and ignoring the devil. Therefore, we will simply assume that from a wholly scientific point of view the details of the clay crystal hypothesis will one day be filled in.

In fleshing out a Darwinian account of evolution, clay has several appealing features. First, there is a lot of it. Second, it is not organic, and thus there is no danger of question-begging. Third, while clay may look simple, under the eye of an electron microscope it reveals a sophisticated crystalline structure. So, since crystals "grow," might they not also "evolve" into more and more complex structures?

Before addressing this question directly, let me anticipate an objection. In chapters 2 and 3 we distinguished between the way trees grow and the way clouds "grow." There we said that clouds only "grow" in a metaphorical sense. The difference between trees and clouds is that trees are heterogeneous whereas clouds are homogeneous. Divide or add to a cloud and you get either a smaller or larger cloud. But when you divide a tree in half, you don't get half-size trees—all you get is firewood and mulch. Wouldn't this same sort of objection hold to a hypothesis that clay crystal might grow? Perhaps crystals can "grow" in a metaphorical sense, but they can't grow in the same sense as a tree or dog.

Cairns-Smith is has a good response to such an objection. The thing about crystals that make them an excellent candidate for natural selection is twofold. First, they are organized in a regular pattern. These patterns are both recognizable and predicable. Second, there are also naturally occurring flaws in crystals. Such flaws are not predicable, but once they occur, they tend to get repeated. As an illustration, consider a bricklayer paving a driveway in a regular pattern. Without noticing it, and for no reason other than it was a chance mistake, one of the bricks laid is "half a bubble off." As subsequent bricks are laid (and as long as there are no further irregularities), this same "flaw" will be reproduced in the rest of the row. In other words, the patterns in both crystals and the driveway are the product of both chance and necessity.

Now the thing that is both scientifically and philosophically interesting about the coexistence of chance and necessity is that these are the necessary and sufficient material conditions for the flow of information. If, as the result of a flaw in the central processing unit, every key on the computer that Fred strikes prints an "x," then it would be impossible for Fred to use his computer to communicate information. However, if just the 0 and the 1 key worked in a regular fashion, then it would be difficult, but not impossible, for Fred to communicate with his computer. He could, for example, communicate using Morse Code.

The requirement for at least two working keys for all forms of communication illustrates the need for chance or randomness. As long as the sequence of 0s and 1s is not determined by the CPU, that is, as long as from the point of view of physics the occurrence of a "0" or "1" is equally possible, only two keys are need to transfer information.

On the other hand, the flow of information also requires stability and/or regularity. The physics of the working keys on any keyboard must be such that hitting a single key produces the same results on a regular basis. If upon striking the "0" on the keyboard, it was equally likely that a "0" *or* a "1" would be produced, then, once again, communication would be impossible.

Crystals of clay have both of these physical properties. First, their crystalline patterns are naturally reproduced in a regular and predictable fashion. Second, any random, accidental, or chance flaw in a single crystal will also be passed on to succeeding generations of crystals for purely chemical reasons. Crystals require "catalysis" to initiate the crystallization process. Like the single brick laid "half a bubble off," flaws in crystals acting as catalysis are reproduced. The stage is now set for Dawkins to tell his story. He tells it so well that he deserves to be quoted at length.

Suppose that a variant of a clay improves its own chances of being deposited, by damming up streams. This is an inadvertent consequence of the peculiar defect structure of the clay. In any stream in which this kind of clay exists, large, stagnant shallow pools form above dams, and the main flow of water is diverted into a new course. In these still pools, more of the same kind of clay is laid down. A succession of such shallow pools proliferates along the length of any stream that happens to be "infected" by seeding crystals of this kind of clay. Now, because the main flow of the stream is diverted, during the dry season the shallow pools tend to dry up. The clay dries and cracks in the sun, and the top layers are blown off as dust. Each dust particle inherits the characteristic defect structure of the parent clay that did the damming, the structure that gave it its damming properties. By analogy with the genetic information raining down on the canal from my willow tree, we could say that the dust carries "instructions" for how to dam streams and eventually make more dust. The dust spreads far and wide in the wind, and there is a good chance that some particles of it will happen to land in another stream, hitherto not "infected" with the seeds of this kind of dam-making clay. Once infected by the right sort of dust, a new stream starts to grow crystals of dam-making clay, and the whole depositing, damming, drying, eroding cycle begins again. [17]

Now what's an Aristotelian to make of such a hypothesis? True, the theory is highly speculative from a scientific point of view, but that in itself is no objection to the claim that such an account demonstrates that final causation is both fruitless and unnecessary to understanding the origin of life. Nowhere in the account of Cairns-Smith was any mention made, either implicitly or explicitly, of goals or purposes. Everything mentioned could at least in principle be captured on a camcorder. Furthermore, if Cairns-Smith's theory, or something like it, turns out to be true, then a slow, smooth, gradual transition from nonliving to living will have been established.

Without denying the truth of anything said in the last paragraph, there is still no threat to the Aristotelian account of final causation. Dawkins's liberal use of quotation marks should be our first clue.[18] His entire theory presupposes the flow of in-*form*-ation. Cairns-Smith makes this explicit. He says, "In biology both goods and messages are passed on from one generation to the next. But it is the messages that are the most important inheritance: only they can persist over millions and millions of years. This distinction between goods and information is a case of the ancient distinction between *substances* and *form*. While a message may have to be written in some material substance, the message is not to be identified with that substance. The message as such is form."[19] What more could an Aristotelian want? Even the emphasis appears in the original!

However, elsewhere Cairns-Smith's philosophical interpretation of his theory is not so friendly to Aristotle. He writes, "Life, then, is not some absolute quality that would have suddenly appeared, it would have emerged gradually during early evolution. Between the first evolving entities . . . and later forms that did so more cleverly, there would have been no hard line. But who cares? When you can see what is going on in such a progression you lose interest in erecting picket fences. As I said, 'life' is a fuzzy idea—and it is best left like that."[20] It seems that if he is correct about this, then at least one of the five ontological distinctions we insisted upon so strongly in chapters 2 and 3 has been destroyed.[21]

In the remainder of this chapter we will try to show why this is not the case. Our argument, once again, hinges on the distinction between the ontological and the epistemological point of view. What really exists and what we can know are not the same. From the ontological perspective of chapters 2 and 3, even if Cairns-Smith's theory is true, nothing in it destroys a hard-and-fast *ontological* distinction between the living and the nonliving. It is true, however, that in many cases it is difficult, if not impossible, to *know* whether a particular specimen is to be classed with the living or the nonliving. If Cairns-Smith's theory is correct, this epistemological difficulty will be exacerbated.

Aristotle's argument goes like this: The distinction between the living and nonliving rests on the distinction between that which is heterogeneously ordered and that which is not.[22] (Heterogeneous ordering is a necessary, but not a sufficient, condition for life. Automobiles are heterogeneously ordered, but they are not alive.) Cairns-Smith and all other evolutionists explain the heterogeneous ordering of living organisms in terms of the information passed between genes and the cells that compose the functionally distinct parts of an organism. Therefore, the distinction between the living and nonliving can only be "fuzzy" if the distinction between that which is and that which isn't information is itself fuzzy. Our conclusion, then, is that while the *amount* of information contained in any physical message can vary by degree, the existence or nonexistence of the information *itself* is an all-or-nothing affair.

Ontologically speaking, information is like pregnancy—a woman either is or isn't pregnant. It makes no sense to say that one is "a little bit pregnant." Epistemologically speaking, information is also like pregnancy. Just as a woman is not always able to pinpoint the precise day that she became pregnant, *knowing* whether something is information may not be easy to determine. In fact, information may be so masked by "noise" that a person might never be able to determine with certainty whether or not a particular physical pattern did or did not embody information. If a woman gives birth in July, however, it is pretty safe to conclude that she was pregnant in January, even if no one knew it at that time. So too, while we may today be very unsure about how to classify clay crystals, if in twenty years scientists have been able to establish a causal chain between a particular type of clay crystals and the first single cell organism, then our uncertainty would be largely eliminated—clay crystals will have become the original biological species.

Let us illustrate these points by considering less controversial examples. Think, for a moment, about the portable signs highway workers use. These signs are often made out of a matrix of light bulbs, some of which are lit while others are not. By lighting a particular set of lights, words are spelled.

Ontologically speaking, the necessary conditions for being a word are clear—the pattern of lights (or whatever other physical medium is used, from chalk dust on black boards to patterns of driftwood on a beach) must be the result of the intentional acts of a person. Wind and waves (or any other nonintentional acts) can create patterns that look physically exactly like words, but they only have the *shape* of a word. Information requires the proper *form*.

Epistemologically speaking, however, the necessary conditions for being a word are fuzzy. Suppose one sees a pattern of lights several thousand yards down the highway. At that point, it is unclear whether the pattern spells "STOP" or is simply an unusual pattern of taillights on the cars down the road. At first it may be impossible to *know* which it is. But as we continue down the road, we may become more and more sure that this really is a word intended to communicate information. Finally, when we arrive at the sign, we will be certain.

The point we want to draw is simple but crucial. While our *knowledge* about what we are seeing may be fuzzy (is it really a word or just an unusual pattern?), the *thing* we are seeing is not fuzzy—it either is or isn't a word. This point is so important that we need to consider a possible objection.

The objection goes like this: Suppose that fifty lights are lit to spell the word "STOP." If one of them burns out, we will still have a word. If two lights are burned out, we will still have a word. But if forty-nine lights are burned out, we will not have a word. Yet, any place we draw a line will be arbitrary. Therefore, the boundary between really being a word and not being a word must be fuzzy.

The objection is well stated and we will not be able to fully answer it until the next chapter. There we will make the distinction between words and concepts explicit. For now, we will simply return to the distinction between shape and form. We have seen several times that being in the shape of a word doesn't make something a real word. The converse is also true—for a physical pattern to lack the shape of a word doesn't mean that the *form* (i.e., intention or concept) is not present, though it does mean that the *form* of the word will not be clearly communicated.

In the jargon of information theory, information may be "going out," but if there is too much noise, no information will be received. In the objection considered above, burned out light bulbs are "noise" that obscures the *communication* of information. Again, the information itself either exists or it doesn't exist, but whether the information is or is not being communicated is an epistemological (not ontological) matter.[23]

With these examples and distinctions in mind, let us return to the original issue. Suppose Cairns-Smith's theory concerning the origin of life (or some similar theory) is one day firmly established by scientists. Would not the possibility of providing a wholly *physical* account of each step in the gradual transition from nonliving clay crystals to living single-cell organisms make obsolete Aristotle's ontological categories?

The simple response is to reject the question on the grounds of incoherence. Once again, we must remember that Cairns-Smith presupposes that clay crystals can embody information. Since information is not a *physical* property, no account of evolution that presupposes the inheritance of traits by means of a *code* is a wholly *physical* account. Whether the carrier of the code is a mineral or carbon-based life form is irrelevant.

Still, this response seems too simple. It doesn't treat the particulars of Cairns-Smith's theory with due respect. If Cairns-Smith is correct, then it seems that what began as nothing more than a random physical flaw in an individual clay crystal that contains no more information than a crack in a rock can, over time, *become* information. It is this element of *becoming* that causes havoc for the ancient theory of natural kinds.

To help us think our way through this objection, let's return to the beach with a slightly modified version of a highway worker's sign. The only difference is that instead of lit light bulbs, this time we will be considering fairly large round stones.[24] The example goes like this: Over a period of many years, Fred and Sally make repeated trips to their favorite beach. Before hiking down the many stairs to the sand, they like to view the whole beach from the bluffs. Like many beaches, there are large round stones distributed in a random fashion up and down the beach. At first, Fred and Sally pay no attention to these. After a couple of years, a rather unusual pattern of round rocks begins developing at the south end of the beach. After a few more years, the pattern begins to look more and more like words. Finally, though neither Fred nor Sally could pin point the precise trip at which they reached their conclusion, they now see clearly a pattern of rocks that looks like:

MADE BY GOD

Now, they didn't observe the actual process by which the rocks were shaped into the pattern they now see, so they begin speculating about the origin of this unusual pattern. Being the hard-nosed skeptical type, they immediately rule out the possibility that these rocks are a real message from God. They settle on two other alternatives: this is a long-term project by a church youth group or this is an incredibly unusual random coincidence.

In an important sense, however, the latter alternative—it's an incredibly unusual random coincidence—is not really an explanation of the phenomenon. Rather, it is the assertion that phenomena like this do not rationally require an explanation. To say that something occurred by mere chance or coincidence is not to provide an explanation, but instead, it is to assert that the event or object in question neither has nor demands an explanation. Since Cairns-Smith *is* claiming to explain the origin of life, this alternative would not be analogous to his project.

The second alternative—it's a long-term church youth group project—is a better analogy because it captures his notion that something can gradually *become* information.[25] Before we examine this possibility further, we must first distinguish the difference between words, concepts, and physical things.

Word are physical things—either visually or audibly observed patterns. They are not *just* physical things; they are physical things with a distinct *form*. Where do these forms come from? They are the *concepts* that persons intentionally impose on physical patterns. According to Aristotle, concepts only exist in the *immaterial* minds of humans.

We have said repeatedly that forms are not *in* objects the way dirt is *in* a rug. So too, concepts are not *in* words the way a virus is *in* a body. Viruses enter a body at a particular time. Concepts do *not* enter physical patterns (words) at a particular time, say when fifty-one percent of the pattern is completed. The most we can say is that the concept must precede or be simultaneous with the beginning of the pattern. Phonemes are only words if they are preceded by a concept. If the phonemes are articulated very slowly (say over a ten-second period) there is no middle point, fuzzy or clear, at which the concept turns meaningless sounds into a word.

Similarly, if what begins as an *apparently* random flaw in a clay crystal over millions of years results in a single cell organism, then there can be no midpoint, fuzzy or clear, at which the pattern of flaws in the clay *become* information. Information was either present at the start or it will never be present. Since everyone assumes that information is present at the end of the process, that means that we must also assume that it is present at the very beginning of the process as well.

Does this mean that some day we may discover that clay crystals are really alive? In a word—yes. While this may sound paradoxical, it is not at all difficult for Aristotelians to include noncarbon-based beings on the organic side of the ontological divide between the living and nonliving. Only people who write job descriptions for organic and inorganic chemists will have to seriously rethink their work.

Summary

Nothing said in this chapter has been intended to *prove* that Aristotle's ontological categories are real.[26] The proof of that stands or falls with the ability of Aristotle's philosophy to make better sense of the ordinary observations made by all people in all places than competing alternatives.[27] The focus of this chapter, however, has been the *special* observations made by modern science. Thus, the sole intent here has been negative—showing that the discoveries and advances made by modern biology do not *dis*prove Aristotle's philosophy.[28]

8

The Challenge
of Artificial Intelligence

Calling the Materialist's Bluff

Arguments for immaterial minds must be indirect. The logic of indirect arguments in both science and philosophy is discussed, and their similarity is noted. The primary difference is that in science indirect arguments are based on observations not made in the ordinary course of daily life. Instead, they depend upon experimental or deliberately and painstakingly sought-for data. In philosophy, however, indirect arguments are based on observations made by all people, during all historical eras, and in all cultural settings. Since the distinction between ordinary and extraordinary observations is fuzzy, so is the distinction between the logic of indirect arguments in the sciences and in philosophy.

The premise of the indirect argument for immaterial intellects is that only humans understand words referring to things that cannot be perceived. Some obvious examples of the unique linguistic abilities of humans are listed, and a promise to refine the distinction in the next chapter is made.

Alan Turing created a test—what he called the "Imitation Game"—to answer the question, Can computers really think? John Searle has argued that the test is not valid, but Aristotelians agree with Turing. If a computer is ever programmed to use language in a fashion that is indistinguishable

from the way humans use language, then Aristotle's argument for an imma-
terial intellect will have been refuted.

While Aristotelians believe that the Turing Test really measures what it
sets out to measure, however, the test cannot be "machine graded." For Tur-
ing's test to work as he intended, he simply rules out biologically "cloned"
machines. The problem is that such dismissal brings in through the back
door all the difficult philosophical issues Turing tried so hard to exclude from
the front door.

When Turing first proposed his test, he included a prediction that within
fifty years a computer would be able to pass the test. His time is now up, and
cognitive scientists are nowhere near success. In fact, as it became clear how
difficult it would be to pass the test, a "modified" and much simpler test was
proposed. It would appear that the simplified test could be passed using the
"brute strength" of a computer, but it cannot.

In sum, cognitive scientists are not significantly nearer to programming
a computer that duplicates the linguistic abilities of an average five-year-old
child than they were fifty years ago. Contrary to conventional wisdom, the
force of the indirect argument for the immaterial intellect has increased, not
decreased, with the passage of time.

Indirect Proofs

Imagine a fairly big black building—big enough to house many people and much machinery. Neither you nor anyone you have spoken with has been inside the building, and it has no windows. It does, however, have two doors—one marked "Receiving" and the other "Shipping." At the receiving door, trucks arrive daily with raw materials—plastics, metal, paint, and other unformed stuff. From the shipping door, trucks depart with finished automobiles. On this basis, without any *direct* information about the inside of the building, a justifiable inference can be made—there are people and/or machines in the building making cars.[1] The fact that no one has ever directly observed the inside of the building is irrelevant. Here we can say that you shall know them by their fruit. That is, unseen causes can be inferred from seen effects.[2]

Indirect arguments are common in the sciences. Electrons, though wholly material, are too small to observe directly. Only the "traces" (effects) they leave in "cloud chambers" can be observed. Philosophers also use indirect arguments. Immaterial intellects cannot be observed— not because they are too small, but because their mode of existence is not revealed by the senses. Even one's own intellect is invisible to intro- spection. Yet being unobserved or even unobservable, by itself, doesn't mean that they don't exist.[3] It simply means that any arguments in favor of their existence must be indirect.[4] To justify a claim that humans are endowed with immaterial intellects, a philosopher would have to be able to point to some behavior (effect) that cannot be produced by any other material entity. Only then would belief in immaterial intellects be rationally justified.

Even if a philosopher can identify actions that cannot *presently* be explained as the effects of material entities, this would not justify positing the existence of immaterial objects. The scientists of Galileo's time were unable to explain the tides, though that hardly justifies a pagan theologian's claim that the tides were the product of Neptune's actions. To maintain rationality, we must agree about where the burden of proof lies.

It would be irrational to argue that one-eyed, one-horned, flying purple people eaters might exist because no person has proven that they don't! The burden of proof falls on the person arguing *for* the existence of a thing or abilities, not on the person who denies their existence. The principle is simple: Existence requires an explanation; nonexistence doesn't. In a dispute about the existence of immaterial intellects, the burden of proof falls on the person affirming their existence, not on the person who denies their existence. The mere fact that materialistically-minded philosophers cannot presently *disprove* the existence of immaterial mind is not itself an argument in favor of immaterial minds. Aristotelians openly acknowledge that the burden of proof rests on them.

But there is a wrinkle with indirect proofs. Scientists now claim to have proof of planets circling stars outside of our own solar system. Their evidence is indirect since it is impossible to observe planets so far away. All they have observed is a "wobble" of a star. They then argue that such a wobble can only be explained by positing a planet or planets whose gravitational field is affecting the motion of the star. The wrinkle is this: What's to stop a skeptic from arguing that though we *presently* know of no other factors that might cause stars to "wobble," someday we will have the alternative explanation, and hence, there is no good reason to believe in the existence of intergalactic planets?

From a wholly logical point of view, we are left with a dilemma. We've said that it is existence, not nonexistence, that requires an explanation and hence locates the burden of proof. Therefore, the burden of proof lies with the scientists who are asserting the existence of unobserved planets, not on the one denying their existence. Yet, with indirect arguments, ruling out alternative explanations is crucial—that is, one must prove that some other explanation doesn't exist. Obviously that's hard. How does one prove there aren't good arguments in favor of one-eyed, one-horned, flying purple people eaters? Besides, doesn't the question itself violate the principle that it is existence, not nonexistence, that must be proved? How can we place the burden of proof on the affirmative side and at the same time require them to prove that no other explanations exist? Isn't this requiring the "proof" of a negative and hence proof of nonexistence?

The solution to the dilemma is time. Like good red wines, indirect arguments improve with age. When Charles Wilson first argued for the existence of subatomic particles (i.e., electrons) by pointing to streaks in a "cloud chamber," his argument was interesting but not conclusive. Until other scientists had consistently failed to provide alternative explanations for the observed streaks, skepticism concerning subatomic particles was defensible. But today, many years later, for someone to argue that Wilson's experiments prove nothing because there *might be* some other explanation for the streaks is unfounded skepticism.

Of course, the introduction of the passage of time in the evaluation of indirect arguments doesn't solve all problems.[5] Since time constitutes a continuum, the logician will always be faced with the question of where to draw the line. If a month after the publication of Wilson's experiments skepticism was justifiable but today it is not, then there must be some point where this change in the evaluation of Wilson's argument occurred. In point of fact, there is no nonarbitrary point where a line can be drawn. So, if skepticism was justifiable a month after his experiments, it must also be justified today, or at least that is the way skeptics argue.

While such skepticism is common today, classical logicians saw through such sophism. Though there is some vagueness on either side of all lines drawn on continuums, this does not mean that vagueness infects the entire continuum. Colors constitute a continuum. Nonetheless, red and orange are different colors even though on a color wheel there is no nonarbitrary point where we can say that to the left of the line lies red and to the right of the line lies orange. The fact that a line is "arbitrary" doesn't mean that it is irrational. By definition, lines on a continuum do *not* divide nature at its joints. The complaint that a line drawn on a continuum is "arbitrary" cannot logically be understood as a complaint about the line; it can only be understood as a complaint that nature includes continuums!

Another difference between the indirect arguments of scientists and philosophers is the nature of the observed phenomena. While indirect arguments always begin with an observable phenomenon, the observed phenomena in philosophy are typically quite ordinary (as we have been saying, "common sense"), whereas in the sciences they are typically *unusual* (or as we have been saying, "special"). For electrons, it was the streaks in Wilson's cloud chamber. For the existence of planets outside of our solar system, it was the observation of "wobbles" in stars using the most powerful of telescopes. Both of these cases required specially constructed tools.

Of course, since the distinction between ordinary and extraordinary observations is fuzzy, so is the distinction between science and philosophy. Thus, once again, we will have to consider science and philosophy as extremes on a continuum rather than two discrete and distinct subjects.[6] As a general maxim we can still say that in philosophy the observable phenomenon from which indirect arguments begin is open to all. In one sense, this makes the evaluation of indirect arguments in philosophy easier. They are easier to evaluate because the premises of indirect arguments in philosophy are immediately verifiable by *anyone*, and thus are hardly open to doubt. In another sense, the evaluation of indirect arguments in philosophy is more difficult than their cousin in the sciences.

The difficulty with indirect arguments in philosophy is that the ordinary is often overlooked. Like the proverbial fish that doesn't believe water is wet, we sometimes miss obvious implications just because they are obvious. This inability to see the obvious creates a second difficulty. It is often hard to persuade people that ordinary observations can justify extraordinary conclusions.

To overcome such difficulties, it is good to preface the evaluation of any indirect argument in philosophy with a reminder of the relativity of the terms "ordinary" and "extraordinary." One generation's extraordinary is another generation's ordinary. Sending a man to the moon seems ordinary today, but a mere generation ago it seemed extraordinary. Talk of "invisible fields of force" that communicated images and sounds around the world (radio waves) would have appeared to be sheer superstition to the materialists of Hume's generation. Today the existence of television images from the moon and beyond is taken for granted. Prior to Newton, the possibility that the planets were composed of ordinary matter no different in kind from ordinary dirt and rocks was unthinkable. How could something so heavy as Earth be kept in perpetual orbit around the Sun by a force that acted without making physical contact? Newton himself was dubious about "action at a distance,"[7] but two centuries after Newton, the concept of gravity—invisible fields of force that can act without making physical contact—seems obvious to grade school children. These sorts of examples can easily be multiplied. Why should we then be puzzled when philosophers draw "extraordinary" conclusions from quite "ordinary" premises?

So, when it is suggested that immaterial minds are too strange to be worthy of serious philosophical investigation today, we must remember that nothing is, objectively speaking, ordinary or extraordinary, common or strange, typical or bizarre. Instead, such words denote little more than the subjective judgments of people living in a particular era or working in a particular culture. Since there are few philosophers today consciously working in the Aristotelian tradition, Aristotle's conclusions naturally seem "bizarre" to outsiders, but this hardly constitutes an argument against Aristotle.

Nonetheless, contemporary Aristotelians are quite willing to assume the burden of proof when it comes to the existence of immaterial intellects. They only protest against an irrational begging of the question that rules out the even the *possibility* of immaterial existence prior to an examination of the arguments. Philosophical argument, if it is to be worth anything, must not be limited to the prejudgments of the current generation. The immaterial intellects that today's philosophers deem extraordinary, previous generations of philosophers deemed relatively ordinary. What could be more common than something every living person uses daily?

The fact that immaterial minds have never been "scientifically observed" is also irrelevant—many "scientific" entities like electrons, black holes, planets outside of our solar system, and the operation of natural selection haven't been "scientifically observed" either, at least if that means directly observed. Arguments for the existence of immaterial minds and the arguments for electrons and black holes are logically the same—they must all be indirect. That is why we included this review of elementary logic. It was necessary because we are about to consider what most philosophers today believe is the most dubious of Aristotle's claims, i.e., that humans, and nothing else, are endowed with immaterial intellects. Since any argument concerning immaterial entities or abilities is necessarily going to be *indirect,* it is crucial that we agree on the *logic* of indirect arguments applied to noncontroversial cases before we tackle a really tough case like the one we will consider presently.

The Turing Test

It is time to say something nice about Descartes. While contemporary Aristotelians trace much of the confusion of modern philosophy back to him, they fully endorse his contention that the use of language is *the* distinguishing characteristic of humans. Aristotelians and Cartesians are in complete agreement that the ability to use language is unique to humans. No other animal is capable of using language the way humans do. While other animals are clearly able to communicate, think, and make inferences, humans use words in a way that is different in *kind* from the way animals use signs to communicate or make inferences. To review, here are some of the unique ways humans use languages that we have already considered. We use language to:

- Define *what* things are by distinguishing between accidental properties and essential natures.
- Distinguish between the intension and extension of terms.
- Distinguish between cause and coincidence.
- Classify objects using subjunctive conditionals, e.g., humans know how to classify a baby born with a feather on its back even if no such baby exists.
- Reason about the un-*image*-able (chiliagons).
- Reflect upon our own existence (self-consciousness).

The distinction between the way animals use language and the way humans use language will be refined in the next chapter. For now, we will stick to these previously discussed points.

Alan Turing was a famous British mathematician. He was sure that Aristotle was wrong about the existence of immaterial minds, but he knew enough logic to understand that arguments in favor of immaterial minds were all indirect. Immaterial intellects, if they exist at all, exist "in" black boxes that can never be opened. So, following the principle that by their fruit (effects) you shall know them, Turing formulated what he thought would be a decisive proof that immaterial intellects don't exist. The central idea of his argument has come to be called the "Turing Test." It works like this: Create two "black boxes" with input and output slots. Then find pairs of Aristotelians, Cartesians, or any other philosophers who are firmly committed to the existence of immaterial minds and place one of them in one of the black boxes. In the other black box, place a computer. Finally, let the other Aristotelian, Cartesian, or other committed philosopher place a typed question in the input slots of either black box. If the philosopher was unable to consistently "unmask" the computer and find his philosophical partner, then the computer will have passed the "Imitation Game." Furthermore, Turing claimed, when a computer passes the test, it will no longer be rational to argue that there is an essential difference between the "mind" of a person and the "mind" of a computer. Since computers obviously lack an immaterial intellect, so must humans.

Now some philosophers, most famously John Searle, have argued that the test is invalid. Even if a computer could be programmed so that its answers were indistinguishable from human's, this would not show, according to Searle, that computers *understand* their responses. It is quite possible that a computer might one day be programmed so that it could type out appropriate responses to all questions, but that in itself proves nothing. When the computer typed the appropriate response, it did not *understand* the meaning of words it typed. All it did was mechanically manipulate symbols that were totally unintelligible to it.[8]

We mention Searle's argument only to set it aside. Like Descartes, Aristotelians believe that the ability to use a natural language decisively distinguishes humans from everything else. Aristotelians have no quibble with the principle that positing an unobserved entity is *only* justifiable if the effects observed cannot be explained in any other way. If a computer can be programmed to engage in written conversions in such a way that its responses are not discernibly different from humans, then the indirect argument for immaterial minds collapses, as there would no longer be something that could not be explained in wholly material terms.

We are not convinced by Searle's argument that, even after passing the Turing Test, computers nonetheless would lack "understanding." Imagine a teacher who suspects a student was cheating on a test. The standard test of teachers for unmasking cheaters is to ask the same sort of questions in different ways. If the student still is able to answer all the teacher's question satisfactorily, then it would be pure prejudice for the teacher to maintain that the student cheated. If a student can answer questions about an idea asked in several different ways, then the student must *understand* what he or she is saying and not "parroting" someone else's answers. In short, Aristotelians have no quibble with the validity of Turing's test.

Is the Turing Test Objective or Subjective?

Aristotelians, however, do have a quibble about the *nature* of the test. Turing and many others seem to think that the test is wholly objective in the sense that statistical analysis of the outcomes is all that is necessary to determine whether the test has been passed. The point of Turing's proposed test was to move the question, What's the difference between minds and brains? from the realm of endless philosophical discussion to the realm of questions that are, at least in principle, objectively decidable. Of course, Turing didn't think that "objectively decided" questions would produce universal consent, but he did think that if scientists and engineers actually built a machine that could pass his test, then only obscurantists would continue to contend that minds are more than brains.

Our point here is that there are really two issues that must be made "objectively decidable" for questions about minds to be removed from the realm of philosophical discussion. First, what does it mean to say that something is capable of rational thought? This question, Aristotelians believe, *is* objectively decidable in Turing's sense.

But Turing's test presupposes an answer to a second question that is not objectively decidable without much philosophical discussion. That second question is, What does it mean to say that something is a machine? If we can't answer that question, we obviously don't know what it means to "build a machine." Mining silicon and turning it into a computer is certainly "building a machine," but is a husband and wife deciding that it is time to "make a baby" also a case of "building a machine"? Now the point of this question is *not* to answer it in either the affirmative or negative, but only to make clear how the Turing Test answers one philosophical question only by raising a different philosophical issue.

In fact, Turing himself anticipated this sort of objection. Even before cloning was physically possible, Turing recognized that if biologists one day "grew" a human being from a single cell, presumably this person would be able to passing the Turing Test. Turing realized, however, that passing his test *in this way* would not put to rest the endless philosophical discussions about the body/mind problem. Those who contended that minds are more than brains would obviously not concede defeat at such a development. They would simply contend that "cloned people," just like people born in the normal fashion, have both a brain and an immaterial mind.

Turing's only response to this anticipated problem was to dismiss it. "Biological machines" are simply not allowed by Turing to participate in his test. What we wish to point out here is simply that distinction between "biological machines" and nonbiological machines brings in through the back door all the difficult philosophical issues we discussed in the previous chapters that Turing tried so hard to exclude from the front door.

Turing's Prediction

Turing wrote his article in 1950. In this justly famous essay, he not only proposed his test, he also outlined a process for programming computers to pass the test. Finally, he predicted that in fifty years his challenge would have been met, and that in the future only historians will be discussing arguments about immaterial minds. So how are the computer designers and programmers doing? In a word, poorly. No one is even close to creating "artificial intelligence," that is, programming a computer so that it can pass the Turing Test.

In fact, as the difficulty of satisfying the full-fledged Turing Test became more apparent, advocates of AI (artificial intelligence) began discussing intermediate steps in what came to be called the Modified Turing Test. The basic design is the same, but now there were rather strict restrictions placed on the questions and answers. First, all questions and answers must be four words or less. Second, all words used in questions and answers must be found on an agreed upon list of eight hundred words of basic English. Third, there would only be a series of forty questions and answers.

Now with such a restriction, it would seem that "brute force" would enable a computer to pass the simplified test. Here "brute force" refers to programming a computer with all possible combinations of meaningful first questions and then writing appropriate responses to each. Since each initial question is limited to four words out of a total list of only eight hundred, the number of possible first questions is large (something less than eight hundred to the fourth power) but finite. Once all first questions are answered, the computer is then programmed to do the same for each second question. Of course, now the number of responses necessary is even larger (eight hundred to the fourth power itself raised to the fourth power). But again, the number is finite and it is not conceptually impossible for computers to handle so many possibilities. The "brute force" solution to the Modified Turing Test simply repeats this process for all forty questions.

While it would be prodigiously boring to actually carry through such a program, it nonetheless appears to be a plausible strategy.[9] Though it is obvious that the number of programmed responses required to implement a "brute force" solution grows exponentially at each new set of questions, the defenders of AI continually remind us that the power of computers is also growing exponentially with each new generation. Again, while no research team would find such a project a worthy intellectual challenge, it seems to present no *conceptual* obstacles.

Better mathematicians, however, like Turing himself, understand that this would be a futile strategy for attacking even a highly restricted test. The number of seconds that have elapsed since the "Big Bang" is around 10^{19}. The number of "parroted" responses in a brute force solution to a Modified Turing Test is around 10^{30}! It isn't only the Luddites who are skeptical of claims that a "technological" breakthrough will someday enable a computer to pass a Modified Turing Test.

Even if we ignore these wholly quantifiable issues about the size of the difficulty, we must not forget that passing a Modified Turing Test is qualitatively different from passing a full-fledged Turing Test. The wonder of human language is not that there is an incredibly large number of different sentences (and hence, questions and answers) that can be formed; it is that there is an *infinite* number of different sentences that can be formed. Though the tune is getting old, it still rings true—since shape is not form, there can be no wholly *computational* solution to the Turing Test.

Promissory Materialism[10]

Our conclusions, again, are fairly modest. The unique abilities of humans to use natural languages constitute an indirect argument for an immaterial intellect. Furthermore, the argument originally propounded by Descartes has become stronger—not weaker—with the passage of time. Materialists have frequently written promissory notes, but Turing is the first to have attached a due date. The date has come due, but there is no cash to cover the note. Cognitive scientists are not significantly nearer to programming a computer that duplicates the linguistic abilities of an average five-year-old child than they were fifty years ago. Contrary to conventional wisdom, the force of the indirect argument for the immaterial intellect has increased, not decreased, with the passage of time. Therefore, we conclude that a serious investigation of the Aristotelian arguments for an immaterial intellect is in order, which is what we provide in the next chapter.

9

The Inadequacy of Materialism

No Soul, No Words

Though words are found everywhere, they are really quite extraordinary. Most people, along with many philosophers, fail to appreciate the amazing character of words because they have never asked what a word is. Examples of words are everywhere; definitions of words are rare.

Any philosophically adequate definition of words must capture the distinction between natural signs and intentional symbols. Natural signs name observable causal relations that do not depend upon the intentional actions of humans. Intentional symbols name formal relations that depend wholly on intentional acts since there is no shape that is the form (meaning) of a word.

Used as intentional symbols, words have extraordinary powers. We do not deny, however, that in special circumstances humans sometimes use words as natural signs.

With this distinction, we can make precise the difference between the way animals and humans use "language." Animals are fully able—in many cases, more able than humans—to read and understand natural signs, but only humans are able to read and understand intentional symbols.

Words embody concepts. Concepts are meanings that exist as a universal (not as a particular thing) in the immaterial intellect of humans, but it is important to note that not all mental objects (e.g. images and feelings) are immaterial.

Behaviorist philosophers have attempted to reduce concepts to behavioral dispositions. Their attempts, however, fail for two reasons. First, their argument is viciously circular. Second, they have confused the way we know the mental states of people and animals with the way the mental states of people and animals exist.

Finally, the (long awaited) argument for an immaterial agent intellect is produced. We close with a couple of philosophical parables to help us understand what is literally un-image-able and a response to objections.

Natural Signs and Intention Symbols

"The cause of the present difficulty," Aristotle writes at the beginning of the *Metaphysics,* "is not in the facts but in us. For as the eyes of bats are to the blaze of day, so is the reason in our soul to the things which are by nature most evident of all."[1] Here we have a classical expression of the fact that sometimes we don't see things that are as obvious as the nose on our face. Paradoxically, we often overlook the obvious in favor of the esoteric, foreign, and obscure.

Words are a good illustration of this. Because they are so common, provincial, and obvious, we seldom take the time to appreciate their wonder and power. Part of the reason we don't realize the awesome nature of words is that we rarely take the time and expend the effort necessary to understand *what* words are.

So what is a word? First, we must distinguish two closely related and commonly confused relations—the causal relation between natural signs and what they signify, and second, the noncausal relation between intentional symbols and what they intend. Here are some examples of natural signs:

- Clouds are a *sign* of rain.
- The yellow hue of her skin *means* she has hepatitis.
- The explosion of the pressure cooker is the *reason* spaghetti is plastered on the ceiling.

Natural signs exist because cause and effect relations exist in nature. When these natural relations are understood, we speak of signs, meanings, and reasons. We also speak of signs, meanings, and reasons when no natural (cause and effect) relation exists, but instead, a wholly *intentional* relation exists. For example,

- Drawing a cigarette in a circle with a line through it is a *sign* to prohibit smoking.

- "Procrastination" *means* the tendency to put off work or other undesirable tasks.
- Human understanding of universals is a *reason* Plato believed our souls to be immortal.

In each of these cases, the relation between the sign and the signified, the word and the meaning, the concept and the belief is a nonphysical relation. There is nothing about the physics of ink molecules on wood, paper, metal, or plastic that *makes* a circle with a line though it a symbol. Without the *intention* of the maker to create a symbol to prohibit smoking, a picture with a circle and a line would not *be* a symbol.

Similarly, the specific acoustical disturbances that make up the sound "procrastination" do not *physically* produce a meaning. As we have said many times before, there is no shape that is the form (meaning) of a word.

In the last example, the relation between "understanding universals" and the "immortality of the soul" is one of premise and conclusion, not cause and effect. The premise does not physically cause assent to the conclusion. If it did, shouting the argument in the presence of materialistically-minded philosophers would eventually cause them to believe that they were wrong and that the soul really is immortal. Of course, this isn't the case. Rational arguments do not physically compel. In all of these cases, the relation is wholly intentional or formal, and hence, it cannot be understood in material terms.

There is, however, a qualification that should be added to this last sentence. There are special circumstances in which an intentional symbol *functions* as a natural sign. Pavlov famously demonstrated that dogs could be conditioned to salivate at the mere sound of a bell. In essence, Pavlov's conditioning established a causal relation in dogs between the ringing of a bell and the presence of food. In our terms, a ringing bell became a natural sign for food; it was not an intentional symbol for food. Given the laboratory conditioning of these dogs, their physiological response of salivating was no different than ordinary dogs barking in fearful situations. When the evolutionary predecessors of domestic dogs barked in the wild to warn other members in their pack of danger, their barks were not an intentional symbol of danger the way ink in the shape of "Danger" is an intentional symbol of danger. Rather, barks are a natural sign of danger. In the same way that the ringing bell became a natural sign of food to Pavlov's dogs, the barking of a member of a pack of dogs became a natural sign of danger to the other members of the pack.[2]

In nonphilosophical contexts no harm is caused by using the word "means" to refer to the relation between both causes and their effects (natural signs) and symbols and the meaning (intentional symbols), but in philosophical contexts, it is absolutely crucial that we be conscious of this ambiguity. To say that one dog's bark *means* danger to the other members of the pack is no less a legitimate use of "means" in ordinary contexts than to say that procrastination *means* the tendency to put off unpleasant tasks. The only point we wish to insist upon here is that these two uses of the word "mean" are equivocal. The meaning of causal signs and the meaning of intentional symbols refer to two distinct *kinds* of relations.

We should also be clear that these two distinct meanings of "mean" are not coextensive to their application to animals on the one hand and humans on the other. Humans, no less than dogs, can be conditioned to respond to a certain stimulus in a wholly causal and predictable fashion. This sort of conditioning can take place either in the laboratory of a psychologist or in the ordinary world in which we live. For example, after many years of marriage, husbands and wives often perform actions that produce a conditioned response in their mate. Such actions can be either nonverbal or verbal. Some farm wives used to ring a bell to call their husbands to dinner, others simply yelled "Dinner!" Over the years, many husbands undoubtedly developed a conditioned response to a ringing bell or a shout of "dinner" just like Pavlov's dogs. In other words, there are special situations in which "dinner" functions not as a word (intentional symbol) but rather as a cause (natural sign) to produce an effect, but such situations are atypical. In the vast majority of cases, words function as wholly intentional symbols where their meaning is independent of the physical response they produce in others.[3] It is in these typical situations that words are awesome.

Finally, we must remember the difference between distinctions of kind and distinctions of degree. People frequently speak of "rudimentary," "incipient," or "elementary" languages. This is especially true of animal behaviorists. Yet all of these imply that the distinction between natural signs and intentional symbols is one of degree, not kind. The only way this distinction can be one of degree is if everything else we have said about the distinction of form versus shape, essential nature versus accidental characteristics, extension versus intension, and perceptual versus conceptual knowledge is totally wrong. Otherwise, it is simple confusion on the part of animal behaviorists to speak of the rudimentary, incipient, or elementary linguistic abilities of nonhuman animals. Nonhuman animals either can or cannot use language as intentional symbols to refer to that which cannot be perceived.

The Wonder of Words

What is so wonderful about words? It is that words (and all other intentional symbols) are the very place where the immaterial realm of the intellect affects, and is affected by, the material realm of nature. When words are functioning as intentional symbols, immaterial concepts have become "embodied."

Once again, we must exercise extreme care in our definition of "concept." There are four parts to the definition of concept as used by Aristotle.

First, the meaning of a word is identical to the concept it conveys. Concepts are the mental tools we use to answer questions like: "What is that?" If a child points to a rabbit and asks—"What is that?" —the correct answer would be "rabbit," "conejo," or "lapin," depending on which language the child understands. While these are three different words, the *concept* they intend is the same. The converse is also the case. Not only are meanings concepts, concepts are meanings. In short, concepts and meanings are identical.[4]

When Aristotelians say that concepts *are* meanings, they are not saying that concepts *have* meaning. It is common to say things like "Democracy didn't have much meaning in Nazi Germany" or "Freedom was without meaning in the Soviet Union." Obviously, when we utter sentences like this we are not suggesting that a person physically located within the geographic boundaries of Germany during the years of Hitler's rule would have difficulty understanding the meaning of the word "democracy." All we mean is that Germany, during Hitler's rule, did not practice democracy in the fullest sense, even though Hitler came to power as a result of a popular election. Similar things could be said about freedom and the Soviet Union.

In other words, to say that concepts *are* meanings is simply to say that concepts are the definitions of things. The concept of a house—a shelter in which people live—is what *makes* something a house. Using the distinctions of the first part of this book, we can say that concepts are the essences or forms of things. Of course, when we say that the concept of a house is what *makes* something a house, we are not referring to either the architect, contractor, carpenter, or physical material out of which houses are composed.

Once again, we must be careful of equivocations. "Makes" has two distinct meanings. First, it can refer to either the material or agent that *causes* a thing to come into existence. Second, it can refer to the essence (form) of a thing that *constitutes* its distinct nature (definition). Thus, in the previous paragraph when we said, "The concept of a house is what *makes* something a house," we were using "makes" to refer to the definition of a house, not the cause of its existence. When we speak of the definition of a house, we are using this term in the full Aristotelian sense in which words define *things*, not just other words.

Second, concepts exist as universals; things exist as particulars. A universal is that which all members of a species, group, or class have in common. Every hammer is a tool designed for pounding, and every animal is a living being capable of consciousness. Universals are the concepts (essences) that humans are able to abstract from groups of individuals. Here "abstract" does not mean either vague or ambiguous, nor does it mean abstruse. It simply means "to draw out or separate." Humans abstract a concept from a thing when they consider separately one of its essential aspects or properties.[5]

Suppose a child who is just learning to talk points to a tree and asks, "What is that?" The parent says, "That is a tree." In this response, the parent is using the word "tree" to instill in the child a universal concept. The individual tree to which the child is pointing has a particular shape, size, and color. The universal concept of a tree, however, has no shape, size, or color. If it did, it would only refer to the single (or small number of trees) that had precisely the same shape, size, and color of the tree at which the child is currently looking. "Tree," however, refers to a whole range of objects that come in all varieties of shapes, sizes, and colors. The universal concept of "treeness" is the essential nature (form) of a tree that the mind draws out by a process of abstraction, while at the same time it ignores the particular shapes, colors, and sizes of individual trees.

Third, while all concepts are mental objects, all mental objects are not concepts. Our minds are populated with many things besides concepts, for example, feelings and images. A baby can *feel* love long before he or she has a concept of love. So too, babies have *images* of rabbits before they understand what a rabbit is, i.e., before they have a concept of a rabbit.

Understanding the distinction between feelings and concepts is not especially difficult, though we often fail to observe the distinction in practice. Puppies presumably feel loved by their mothers just as do many babies, but human babies, unlike puppies, can mature to a stage in which they not only have feelings of love but they also know what love is.

It is difficult to maintain this distinction. We live in a culture in which concepts are often reduced to feelings. For example, many people now seem to believe that if Fred *feels* offended by something Sally said, then Sally must have said something offensive. Earlier generations' concepts of "offensive" was objective—there was an agreed upon set of actions that were considered impolite, and no single individual could add or subtract from that set at will. Today "offensive" refers primarily to a unique subjective state of individuals, and hence, we no longer have a concept of offensive.

The distinction between concepts and images is more troublesome.[6] Remember our previous discussion of chiliagons (thousand-sided objects)? There is an obvious difference between an *image* of a chiliagon and a *concept* of a chiliagon. Most people have little difficulty forming a fairly clear mental image of a five-sided object, but no person sincerely claims to be able to form a clear mental *image* of a thousand-sided object. Nonetheless, it is not especially difficult to form a clear *concept* of a chiliagon. As we said earlier, a good carpenter could, for example, easily calculate the angles at which to cut the perimeter of a large thousand-sided house. He would simply reason that since a four-sided house must have its perimeter cut at 90 degrees (360 divided by 4); a thousand-sided object must have its perimeter cut at .36 degrees (360 divided by 1000). Examples like this illustrate the fact that humans are able to reason about things using concepts that are utterly un-*image*-able.

Finally, while concepts exist and are real, they do not exist the way material things exist. Rabbits exist in nature; our concept of a rabbit only exists in our mind. Rabbits exist whether or not anyone is thinking about rabbits; they exist independent of our thinking about them. Concepts of rabbits only exist when a person is thinking about rabbits; their existence is wholly dependent upon a person's mental state. Rabbits have weight, size, shape, color, etc. The concept of a rabbit has no weight, size, smell, color, etc.

In short, concepts, as they exist in people's minds, are immaterial, and not just in the sense that the properties of physical things are not themselves physical. While the whiteness of a white car is not strictly speaking a physical thing, it is a property of physical things that can be captured on a camcorder. To say that concepts are immaterial in the sense intended here is to say that individual concepts are neither the cause nor the effect of any particular *kind*[7] of thing that is physical. In other words, there is no predictable sequence of events capable of being captured by our super-camcorder in which a concept and a thing are causally related or even constantly conjoined. Therefore, concepts can only be known indirectly; they can never be experienced or observed. For example, we only know that children have a concept of an animal when they are able to answer appropriately an indeterminate set of questions about animals. Or adding to the discussion of the last chapter, we know that either a child or a computer has understood the concept "animal" when they can pass the Turing Test.

Concepts As Tools

The fact that concepts are immaterial has caused them to be both hated and loved by philosophers.

For Plato and Descartes, they were an object of love. Plato's preference for the world of preexistent Ideas led him to argue that "dogness" somehow existed prior to dogs and in fact was more real than individual dogs. According to Plato, true knowledge of dogs was to be discovered in the study of the Idea of dogs, not dogs themselves.

Descartes's notion of "clear and distinct" ideas had similar implications. As we have already seen, according to Descartes, all human beings had direct access to the realm of mental ideas and images. In fact, the realm of ideas and images is the *only* realm they had direct access to. *Actual* dogs were only an inference made from our mental images of dogs via our clear and distinct idea of a good God and an argument that such a God would not permit us to be deceived by our clear and distinct ideas.

Aristotle, however, would have nothing to do with such an elevation of the realm of ideas and the corresponding depreciation of the natural realm of physical dogs and cats, nor would he be willing to say that our concepts are open to direct observation. Because they are immaterial, it is obvious that concepts cannot be seen with physical eyes. Furthermore, Aristotle was insistent that concepts cannot be seen by the "mind's eye." In short, concepts are not subject to either introspection or extrospection. Concepts, Aristotle consistently taught, are never *that which* we understand. Rather, they are always *that by which* we understand.[8] Like good eye glasses, concepts work best when they are *not* seen.

While concepts are mental objects (or better—mental tools), they are not mental objects the way pains and other feelings are mental. A pain in the back cannot be directly observed by the doctor, but it can be directly observed by the patient. Everyone is at one time or the other directly conscious of pain. Concepts (except perhaps in certain sorts of mental illnesses) are never something that we are conscious *of*. Again, like a good pair of clean and unscratched glasses, concepts are that *by* which we see, they are not that *which* we see. When we can see our glasses, that is, when they are dirty or scratched, then we are inhibited, not helped, in seeing the world beyond our lenses. So too, concepts are tools we use to understand the world in which we live. They are not the *things* that we understand. Though we often speak (loosely) of having difficulty understanding the concept of quarks, what we really mean is that it is hard to understand quarks.

Not All Mental Objects Are Immaterial

We made it a point earlier to argue that all mental objects are not concepts. Furthermore, Aristotle and Descartes drew quite different lines separating the material and immaterial realms. According to Aristotle and Aquinas, all mental objects are not immaterial. For them, the realm of the mental or of consciousness is *not* coextensive with the realm of the immaterial. As we just said, pains and other feelings, images, and even our habitual reaction to events that are constantly conjoined are, according to Aristotle and Aquinas, mental phenomena that are in principle reducible to physical events and their properties. Only when abstracting concepts or reasoning about concepts did they believe that an immaterial mind was necessary. This has largely changed since the time of Descartes.

Today, when philosophers ask whether the mind is a material or immaterial entity, they typically lump feelings, images, pains, and concepts into a single category called "consciousness." Many philosophers today believe that science can give a wholly naturalistic (i.e., materialistic) account of consciousness, while a few do not. It is virtually impossible, however, to find a contemporary philosopher (outside of the few remaining Thomists like Maritain, Gilson, and Adler) who answer this question the way Aristotle and Aquinas did. Aristotelians and Thomists have always believed that feelings, images, and even pains were solely the result of causal relations and are in principle wholly explainable in physical terms. Only concepts required an immaterial explanation for reasons we will examine in a moment.

Descartes initiated this conflation of concepts and all other "mental objects" into the single category of something called "consciousness." But as either an innocent error or, in a strange sort of way, an implicit fear of Aristotle's arguments, the error has been perpetuated by contemporary materialists. By treating concepts as simply one undistinguished member of a large group of things called "mental objects," it becomes easier to accommodate concepts in a wholly material metaphysics. As we just said, even Aristotelians give a wholly materialistic account of "consciousness" when it only includes feelings, memories, images, and pains. Thus, it makes sense that today's materialists would treat concepts as if they were simply one of the many indistinct mental objects included in "consciousness." After all, if four out of five members of a class can be explained in wholly material terms, then isn't it just a matter of time before the fifth and final member will also be explained materialistically?

The problem with this sort of reasoning is that it assumes that the Cartesian definition of "consciousness" really divides nature at its joints. Only then would it be reasonable to conclude that all members of a class will eventually be discovered to share a wholly materialistic explanation. But Descartes's definition of consciousness, if Aristotle and Aquinas are correct, is nothing more than a "social construct," and hence nothing of any philosophical or scientific interest follows from the argument of the previous paragraph.

Here is an analogy: Suppose a new word, "Ork," is created. This new category includes (i.e., its extension)—computers, programmable coffee pots, automobiles, railway trains, sophisticated time-keeping devices in hospitals, and pendulum-powered cuckoo clocks. One day someone says, "Computers, programmable coffee pots, railway trains, and sophisticated time keeping devices might not work in the new millennium." Interesting observation. Someone else then reasons, "Well, since everything just mentioned is an ork, and since my pendulum-powered cuckoo clock is also an ork, maybe it will not work in the new millennium." Obviously, such reasoning is silly because the category of "orks" is nothing more than a human invention. Aristotelians claim that "consciousness," as Cartesians use the term to include images, feelings, memories, perceptions, *and* conceptions, is itself a human invention that has no basis in reality.

Let us summarize this portion of the argument. If concepts really *were* nothing more than natural signs and in the same category as all other mental events, then our conceptual understanding would be reducible to either physical events in the brain or to dispositions to behave in a particular fashion. But concepts are not simply natural signs. Therefore, all attempts to reduce them to either brain processes or behavioral dispositions will fail.

We will first consider the reduction of all mental processes to behavioral dispositions.[9]

Two Reductionist Theories

Behaviorists argue that "mental objects," including concepts, are not things, but instead, they are names that signify dispositions to behave in a particular way. Suppose someone thought that the word "brittleness" named a *thing*. If they then asked, "*Where* is the brittleness in this piece of glass?" such a question would be impossible to answer, but not because the question was profound or because there was still much to be learned about glass. The question is only difficult to answer because it is confusing. "Brittle" means "easy to break or shatter," and "brittleness" is nothing more than the adjective turned into a noun. But the fact that we can turn an adjective into a noun does not mean that there is some "thing" which the new noun names.

Similarly, say behaviorists, philosophers and common folk have asked confusing questions about what words like "concept" and "intellect" signify. Because these words are grammatically nouns, people have mistakenly concluded that they must refer to things. Hence they have asked questions like "Where are concepts?" or "How does the intellect act on the brain?" Unable to discover good scientific answers to such questions, confused philosophers have concluded that there must be some nonmaterial realm in which such things reside.

Contemporary behaviorists respond that such reasoning is grounded in a "category mistake."[10] "Concept" and "intellect" do not name things. Rather, they function like adjectives to refer to the dispositional properties of humans. Questions about concepts and intellects are only hard to answer because the questions themselves are confused.

Now there is confusion here, but much of it lies with the behaviorists. The first problem is that behaviorists have confused natural signs with intentional symbols. "Brittleness" can be analyzed in wholly dispositional terms because there is a common and typical behavior of all things that are brittle—they break when struck by a hard object. Words and concepts, however, cannot be analyzed in wholly dispositional terms because there is no common and typical behavior of people who understand a word or concept. Different people respond to words in all sorts of different ways, even when their understanding of the word's meaning is the same.

For example, men and women have the same understanding of the words "men" and "women." Yet, when they observe these words on restroom doors, they respond quite differently. Unlike glass that typically breaks when struck by a hard object, there is no typical response of humans upon seeing the word "Men" posted on a door.

Now a behaviorist would respond that these differences of behavior can be accounted for by the fact that men and women are different, just like tempered and nontempered glass. Men are disposed to act in one way when they see the word "Men" posted on a door and women are disposed to act differently.

But is this true? People are only disposed to act in the same way to "verbal stimuli" if they share the same beliefs, priorities, and desires. For example, a free-thinking and unconventional woman who knows exactly what the words "men" and "women" mean might refuse to stand in a line at the women's restroom during the half time of a football game and instead use the men's restroom as a symbolic protest against irrational standards of public decorum.

At this point, behaviorists might argue that a person's beliefs, priorities, and desires should themselves be analyzed in behavioral terms. That is, we need to distinguish the behavioral dispositions of freethinking women from those of more conservatively-minded women in the same way that we distinguished between tempered and nontempered glass.

But now the behaviorist's argument has become viciously circular. To see why this is so, two examples are required. First example: Consider two soldiers starting a long march. Both Peter and Paul read and *understand* in the same way the words on the sign—"Contaminated Water." Peter desires good health and hence refrains from drinking the water. Paul is tired and wants an excuse for returning to camp, so he drinks the water. Thus, once again, "understands the sign," cannot be analyzed in behavioral terms.

Okay, so let's try to analyze *desires* in behavioral terms. Second example: Doug and David are tired of marching and want to turn back. Doug understands English and sees the sign that says "Contaminated Water," so he drinks. David does not understand English, so even though he sees the sign, he does not drink because what he sees produces no such disposition. Even though their desires are the same, their dispositions are different because they have different understandings.

In conclusion, people with the same desires are only disposed to act in the same way *if* they have the same understandings, and people with the same understandings are only disposed to act in the same way *if* they have the same desires. The circle is vicious.[11]

Of course, if we posit two individuals with an *identical* set of understandings and desires, then they would be disposed to act in the same way. But now, "identical" functions like the "strong enough" in the weight lifter's boast: "If I were strong enough, I could bench press a Mack truck." Similarly, it is true, but vacuous, to argue that if two individuals had "identical" understandings and desires, then they would be disposed to act in identical ways. There is no way to identify such individuals other than to identify two individuals who are always "disposed to act in the same way." Thus, the sentence, "Two people with identical understandings and desires will be disposed to act in the same way," becomes equivalent to the trivial tautology—"Two people who are disposed to act in the same way are disposed to act in the same way."

The second confusion surrounding the behaviorist analysis[12] is that they have confused the way we *know* the mental states of people and animals with the way the mental states of people and animals *exist*. Behaviorism is thus one further instance of the post-Cartesian tendency to confuse epistemology with ontology. It is true that we can only know of someone else's mental states *through* their behavior (including verbal responses), but people's beliefs and pains are not their behavior. In effect, the behaviorist argument is that behavior *constitutes* beliefs and pains; the truth is that beliefs and pains *cause* behavior.[13]

The behaviorist's confusion of constitutive relations and causal relations led other materialists to *identify* understanding not with outward behavior but with inner states and processes of the brain. In this theory—usually called the Identity Theory—the relation between brain processes and/or states is thought to be the same as the relation between the Evening Star and the Morning Star. That is, these are simply two different ways to refer to the same object.

This reductionist attempt has the virtue of acknowledging the causal role of ideas and feelings, but in this case the confusion is between final causes and efficient causes. The identity theory assumes that intentional symbols produce behavior *in the same way* that natural signs produce behavior. Our argument will be that intentional symbols do cause behavior, but that these are not *per se* efficient causes, as is the behavior caused by natural signs, but explaining this point will have to wait until chapters 10 and 11.

The Agent Intellect

Words exist on the cusp of the material and immaterial realms. Words are themselves physical things, but they are not *merely* physical. The concepts words embody transcend the material realm, yet the concepts that name the form or essence of things do not exist *apart* from things and thinkers. Concepts that exist "in" words and the essences that exist "in" things do not exist as a *part* of words and things. It is not until the human intellect separates the wheat from the chaff—the form from the shape—that concepts have anything approaching an existence of their own.[14]

Before we say more about the human's unique ability to abstract forms from things,[15] we need to consider once more the fundamental principle of common sense that nothing comes from nothing. In traditional Aristotelian terms, this is the principle that the actual must *precede* the potential. Unless something actually exists, nothing else exists potentially. An actual man can build a house; a potential man cannot. An actual cat can catch a mouse; a merely potential cat does nothing. An actual dollar can purchase a cup of coffee; a potential dollar only exists in the dreams of the homeless.

Yet, there is an ambiguity in the meaning of "precedes." Precedence can be either in *time* or what we will call *rank*.[16] Generals surpass privates in rank, but in order of time, a person is a private before becoming a general. So too, an idea of a potential house exists *temporally* in the mind of an architect before the house is actually built, but a potential house in the mind of an architect shelters no one, not even the architect. The only reason we understand what it is to be a potential house is that we have first understood what it is to be an actual house. To say that nothing comes from nothing means that we must understand the potential in terms of the actual, and not vice versa. We do not understand what it is to be an actual house because we have first understood what it is to be a potential house. Instead, we understand what it is to be a potential house because we have first understood what it is to be an actual house. In order of *time*, a chicken egg precedes any particular chicken, but in order of *rank*, the actual chicken must precede the egg.

So too, in order of *time*, essences (forms) existed in things long before humans existed, but until human intellects conceptually separated a thing's form from its shape, the thing's essence was a mere potential object of understanding. Therefore, in order of rank, it is the agent that performs the separation that deserves precedence.[17]

To explain the human capacity to abstract a thing's form from its shape, Aristotle postulated what he called the agent intellect. The name is descriptive. It is called the *agent* intellect to emphasize the fact that the human soul is not just a passive recipient of observations, but instead, that the human soul actively turns observations into in-*form*-ation. And it is called an *intellect* to emphasize that it is not mere precepts or images (shapes) that are understood, but instead, it is the concepts (forms or essences) that the human soul has grasped.

Finally, Aristotle argued that the agent intellect that is capable of understanding universals (unlike the animal soul that can only know the particulars it observes) is not itself a material organ or the property of a material organ. Since this final claim is so controversial, unfashionable, and contrary to the conventional wisdom of our time, a step-by-step presentation of its premises and inference is in order.

The Argument For an Immaterial Soul[18]

1. All relations are either physical or nonphysical (i.e., intentional).
2. The relation between a word and its meaning is not a physical relation.
3. The person who understands the meaning of a word is active, while the word itself is passive.
4. That which is capable of action must *subsist*.

5. Therefore, the agent intellect that understands words must be immaterial and subsistent.

The first premise is simply an instance of the laws of excluded middle and a stipulation to call the nonphysical relations between symbols and their meaning an "intentional relation."

The second premise merely restates the distinction discussed at the start of this chapter between natural signs and intentional symbols. Natural signs (causes) *do* stand in a physical relation vis-à-vis reference (effect), but intentional symbols are not natural signs. As we have said many times, there is no physical shape that is the form (meaning) of a word. Obviously something that is nonphysical cannot stand in a *physical* relation to something else. Ironically, the second premise merely insists on what materialist critics of dualism have said all along: it is impossible to understand how an immaterial mind could have a *predictable* physical effect on the brain.

The third premise makes explicit what we might call the "direction-of-action" between intentional symbols and people. People *understand* intentional symbols; it is not the case that intentional symbols *understand* people.

The fourth premise restates the Aristotelian principle that nothing comes from nothing, that is, the actual must precede the merely potential. For a thing to act upon something else, it must first *be* (subsist) before it can act.

Finally, the conclusion follows deductively from the premises.[19]

Some Objections Considered

So what are we to make of this argument?

First, it should be considered as a philosophical hypothesis. The agent intellect is postulated for one and only one reason: we have no better way to explain the fact that humans are able to understand intentional symbols. Aristotelians do not pretend that the existence of immaterial and subsistent agent intellects is a conceptual necessity beyond doubt. Conceptual necessities are those truths that cannot be denied without contradiction. Stock examples of conceptual necessities are "Not all twenty-dollar bills are counterfeit" and "Not all statements are false." The statement "Immaterial agent intellects exist" is not such a conceptual necessity.

Unlike wholly conceptual arguments, the philosophical hypothesis we have just outlined is certainly refutable. Many philosophers have questioned the claim entailed in the second premise that understanding the meaning of words or essence of things is not a physical cause and effect relation. But we have already considered the standard criticisms of the second premise throughout the first six chapters, and we have little more to say than to repeat: form is not shape, and there is no shape that is the form of a either a word or any other essential nature. Since words and living beings undeniably exist, and since there is no physical description of what it is *to be* a word or to be a living being, it follows that our understanding of words and living beings cannot be a wholly physical relation. How can the merely physical *understand* the nonphysical?

Though the question is partially rhetorical, it is not intended to be a discussion stopper. Aristotelians will not obstinately maintain their position in the face of all conceivable evidence. After all, many dualists ask, "How can a wholly physical event like the firing of a neuron in the brain be a pain, that is, something that we feel?" On this question, Aristotelians side with the materialists. Both say, "We don't fully understand how this is possible, but we are working on it." Of course, this sounds slightly lame to dualists, as it should if it stands by itself and isn't fleshed out with scientific details. So, lest Aristotelians be accused of hypocrisy, they must be willing to specify the sorts of evidence that would refute their claim that conceptual thought can't be reduced to brain processes.

Here is a list of specifics that, if proven, would refute Aristotle's theory:

1. Demonstrate that nonhuman animals are capable of understanding words as intentional symbols as opposed to causal signs. As we argued in chapter 6, doing so only requires that a nonhuman be taught to respond appropriately to a question or statement containing the word *tomorrow*.
2. Demonstrate that a computer is capable of passing the Turing Test.
3. Produce a logically consistent and philosophically more comprehensive and coherent account of the two fundamental facts of common experience that we have been considering throughout this book—that form is not shape, and that both are real.

Aristotelians, however, will not surrender their position in the face of a mere boast or promise that scientists and/or philosophers will at some future time produce one or all of the above demonstrations.

Two Philosophical Parables

Even if the reader grants all of the above, two gnawing doubts remain: What exactly is the relation among the agent intellect, the human brain, and the forms humans understand? and Is an agent intellect that *sub-sists* any different from Descartes's immaterial mind?

While there is no simple answer to the first question, there are analogies that might help. Here's one: The agent intellect is the principal or primary cause of understanding forms and the brain is its instrument. In other words, the brain is like a violin, the agent intellect like a violinist, and the actual understanding of forms is like the song produced when a violinist plays her violin.

To be an instrumental cause, three conditions must be met. First, both the agent and the instrument of the agent must be *necessary* conditions for the effect produced. If a violinist could produce a violin's song without a violin, then she would be a sufficient condition for the production of song. And if a violin could produce a song without a violinist, then it would be the sufficient condition.

Second, while neither the agent nor the instrument by themselves can be a sufficient condition, together they are a sufficient condition.

Third, there is an inequality of conceptual rank between the two necessary conditions—the agent is the active condition, while the instrument of the agent is the passive condition. While the violinist and violin both need each other to produce a violin's song, they do not need each other in the same way. Violinists *use* violins, but violins do not *use* violinists.

Thus, we can say three things about the relation between the physical body, the agent intellect, and actual understanding: (1) the agent intellect is a necessary condition for understanding; (2) together with the physical body as its instrument, understanding becomes actual; and (3) in the act of understanding, the agent intellect is using the physical body but not vice versa.

The second question is more difficult. In fact, the claim that the agent intellect is like a violinist playing a violin seems to exacerbate the problem of distinguishing Aristotle's position from Descartes's. The relation between a violinist and a violin seems to be no different than the relation between a captain and his ship. Doesn't likening the agent intellect to a violinist turn humans into angels?

No. Agent intellects *subsist*, but they cannot exist fully apart from their bodies. This means that agent intellects are *really* active when joined to the body—they are not mere fluff or foam going along for a ride on a wave (what philosophers call epiphenomena).[20] It also means that they are potentially active after the body dies *if* they are rejoined to an appropriate body once again. Only the agent intellect in union with the body constitutes a fully existing human being.

Another music parable may help. When Beethoven first composed and played the "Ode to Joy," a new song came into existence. This song, when it is being played, is composed of form and matter. The form of the song is the unique set of mathematical relations that exist between the notes. The matter of the song is the acoustical disturbances that are created by the musical instruments. Each time the instruments are finished playing, the song (which is the union of form and matter) also ends. Therefore, if the earth and all its musical instruments are destroyed once and for all, Beethoven's "Ode to Joy"—as a substantial unity of form and matter—will also be destroyed. Yet, even the total destruction of the entire physical universe will not destroy the mathematical relations that Beethoven created that make the "Ode to Joy" the particular song that it is. This set of formal relations is incorruptible, even though the substantial unity of form and matter may never exist again.

Similarly, all human beings begin at birth to create a set of understandings about themselves and the world in which they live. Together with these beliefs and opinions, the choices people make create a set of attitudes and habits that partially determine all their future choices and actions. These two elements—belief and opinions, attitudes and habits—make each human being the unique person he or she is.[21] This set of understandings and choices constitute each person's *individual* "form." In other words, being a rational animal makes us *what* we are—human beings. Our individual set of understandings and choices makes us *who* we are. It is this set of beliefs, opinions, attitudes, and habits that *subsists* even after the body dies. Apart from a body, however, no human being actually exists.[22] Only if, by some supernatural act, an individual's subsistent set of understandings and choices is reunited with a body will that individual obtain immortality.

Aristotelians Are More Than "Cowardly Dualists"

Committed dualists will probably remain unsatisfied. "How," they will say, "is this Thomistic reading of Aristotle all that different from Descartes's? This notion of a subsistent (though not fully existing) agent intellect seems suspiciously vague, nor does your equivocal defense of the immortality of the soul do full justice to our spiritual dignity. To tell the truth, after all your Descartes-bashing, your conclusion sounds more like a cowardly defense of dualism than a third, distinct alternative to materialism."

These observations deserve a response.

First, let us again remember that Aristotle and Descartes drew quite different boundaries between the material and immaterial. Descartes's lumping of all thoughts, feelings, images and beliefs into a single category now called "consciousness" has serious and subversive implica-

tions with regard to the "spiritual dignity" of humans. Cartesian dualists are caught on the horns of a dilemma. If it really is consciousness
that distinguishes humans from all other animals, then dualists must
follow Descartes and maintain that dogs and cats feel no pain when
kicked or hit by a car. But is it really a defense of human dignity to argue
that across all times and cultures our species has been completely mistaken about other animals' ability to feel pain? On the other hand, if
dualists retain the common sense conviction that dogs and cats *do* feel
pain, then by Descartes's argument dogs and cats must also have an
immaterial soul. What then is the difference between the "spiritual"
nature of humans and dogs or cats?

Second, the charge that Aristotle's conception of the soul is no more
than an equivocal defense of immortality, it must be admitted, is at least
half true. A few paragraphs earlier we said that the unique set of beliefs,
habits, and attitudes that each of us create for ourselves establishes *who*,
as opposed to *what*, we are. We also compared the unique set of beliefs,
habits, and attitudes that we die with to the set of mathematical relations that exist among the notes in a song. Both exist as a set of purely
formal relations that, once created, are impossible to destroy, but a set
of notes, by themselves and apart from any instantiation as actual sounds,
has only a poor and shadowy sort of existence. So too, the formal relations that exist among the beliefs, habits, and attitudes that we die with
can never be destroyed. As is often said, the memories others have of us
are immortal, but existence as a "memory" is a poor and shadowy sort
of existence.

As a pagan, Aristotle could carry the argument no further, but Thomists
lay claim to a further resource, namely, divine revelation. True, they say,
my existence in the memory of other people is not real existence as a
human being, but we believe that God, at the end of the age and by his
supernatural power, will reunite with a new body this subsistent set of
formal relations that each of us had at the moment of our death. It is
only then, with this new, resurrected body, that we will again exist as a
human being.

Clearly this last paragraph mingles philosophical and theological
arguments in a fashion contrary to our promise at the start to remain
wholly philosophical, so all talk about an omnipotent God resurrecting
the dead must be understood hypothetically. That is, *if* we assume for
the sake of argument that the Biblical claims concerning the resurrection of the dead are true, what follows that is of philosophical interest?

Philosophically it appears that the Thomistic understanding of human
nature is subject to the same sort of criticism it just leveled at the Cartesian—namely, dogs and cats are not really different from humans because
they too create their own unique set of formal relations that subsist for-

ever. If a set of musical notes constitutes a set of formal relations that cannot be destroyed, and if each person's beliefs, habits, and attitudes also constitute a set of subsistent relations, then wouldn't the beliefs, habits, and attitudes of a particular dog, say Lassie, also constitute a unique and "immortal" set of formal relations? In short, if humans have immortal souls, doesn't Lassie also have one?

The philosophical answer is "no," and here the resources Thomists find in Aristotle *are* sufficient. Dogs and cats are certainly conscious in the sense that they have feelings, memories, and awareness of the world in which they live. There is no evidence, however, that any nonhuman animals are self-conscious. The reason is simple. To be self-conscious, an animal must not only demonstrate that it is capable of having wants, knowledge, and beliefs. It must also demonstrate reflexive knowledge, i.e., that it *knows* that it knows, or that it *knows* what it believes. But reflexive knowledge presupposes conceptual understanding, and as we argued in chapter 6, there is no evidence that any nonhuman animal can understand even a simple concept like "yesterday" or "tomorrow."

The lack of conceptual understanding and the corresponding lack of self-consciousness has immediate and direct philosophical implications concerning the possible resurrection of nonhuman souls. Given the non-rational nature of dogs, the best God could do would be to create a *duplicate* of Lassie, i.e., a dog with the precise set of beliefs, knowledge, and preferences that Lassie had when she died. Not even an omnipotent God could *resurrect* Lassie the way Christians believe he will resurrect humans. Lassie, being a nonhuman animal, lacks conceptual understanding and therefore could never *know* that she is the same dog that she was when she died. Such knowledge presupposes the understanding of "yesterday." Though this is a fairly simple concept, for all the reasons we have already given, "yesterday" is clearly a concept that transcends any sort of knowledge that might be captured by the most sophisticated camcorder or the smartest of nonhuman animals.

Unlike nonrational animals, humans have both perceptual and conceptual understanding. This makes us capable of self-knowledge, and for animals capable of self-knowledge, a reembodiment of a subsistent set of beliefs, habits, and attitudes would be more than the creation of an exact duplicate. Conceptual understanding makes genuine resurrection possible. Persons who awake in the new heavens and new earth with exactly the same set of beliefs, habits, and attitudes they had before will know immediately that their hope for their *own* resurrection has become a reality.

But issues concerning the possibility of personal immortality jump the gun just a bit. The real philosophical difference between Cartesian and Aristotelian souls, and this is our third point, is found in the difference between the way they *act* here on earth. Descartes's dualism requires "gaps" in the nexus of physical causes. Without a pineal gland or some other "place" to connect, Cartesian minds would be totally ineffectual. Aristotle's agent intellect acts on bodies in a quite different way. While Cartesian minds and Aristotelian agent intellects are both immaterial, only agent intellects are able to act on bodies without requiring an exception to the principle that every physical event has a physical cause. The last two chapters flesh out this point.

10

The Bogy of Mechanism

Why Our Actions Will
Always Be Unpredictable

Clouds are not clocks, and even though the motion of both clouds and clocks is wholly determined by antecedent physical causes, only the motion of clocks is mechanistic and predictable. At least that is what people thought prior to Descartes.

Once again, Descartes's philosophy overturned common sense when he convinced the philosophers that the distinction between clouds and clocks is bogus. The pervasive effect of Descartes's mechanization of all material substances is illustrated by Laplace's boast that a future Isaac Newton with sufficient data could have precisely predicted the present state of British flora and fauna as it would exist in the nineteenth century.

Four arguments against Descartes are presented. (1) The complexity of the causal factors responsible for the motion of clouds makes Laplace's boast true, but vacuous. (2) There are thresholds in nature (nonlinear systems) that magnify minor errors and create what has been dubbed the "butterfly effect." (3) There is a gap between measurements and reality that mirrors the distinction between epistemology and ontology. (4) Self-prediction is conceptually incoherent, and hence it is conceptually impossible to predict any event that humans can affect.

Finally, the difference between clouds and clocks is explained in terms of the Aristotelian distinction between per se *and* per accidens *efficient causes. This distinction is illustrated with a story about a geologist and his daughter.*

Chapters 6 through 9 focused on human understanding—*how* we know what we know. An Aristotelian theory of knowledge, we argued, transcends a wholly scientific understanding of the universe without contradicting any well-established scientific truths. We might say that our epistemology is ascientific without being unscientific. Science does not explain everything about the universe and our place in it, but what it does explain cannot be ignored or contradicted.

Finally, we concluded by saying that *who* we are (as opposed to *what* we are) is a subsistent set of understandings and priorities. By "subsistent" we mean that voluntary human actions create a unique person with a set of understandings and priorities that cannot be destroyed, though they can, and do, become inoperable at the death of the body. Whether our unique understandings and priorities will some day be rejoined with a body is a question for theology. (We noted in passing, though, that the theory of human nature outlined in this essay is clearly consistent with the Christian hope for the resurrection of the body.)

In the last two chapters, we will focus on how a subsistent set of understandings and priorities is created. To do this, we will outline an Aristotelian theory of human choice. Once again, we will permit ourselves to transcend a wholly scientific understanding of who and what we are, but we will not allow ourselves any assumptions or postulates that contradict well-established scientific truths.

Our goal will be to demonstrate that rational agency and freedom of choice mutually imply each other. An immaterial intellect must transcend the laws of nature, or its actions would be bound by physical laws of cause and effect. If causal laws *mechanically* determined the intellect's actions, then (contrary to the argument of the previous chapter) it would not be immaterial.

On the other hand, a will that is free in any desirable sense must, in some fashion, work in tandem with rationality, or its actions would simply be capricious. A will that *simply* contradicted the physical laws of cause and effect without any transcendent controlling principle would be no different than the "randomizer" that is built into many computers.

Before we try to clarify the connection between rationality and human freedom in the next chapter, we must address what one contemporary philosopher called the "bogy of mechanism."[1] This is the fear that modern science will one day demonstrate that everything humans do is *really* determined by mechanical causes that are as predictable as a clock. Such a conception of human's essential nature runs deeply contrary to our common-sense conviction that much of what we do is determined by our free choices and is *up to us,* as opposed to our genetic makeup and/or environment.

Though our ultimate goal is to explain and defend human freedom, in this chapter our goal is much more modest. Here our task will be to understand what is meant by the term "mechanism" and how this term relates to physical causes. Many scientists and philosophers treat "mechanism" and "physical causes" as virtually synonymous. They believe that if an event has a physical cause, then it is *ipso facto* "mechanical" and at least in principle predictable. Aristotelians disagree. They argue that there are two distinct kinds of physical efficient causes—one mechanistic and predictable, the other not mechanistic and not predictable. Aristotle and Aquinas called mechanistic physical causes *per se* efficient causes. They called nonmechanistic physical causes *per accidens* efficient causes.

A good place to begin an exposition of the distinction between *per se* and *per accidens* efficient causes is by considering the motion of clouds and clocks. First, a caveat—our discussion is limited to *normal* cases. In the case of both clouds and clocks this means that we are assuming that their motion is wholly determined by physical causes. Whether God, the gods, or other occult forces could or would directly intervene in the physical realm is not presently our concern. Such intervention would be miraculous, and it is precisely such events that we wish to leave on the shelf by limiting the discussion to normal cases.

Even if we agree to limit our discussion to normal cases where only physical causes are active, however, common sense does not place clouds and clocks in the same category. Clocks are mechanistic. In fact, they are a paradigm of the mechanical and predictable, but the motion of individual clouds is anything but predictable and certainly not mechanistic. At least that is what people thought prior to Descartes.

Once again, Descartes's philosophy overturned centuries of common sense. His *Discourse on Method* convinced many scientists and philosophers that the common distinction between clouds and clocks was bogus. Those who took the "epistemological turn" with Descartes argued that since the motion of both clouds and clocks are wholly determined by physical causes, it is only human ignorance and lack of precise data that makes the motion of clouds more difficult to predict than the motion of clocks. Though scientists may not *presently* be able to precisely predict what clouds will do, there is no reason to project such limitations into the future. As meteorologists obtain more accurate and complete atmospheric measurements, there is in principle no reason to believe that future scientists will not be able to predict the weather with the same degree of accuracy as common folks predict the motion on the hands of a clock. In short, from Descartes onwards, it has become the conviction of many philosophers and scientists that if an event is determined wholly by physical causes, then it must in principle be predictable.

Truthful Vacuity

One rough contemporary of Descartes, French Enlightenment philosopher and scientist Pierre Simon Laplace, is famous for his boast that a sufficiently intelligent scientist at the dawn of creation, given sufficient data, could have predicted the state of British flora and fauna in the nineteenth century.[2] What are we to make of such an incredible claim?

First, while we must keep an open mind, a touch of skepticism is healthy. True, in the past, overzealous and misguided disciples of Aristotle have attempted to obstruct the advance of science. Since such obstructionism did not work at the birth of modern science, what reason is there to believe that it will work now?

At the same time, we should remind ourselves that the converse is equally true. The history of science is riddled with boasts made concerning the "conclusive findings of modern science" or the soon to be produced results of modern research, when in fact one era's "conclusive findings" become the next generation's embarrassing footnote, and the "soon to be produced results" have never been produced. Remember the confident statements by previous generations concerning the ubiquity of ether. In 1929 the *Encyclopedia Britannica* reported, "There is now no doubt of its existence."[3] And as we pointed out in chapter 8, time has run out on Turing's date-specific prediction that computers would duplicate a human's linguistic ability, and it was not a "mere technicality" that falsified his prediction. When confronted with an extravagant claim about future findings from either philosophers or scientists, a good place to begin is with a retort—"I'll believe it when I see it!"

But even if modern science is nowhere near actually demonstrating the truth of Laplace's boast, we must try to understand its intent. In Laplace's case, it is not hard to see what he was trying to do. He made no effort to hide his contempt for theologians and the vacuity of their doctrines, nor did he try to disguise his faith in the omnipotence of Newtonian physics.[4]

But Laplace got it exactly backwards. An omnipotent Creator might have been able to "predict" the status of nineteenth-century British flora and fauna at the dawn of time. It is wholly vacuous, however, to boast that a Newtonian scientist armed with sufficient data could have done the same.

Alan Turing's prediction concerning computers was date specific. Furthermore, there was a fairly clear test for determining whether or not programmers had succeeded or failed. Laplace's boast, on the other hand, includes neither a date nor a test. In this respect, we have another case of a bodybuilder boasting that he could bench press a Mack truck if he were sufficiently strong. Again, the problem with such a boast is not that it is unlikely or even false that a mere human could ever become "strong enough" to bench press a Mack truck. The problem is that the boast is vacuous because "sufficiently strong" has no meaning apart from the ability to bench press a Mack truck. Again, the meaning of the bodybuilder's boast is simply that if he could bench press a Mack truck, then he could bench press a Mack truck. True, but such ability is hardly something to boast about!

Thus, we are not suggesting that the common-sense truth that clouds are not clocks *contradicts* the claim that a super-smart Newtonian physicist could make accurate predictions about their motion. If a scientist knew *all* the physical factors that affected the weather, even things so trivial as the flapping of butterfly wings, and if her measurements were *exactly* correct, then, given sufficient "computer power," she might very well be able to make accurate predictions about the distant future,[5] but this was not something that Laplace learned by studying Newtonian physics. Rather, the truthful vacuity of Laplace's boast is built into the meaning of his claim—that is, "super-smart" *means* "able to make incredible predictions."

Thresholds and the Butterfly Effect

The mention of butterflies in the previous paragraph was no accident. It alludes to what has recently been dubbed the "butterfly effect." The term comes from the emerging field of "chaos theory" and refers to the fact that something so trivial as the flapping of a butterfly's wings in Russia can determine whether it will rain at the Superbowl three days later.

It is not hard to understand why the weather is so difficult to predict. First, the causal factors that determine the weather are extremely complex, and second, the complexity creates and crosses numerous thresholds. The effect of complexity on the ability of people to make accurate predictions is pretty obvious. The more factors that have to be considered, the more chances for human error to enter the equation. These errors can be either the failure to consider a causally relevant factor or the failure to accurately measure such a factor. (Especially prior to the days of computers, human error was often caused by miscalculation of the data.)

Of course, the complexity of the causal factors that determine the weather is not a recent discovery. Descartes and his followers certainly understood that, but it didn't stop them from boasting because they assumed that little errors in measurements, while not to be ignored, would only produce little errors in the prediction. Similarly, they assumed that when there were thousands of factors that entered into the causal determination of an event, then a failure to consider a single factor would only have a very small effect on the accuracy of the prediction.

Furthermore, as these little errors were corrected, it was assumed that scientists' predictions would become more and more accurate. Though these predictions would never match perfectly with reality, they would approach a perfect correspondence in the same way that the mathematical asymptote approaches the X or Y axis.

Now these are not unreasonable assumptions. In fact, in many cases it is true that little errors in data produce little errors in outcomes, but this is not always true. What chaos theory has made clear is that there are many cases where the old assumptions do not hold. The realization that clouds and many other purely physical systems are riddled with critical thresholds exposes the fatal flaw in Laplace's assumptions. Where critical threshold are involved, or, in the contemporary jargon, when systems are nonlinear, little mistakes at the beginning can have hugely disproportionate results in the end. Neither complexity nor thresholds by themselves make actual predictions impossible, but when both are present, the search for accurate predictions is a delusive and misconceived goal.

So what do we mean by a "critical threshold" or a "nonlinear system"? A simple illustration is two campers being chased by a bear. Both are quite athletic—Bob can jump thirty feet and Ted can jump twenty-nine feet, eleven inches. While there is little difference in their jumping ability, if they are forced to jump a thirty-foot chasm, Bob will be alive and Ted will be dead. The chasm constitutes a threshold. It separates jumpers into two groups—those who can and those who cannot jump thirty feet, and unlike most teachers, chasms don't give "partial credit." Ted is just going to have to face up to the fact that his twenty-nine feet, eleven inches jump earns him the same score as a jump of only nineteen feet, three inches.

Another illustration of the "nonlinear" effects created by threshold is the difference between rolling a bowling ball and throwing a pair of dice. Suppose the prize in a million-dollar lottery was one chance to roll a strike. If the contestant succeeded, she would win a million dollars. Most people selected for such a contest would practice their bowling. But suppose a second lottery offered a million dollars if the selected contestant rolled "snake eyes" on their first throw. It is unlikely that the selected contestant for this second million-dollar prize would begin to practice his dice-throwing technique. Why the difference?

The difference between rolling a bowling ball and throwing a pair of dice is that the bowling ball is part of a linear system, whereas the dice are a part of a nonlinear system. Though all the practice in the world will not ensure a million-dollar prize for the bowling contestant, practice will improve the odds of winning. A novice bowler's rolls exhibit no consistency. An experienced bowler's rolls will be consistently in the "strike zone." Of course, hitting a cylindrical pin with a rolling ball in exactly the right place to produce a strike requires a degree of precision that not even professional bowlers can achieve one hundred percent of the time, but on a round ball and a cylindrical pin there are no "thresholds." Instead, there is a continuum from "fairly close" to "very close" to "extremely close" to "exactly on target."

Dice, on the other hand, are not round. A single die has six stable faces and twelve very unstable edges. A die laid flat on one of its faces will remain on that face. It takes more than a little wind or bump to cause it to change. A die balanced on one of its edges, however, is unstable. The slightest breeze, bump, or other application of force will cause it to fall one way or the other. The edges of the die, in other words, function as thresholds between two discrete and stable states. This means, in contemporary jargon, that the application of the force does not have a linear outcome. In rolling dice, the slightest variation in the forces acting on a single roll can have hugely disproportionate effects. It is the existence of these thresholds that makes "practice" in throwing snake eyes futile. "Close" counts for nothing since it in no way increases the odds in one's favor.

Though they are certainly not as obvious and as easy to define as in our above examples, our day-to-day world is riddled with thresholds where extremely minor variations in causes will have hugely disproportionate differences of effects. Most historians could present several real examples where for want of a nail the horse lost its shoe, and for want of a shoe the rider was lost, and for want of a rider the battle was. . . . Though Virgil was more of a poet than a historian, his account of the "chance" factors that led to Rome's founding rings true. Rome began, Virgil writes, when Aeneas's son innocently went hunting and the nostrils of his hounds caught the scent of a stag sacred to the Rutulians. When the wounded stag "crept moaning into his stall . . . all stained with blood," the hardy country folk immediately took up arms to take vengeance on the furious fiend responsible for the deed. Now a threshold has been crossed that proved "to be the principal cause which started the tribulations to come."[6] Why did the hounds catch the scent of this particular stag and not one of the countless others that inhabited the forest? Virgil attributed it to divine intervention; skeptical moderns would attribute it to chance. But all who are honest will admit that the significance of the outcome is totally out of proportion to the cause.

One final example of the havoc thresholds play with our predictions: In the 1980 presidential election, Jimmy Carter was challenged by Ronald Reagan. During the campaign, Reagan and many others had repeatedly criticized Carter's foreign policy for being "weak" and for being too willing to sacrifice our national interests and honor in the face of challenges from abroad. When the Iranians seized the United States Embassy in Tehran and took American hostages, Carter's (apparent) inaction seemed to confirm everything Reagan was saying.

In fact, later we found out that Carter had set in motion a rescue mission and was only biding his time. By April, American intelligence agents posing as European businessmen had infiltrated Iran and penetrated the ranks of the militants guarding the hostages. Iranian members of the team, by some reports, had even managed to recruit captors as "moles" ready and willing to assist in the escape.

With such groundwork laid, eight helicopters were ready to carry out the rescue. Only six were needed to succeed. Shortly after takeoff, one of the eight developed a rotor problem and was forced to turn back. Halfway through the fight, the helicopters were caught in a "haboob," a rare meteorological phenomenon in which winds generated by a thunderstorm depose clouds of dense dust many miles away. This caused the loss of one more helicopter. Still the mission had the six helicopters needed for success, and success would have certainly made the charges that Carter was a "wimp" look lame, throwing all election predictions out the window. But success was not to be had. The mission was aborted when one of the six remaining helicopter's hydraulic pumps failed as the result of a crack in a ten-cent aluminum nut!

History is determined not only by great men and women, powerful social movements, or marvelous technological inventions; it is also determined by nuts and scents!

Epistemology Versus Ontology (Once Again)

Having illustrated the havoc thresholds play with predictions, let us now consider the havoc played by the confusion of the ontological and epistemological perspective. There is no need to repeat our general critique of Descartes's misguided turn toward epistemology. Those who are fully committed to the epistemological turn will have stopped reading long ago! Nonetheless, there are those (primarily in the sciences) who are still committed to the proposition that reality exists independently of our knowledge of it, and that science's job is to make predictions that match reality. These people, like Aristotle, are *ipso facto* committed to the distinction between ontology and epistemology. Predictions are part of the epistemological realm; matching reality is part of the ontological realm.

Consider again a die lying on one of its faces. Assume that no forces act on it except the wind and that it will remain on that face unless acted upon by a wind exactly equal to or greater than 75 miles per hour. Any wind 75 miles per hour or faster will cause the die to roll, and any wind less than 75 miles per hour will have no effect. Also, let us assume that we are able to actually measure wind speeds to an accuracy of one-tenth of a mile per hour. Finally, let's remember that we have stipulated that there are no "gremlins" or other occult forces that determine the outcome of the rolling of dice.

In situations where the wind varies between zero and a hundred miles per hour, there will be one thousand distinct measurements possible. These constitute the data upon which predictions are made and define the epistemological states of a person predicting whether a wind will roll a pair of dice, but ontologically speaking, there are well over one thousand different speeds at which wind blows. Wind velocities vary along a continuum. In between a wind velocity *reading* of 74.1 and 74.2 there are *actually* (that is, ontologically) many more distinct states.[7]

In all instances from 1 to 74.9 and from 75.1 to 100, our predictor's epistemology and ontology will be in sync—that is, his prediction will accurately reflect reality. However, in the one case where the wind speed indicator reads 75.0, a predictor can have no confidence in his prediction. His epistemological state must remain uncertain. If the *actual* speed of the wind is 75.00 or greater, then the die will roll. But if the *actual* speed is 74.99 or less, then the die will not roll. Since by stipulation any actual wind speed between 74.95 and 75.04 will produce the same reading on the instruments, his predictions will be uncertain, but there is no corresponding uncertainty in reality. (Remember, we have ruled out gremlins and other occult forces.)

The predictability of events mirrors our discussion of information. We saw in chapter 7 that a road sign composed of flashing lights, ontologically speaking, either does or does not contain information. Epistemologically speaking, however, "noise" may make the communication of information fuzzy. Likewise, uncertainty concerning a prediction in a given situation (epistemology) does not by itself imply an uncertainty in reality (ontology). Ontologically speaking, an event may be wholly determined by antecedent physical causes, yet epistemologically speaking the same event may be indeterminate.

Once again, since all this is but a prelude to a discussion of free will in the next chapter, it is important to remember that we are considering *only normal cases*. Too often, skeptical scientists and philosophers view "free will" as some sort of occult force. To be fair to the skeptics, this is not always a misinterpretation on their part. Many philosophers *have* defended a conception of free will that does makes it sound as if there are gremlins within the human soul that causes it to act in a fashion which is inconsistent with the established laws of science. Skeptics should rest assured that this is neither Aristotle's nor Aquinas's concept of human freedom. Arguing that human action is not even in principle predictable does not commit one to occult forces.

The Impossibility of Self-Prediction

At the beginning of this century, most philosophers of science were arguing that predictions and explanations are merely the "flip side" of each other—a scientific prediction was simply the scientific explanation made in advance, and a scientific explanation was simply a prediction "after the fact." In this view, predictions and explanations were essentially the same.

By midcentury, however, serious problems with the alleged equivalence of predictions and explanations were appearing.[8] Today, most philosophers of science no longer believe that the realm of scientific explanations and predictions are coextensive,[9] and in this case Aristotelians are in complete agreement with their contemporary colleagues. Therefore, it is important that we are clear about the difference between predictions and explanations.

Prediction, by definition, takes place before the fact; explanations, by definition, take place after the fact. Much can be explained that could never be predicted.[10] In fact, Aristotelian defenders of human freedom would insist that *after the fact* all free human actions are, at least in principle, explainable in a way that is perfectly consistent with the principle that every physical action has a physical cause. They can do this because explaining and predicting are not simply the reverse of each other. What can be predicted can always be explained, but given the distinction between what is in fact knowable and what in fact exists, many events are in principle explainable in terms of efficient causes that are not in principle predictable.

We have just considered three reasons future scientific discoveries or technological developments will not reduce the whole of reality to a predictable clock: (1) There is the complexity of the factors involved that creates what we have called "truthful vacuity." (2) There are thresholds in nature that magnify minor events and create what has been dubbed the "butterfly effect." (3) There is the gap between measurements and reality that mirrors the distinction between epistemology and ontology. These three arguments have all been grounded in the facts of the matter. Now we will consider a fourth, wholly logical, problem with Laplace's extravagant claim.

If the universe turned out to be much less complex and if there were no critical thresholds, then Laplace might have made good on his boast. This is because our first three arguments against Laplace rest on a contingent truth that might have been otherwise. Thus far we have only argued that Laplace was in fact mistaken; now we will argue that his boast is logically incoherent. Here our argument only turns on the meaning of "prediction." Even if we imagine a universe with very little complexity, no thresholds, and composed solely of "discrete states" so that large epistemological states would perfectly match the ontological state of the universe, predictions of future events in that universe would be impossible.

At least, they would be impossible for any predictor in that universe whose actions had physical consequences. The reason is simple: the prediction of any future event that is in any way contingent upon human action presupposes the ability of predictors to predict their own future actions, but self-prediction is conceptually impossible. People will no sooner *predict* their own actions than square the circle. Here's why.

Scientists can be confident about their predictions to the same extent that they are confident that they are dealing with a "closed system." By a "closed system" we mean a system in which all the causally relevant factors are either known or controlled. Systems in which none of the causally relevant factors are dependent upon or affected by human action we will call *naturally* closed systems. Systems in which at least one causally relevant factor is a human action we will call *experimentally* closed systems.

Very few naturally closed systems exist. The solar system is such a system. There is nothing humans do that affects the motion of the planets, but even here cautious scientists attach a *ceteris paribus* (other things being equal) clause to their predictions. If a previously uncharted asteroid collides with Mars and falsifies an astronomer's prediction about Mars's future location, no one will take this as refutation of Newtonian mechanics. But here we will ignore these sorts of problems and will grant that the solar system, unlike weather systems, is a closed system where we can have a high degree of confidence concerning our predictions.

Most predictions made by scientists, however, concern systems that they themselves have "closed" by controlling the experimental factors being considered. For example, medical researchers make predictions about a drug's effectiveness. They do so after reviewing the results of carefully screened "control groups." After completion of the tests, predictions are then made about the drug's effectiveness for the population at large, e.g., that the drug will lower cholesterol by 64 percent. Of course, since the relevant causal factors affecting the drug's effectiveness are no longer controlled, all medical predictions about how the drug will affect a *particular* patient are in fact quite uncertain.

This is well known and easily understood, but there is a quite different problem that has been defined by Karl Popper and Donald Mackay. They made clear the paradoxical part played by the person or persons who "closed" the system in the first place. For such a person or persons to actually make predictions about what will happen in their experimentally "closed system," they must be able to predict their own effects on the system. The problem, however, is that self-prediction is conceptually impossible because a person can never have up-to-date information about his or her own mental states.

The dilemma for those seeking such information is classically illustrated by Gilbert Ryle's example of a voice instructor mimicking a student's voice and then in a moment of humility mimicking his own mimicry.[11] Once one starts down this path there is no end to the mimicry! Now predictions, if they are to be more than lucky guesses, must always be based on up-to-date data. The paradox is that when people try to collect data about themselves, the very act of collecting the data makes the previously collected data out-of-date. Collecting up-to-date data about one's self is as impossible as a swimmer catching his own waves—the faster he swims, the faster his waves radiate. Therefore, since self-prediction is impossible, any event in a system that is closed by a scientist's own actions will itself be unpredictable.

If one's own actions are unpredictable, then all that they can affect is also unpredictable. Suppose that based on the results of thousands of final exams, a hard-nosed community college chemistry professor predicts that 50 percent of her students will earn a failing grade on the final. After making her prediction, but before administering the test, this professor is herself humbled by what she believes is an unreasonably difficult qualifying exam for her doctorate. As a result, she decides to rewrite her chemistry final more in line with reasonable expectations for freshman chemistry students, and now her prediction is falsified because far fewer than 50 percent of her students fail.

Now some will object that if only she had decided to stick with the original exam, then her prediction would have been true. Yes, but people must always *make* their decisions; they can never *predict* them. Again, the problem is collecting up-to-date information. As soon as people "predict" that they themselves will do X, then there is automatically another factor that will enter into their decision, and their previous "prediction" will be based on obsolete data.

As we have said, there are very few naturally closed systems. In nature, many more events are cloud-like than are clock-like. Most closed systems that scientists study are closed by their own intentional actions. Hence, most *actual* (as opposed to "truthfully vacuous") predictions are the result of a scientist's own intentional actions, which are themselves unpredictable.

The illusion (and fear) of ubiquitous predictability results from lack of philosophical reflection. A scientist creates an experiment (closed systems). Other scientists reproduce the results. New predictions are now possible. The extrapolation is then made that someday one's own intentional action will itself be discovered to be a closed system, but this ignores the fact that it was the (unpredictable) intentional action of humans that "closed" the system in the first place. As C. S. Lewis once observed, "To see through everything is to see nothing."[12]

Per Se and *Per Accidens* Efficient Causes

The point of this chapter has been very simple—clouds are not clocks, and our universe contains many more cloud-like events than clock-like events. Therefore, the fear that modern science might one day prove that humans are really nothing more than complex machines is unfounded. Even if we limit our discussion to events whose causes are wholly physical, there will always be a crucial distinction between mechanistic and nonmechanistic causes, or what Aristotle and Aquinas called *per se* efficient causes and *per accidens* efficient causes.

All that remains is to explain how the truth obvious to all pre-Cartesian philosophers that clouds are not clocks in no way contradicts, demeans, or demonizes the work of contemporary scientists. A final story will illustrate this final point.

A geologist and his daughter are on a camping trip. The daughter has become interested in rocks. Being far away from home, the daughter collects some rocks that don't look much like any she has collected previously. But with a geologist for a father, most of her questions about these unusual rocks are easily answered. On the second day of the trip, she is puzzled by a rock that looks like a sponge and will float on the lake. Her father says that the rock is called pumice, and that it comes from volcanoes.

Now suppose that the daughter finds a rock with a set of cracks perfectly shaped in the form of the letter "C." What will her father say if she asks about the origin of this rock with a C-shaped crack? Will the father be able to provide a scientific explanation of such a crack, just like he was able to explain the origin of pumice and its remarkable ability to float? Obviously not.

Of course, a less confident father who is unwarrantedly feeling a little defensive or is desirous of displaying his scientific prowess might resort to pseudo-scientific jargon. For example, he could reply, "The C-shape cracks were caused by the stochastic processes involved in the differential rates of cooling of the distinct crystalline structure of coadjacent molecules," but such a reply is nothing more than a long-winded and pretentious way of saying that *chance* produced the C-shaped cracks.

Though we made it a point to eschew psychological explanations of belief in terms of fearful and wishful thinking, this pseudo-scientific response in terms of "stochastic processes . . ." is truly worthy of a such an account. There is absolutely no reason a geologist should feel defensive about not being able to answer questions about why a particular rock should have cracks with a particular shape. There is no failure of the father to understand some principle or law of geology that causes him to be unable to answer the daughter's question.

The most likely psychological account for the "stochastic processes" response is misplaced pride. If the father truly believes that he is doing something more than simply appealing to chance, then he has overinflated pride about either his own intelligence or the abilities of his individual discipline. The appeal to "stochastic processes" is no different than the ancient Greek explanation of untoward events in terms of the three Fates.

The fundamental problem with serious appeals to either "stochastic processes" or the Fates is that it turns "chance" into the name of either a person or a thing. When people say that it was *chance* that caused it to rain on the Superbowl, they are speaking truthfully but loosely. Though chance is real, it names neither a person nor a thing. Instead, "chance" refers to a privation. When we say that it was Fred's blindness that caused him to knock over the coffee, we do not mean that Fred's blindness caused his actions the way his heart causes his blood to circulate. Rather, Fred's blindness refers to something Fred lacks that most other people have—perhaps he lacks a link in the optic nerve or a cornea in the eye. In the cases where we explain the presence of a C-shaped crack in terms of "stochastic processes," we are not naming some sophisticated scientific discovery. What we are really saying is that there are no laws of nature (*per se* efficient causes) that explain C-shaped cracks.

Therefore, since chance is neither a person nor a thing, to say that it was chance that caused it to rain on the Superbowl does not literally *explain* the rain. Rather, it is a colloquial way of saying that no person knows what caused it to rain on this particular day at this particular place, or perhaps it means that no person could have predicted that it would rain in Los Angeles three years ago when the officials were selecting a site for the Superbowl.

Explanations that appeal to chance, the Fates, or stochastic processes point to the fact that there are no *per se* efficient causes of these events, but instead that such events have only *per accidens* efficient causes.

Conclusion[13]

Properly understood and applied, real science realizes that there are many questions that it is incapable of answering. This can be for one or two reasons. The first possibility is that the questions are trivial and below it. For example, Why is there a C-shaped crack in this particular rock? The second possibility is that the questions are profound and above the competence of science to answer. While the focus of this chapter has been on the former, the next chapter will discuss the latter.

Finally, we should be open about our motivation. This chapter has largely been addressed to the scientifically minded who are rightfully skeptical about the existence of occult-like forces acting in nature. Throughout this essay, and especially in this chapter, our hope has been to pave the way for the Aristotelian understanding of free will in such a way that even tough-minded scientists might consider it seriously.

In speaking to one side of the issue, however, there is a danger that the opposite side of the debate—the more "spiritually minded"—will conclude that Aristotelians have caved in to the forces of scientific naturalism. To readers with such fears we beg patience. Our position is that human freedom is *consistent* with all the established laws of science, but this is quite different from claiming that scientific laws will ever be capable of explaining free human action. The *per accidens* efficient causes that produce a C-shaped mark in a rock are consistent with the laws of science, but the existence of such a mark can never be *deduced* from the laws of science, nor can they be deduced from the laws of science and something called "stochastic processes."

Similarly, those who believe that humans are neither apes nor angels happily acknowledge that the brain and its functions constitute a *necessary condition* of rational thought in humans. Furthermore, they gladly concede that whatever is finally discovered about the brain, these discoveries will be consistent with all the previous laws of science. Aristotelians are not looking for gaps or gremlins in the neurological functions of the brain. This in no way implies, however, that the laws of science will one day produce a *sufficient* account of human thought and thus nullify our previous arguments for a real ontological distinction between apes and humans. Demonstrating this is the goal of the final chapter.

11

Freedom and Rationality

Can't Have One Without the Other

Free will and rationality go hand in hand. Either without the other is impossible. Unfortunately, most modern discussions of free will focus on the moment of moral choice instead of the ongoing rationality that makes voluntary action possible.

Libertarians argue that humans have the ability to act contracausally. Aristotelians disagree on both metaphysical and ethical grounds. Many modern philosophers also reject the notion of contracausal freedom and argue that human freedom is compatible with physical determinism.

Aristotelians are in agreement with modern compatibilists' conclusions, but they reject their premises, especially their analysis of causation in Hume's terms of constant conjunction.

Classic Aristotelian compatibilism agrees with libertarians that moral decisions are in principle unpredictable. Unpredictability, however, does not require "gaps" in the series of physical causes. The lack of per se *causes is sufficient.*

Rationality is the sine qua non *of freedom. This raises a question: How can the rationality of an immaterial intellect cause even the smallest bit of matter to move? Obviously not by some sort of physical contact—at the pineal gland or any other location in the brain. Instead, the intellect causes bits of matter to be carriers of its intentions by a power analogous to the power of words and the meanings they carry.*

148

In the classical conception of humans as neither apes nor angels, free will and rationality go hand in hand.[1] Either without the other is impossible. Modern discussions of free will have moved far from such a conception. Now discussions of free will center on the idea of moral choice. Like so much else in modern philosophy, Descartes initiated this change, but it was probably Kant who cemented the connection between morality and free will in the modern mind.

Kant believed the Newtonian laws of causality strictly regulate everything that we observe in the physical universe. One of the things that we observe is human beings and their actions. Since humans and their actions are both physical, it follows straightaway that all of our actions are strictly determined. At least, that is all Kant thought that we can *know*, either scientifically or philosophically, but he was quick to add that he "found it necessary to deny *knowledge*, in order to make room for *faith*."[2] Thus, there is another quasi-epistemological realm—that which we can rationally believe. What does this include? According to Kant, we can believe in God, immortality, and moral freedom.

In Descartes's philosophy, the universe is divided into two substances—material and mental. In Kant's philosophy, the universe is divided into two epistemological realms. The first includes all that we can know. He called this the phenomenal realm. The second he called the noumenal realm or things-in-themselves. This realm includes that which we can never know, but which we can legitimately believe. The very fact that we can have no philosophical or scientific knowledge concerning this second realm means that our faith in a noumenal God, immortality, and moral freedom is not irrational.

We will not begin a critique of Kant's philosophy except to note that the epistemological division into phenomena and noumena has always puzzled Aristotelians. If we *know* that the laws of Newtonian mechanics strictly determine everything we see, then how can we *rationally* believe that our actions are morally free? After all, morally free human actions are part of the phenomenal realm. If the entire phenomenal realm is known to be determined, what is it that we *believe* when we say that moral actions are free?

Libertarianism

The response of many thinkers is to acknowledge the puzzle and, if not cheerfully, at least openly, abandon the search for a rational understanding of our world so far as it concerns free human action. These philosophers—often called libertarians—grant that the vast majority of human actions are mechanically determined by the electro-chemical reactions in the brain and central nervous system. Whenever humans are explicitly engaged in making a moral choice, however, libertarians argue that the decision itself is undetermined. Such freedom at the instant of moral choice is often referred to as contracausal freedom. The term is apt. On this conception of freedom, moral choice presupposes a break or gap in the causal sequence preceding a choice and subsequent action.

Libertarians realize that such gaps are scientifically odious. So, to minimize the alienation of scientists, libertarians adopt two strategies. First, they limit the gaps in the causal sequence to explicit moral decisions and then argue that these are fairly rare and thus do not turn the neurological workings of the brain and central nervous system into utter chaos. Second, they argue that the scientific community has embraced similar gaps in the causal sequences in quantum mechanics, and hence there is no scientific reason to believe similar effects are not operative in the human brain.

Aristotelians reject the libertarian understanding of freedom for a number of reasons. First, gaps, no matter how few, are not only scientifically odious, they violate a fundamental principle of all thought— nothing comes from nothing. To argue that some events in the brain, however few, are uncaused is equivalent to arguing that something can come from nothing.

In response, libertarians typically say things like this: The physical changes in the brain during the instance of moral choice do not come from nowhere; rather, they come from the immaterial soul. Now we are right back to a Cartesian dualism of two independent substances, and there is no need to repeat the Aristotelian criticism of this position.

Second, Aristotelians reject the appeal to quantum mechanics. If the orthodox understanding of quantum mechanics is intended to provide a true understanding of *reality,* then it too violates the fundamental principle that nothing comes from nothing. As we have already explained, Aristotelians have no objection to the claim that quantum mechanics is the best *heuristic* tool currently available to physicists for quantifying their observations. However, they totally reject the reigning interpretation of quantum mechanics that reduces ontology to epistemology, that is, the essentially idealist claim that "to be is to be perceived."[3]

Third and most important, Aristotelians reject the conception of morality implicit in the notion of contracausal freedom. Since this is the topic of another essay, our response will be brief.

The fundamental moral problem with libertarianism is that it makes morality an episodic, not integral, part of life.[4] Libertarians conceive of the will's actions as relatively rare events that "overrule" the normal functioning of the human brain. But a person's character is not created by occasional "contracausal choices." Rather, it is created moment by moment throughout the whole of one's life. Iris Murdoch is correct:

> If we consider what the work of attention is like, how continuously it goes on, and how imperceptibly it builds up structures of value round about us, we shall not be surprised that at crucial moments of choice most of the business of choosing is already over. This does not imply that we are not free, certainly not. But it implies that the exercise of our freedom is small piecemeal business that goes on all the time and not a grandiose leaping about unimpeded at important moments. The moral life, on this [Aristotelian] view, is something that goes on continually, not something that is switched off in between the occurrence of explicit moral choices. What happens in between such choices is indeed what is crucial. [5]

The Aristotelian alternative to the libertarian understanding of free will begins by removing the ambiguity in the phrases "in principle predictable" and "determined by antecedent physical causes" that results from failing to distinguish between *per se* and *per accidens* efficient causes. In one sense the actions of animals and volcanoes are predictable, and in another sense they are not. Volcanoes will always spew forth pumice or igneous rocks; they will never produce sedimentary rocks during an eruption. Bees will always live in hives as a community with a female as its leader; they will never live as hermits or with a male for a leader.

As we argued in the last chapter, however, only in a vacuous sense will scientists ever be able to predict when a volcano will produce a rock with a C-shaped crack. The same is true of the particular actions of a particular bee. No scientist will ever be able to predict when a bee's flight will trace an outline of the letter "R," but does the fact that scientists will never be able to make such predictions mean that both volcanoes and bees have a free will? Of course not.

Similar sorts of things can be said about the contention that everything in the physical universe is determined by antecedent physical causes. If "determined" means "the result of law-like regularities," then, once again, the sorts of cracks produced by a volcanic eruption in a particular rock or the precise course that a particular bee will follow in its search for nectar are both undetermined. There are no laws of nature that specify when C-shaped cracks will be produced or when bees will trace the letter "R" during a flight. If "free will" only refers to the *lack* of law-like regularities, then we ought to conclude that volcanoes and bees are free.

The problem with many contemporary discussions of "free will," crudely put, is that the issue has been framed in terms of "shape" when the proper questions concern both shape *and* form. We believe that for a human action to be free it must have the right "shape," i.e., it must be the case that there are no *per se* efficient causes of the action in question. But this is only a necessary condition, and a relatively easy condition to meet. As we argued in the last chapter, our universe contains many more cloud-like motions than clock-like motions. Free human choices are only one of a whole host of actions for which there are no *per se* efficient causes.

Modern Compatibilism

Thus far we have only discussed the libertarian conception of freedom, but there is another modern view that is now dominant among professional philosophers. It is called compatibilism. Compatibilism gets its name from the fact that its defenders argue that free will and scientific determinism are compatible, i.e., the two are not mutually exclusive and hence there is no reason to choose between them. According to compatibilists, the choice need not be free will *or* determinism. Instead, it can be free will *and* determinism.

Aristotelians are in partial agreement with compatibilists. Some readers who remember their introduction to philosophy courses may even have concluded from the previous chapter that Aristotle and Aquinas were themselves compatibilists. There is some justification for such a reading. A quick review of modern compatibilism will provide a useful backdrop for our discussion of classical (Aristotelian) compatibilism.

The goal of modern compatibilism is to demonstrate that we do not have to choose between being faithful to the findings and goals of modern science and maintaining a rational belief in human freedom and dignity. In that sense, modern and classical compatibilists share the same goal—both defend a conception of human freedom that is ascientific without being unscientific.

But we must be clear about how modern compatibilists reach their goal. Their defense of freedom is founded in the distinction between causation and compulsion. Their conclusion is that humans are free if and only if they are able to act upon their own wants and desires. When a bank robber puts a gun to a teller's head and demands money, or when drugs are surreptitiously introduced into a guest's lemonade, or when a brain lesion disrupts an epileptic's neurological functions, these people are obviously not free to act as they choose. But when such compulsive factors are not present, that is, whenever people are functioning without either external or internal constraints, then they are acting freely, according to modern compatibilists.

How does this solve the problem? If determinism is true, then even when there are no guns, drugs, or lesions, people are "constrained" to act according to the neurological states of their brain and central nervous system. Modern compatibilists respond that physical causation, in and of itself, does not involve constraint or compulsion. Observe one billiard ball hitting another billiard ball from every conceivable angle and with the most sophisticated scientific instruments, said David Hume, and nowhere will you discover anything that resembles "force," "necessity," or "compulsion." All that is actually observed is that the first billiard ball is moving, a sound is heard when the two balls collide, and then the second billiard ball starts to move. In short, science only discovers patterns of constant conjunction. Therefore, even if we imagine a super-scientist one day discovering regular patterns to describe all human behavior, that would not (say modern compatibilists) destroy human freedom. Why? Because according to modern compatibilists, normal physical causation, even if law-like (i.e., *per se* causation in Aristotelian terms), involves no force, necessity, or compulsion.

Modern compatibilists also argue that their distinction between freedom and compulsion corresponds nicely to our ordinary beliefs about praise and blame, reward and punishment. Why shouldn't we punish the epileptic who injures someone else during a seizure? The answer seems simple: punishing them would be useless. In this case, punishment does nothing to prevent future seizures, and hence punishment would do nothing to prevent people from being injured when an epileptic has a seizure at an untoward moment.

Punishment is appropriate and effective, however, when a person's actions are the result of normal brain functions. In these instances, the pain of punishment will become causally associated with the brain states that lead to the wrong choice. Assuming a brain that is functioning normally, these negative associations will cause a person to be less likely to make wrong choices in similar future situations, which is precisely one of the things effective punishment is supposed to do.

Classical Compatibilism

There are two major flaws with modern compatibilism that prevent Aristotelians from adopting their strategy. First, their understanding of causation as mere constant conjunction is inadequate. To observe that two events are constantly conjoined is not the same as observing a causal relation. Modern compatibilism makes it impossible to distinguish between mere coincidence and real causation. Numerous events are "constantly conjoined" where there is no real causal connection. Remember Emerson Hall at Harvard University—every time people pass through its doors, they are unable to speak Inuit,[6] but obviously there is nothing about the doors of Emerson Hall that cause a person to forget his native language.

Furthermore, Hume's view of causation (as even Kant recognized) only makes freedom and science compatible by enervating science. If scientists only discover patterns of constantly conjoined events, then we must remain forever skeptical of scientific claims to *explain* natural events. For example, one of Newton's great achievements was to explain why the tides ebb and flow. They do so, he said, *because* of the moon's gravitational field. But if Hume is correct, all that scientists can legitimately say is first the moon moves, then the tides move.

The second major flaw with modern compatibilism is that it extends the realm of freedom so far as to make it of little value. If freedom means being able to act upon one's wants and desires, then obviously humans are often free. But so are dogs, cats, possibly mice, and maybe even ants. The reason is simple: everything that is conscious has wants and desires, the most fundamental being to avoid pain. Since dogs and cats are obviously conscious (unless we take the extreme Cartesian view), it follows that they have wants and desires. Of course, dogs and cats (like humans) are not always free to do what they want to do, but sometimes they are. Therefore, given the modern compatibilist definition of freedom—that is, being able to implement one's own wants and desires—not only do humans have a free will, but so do all other conscious animals.

Many moderns will welcome such a conclusion. Sharp distinctions between humans and other animals strike many people as a prejudicial favoring of our own specie. We have considered such sentiments and the arguments concerning "phylogenetic continuity" earlier and have nothing further to say of philosophical interest. Since the end of this essay is near, we will indulge in an ad hominem. If humans do not have unique freedom and dignity, then why are the vast majority of people justifiably outraged by the practice of human slavery when they have no objection to the harnessing of oxen? Why have all cultures during all historical periods accepted the killing of animals for meat but have never accepted the routine killing of unwanted babies for meat? All people who believe that morality requires us to treat human and nonhuman animals differently are logically compelled to reject modern compatibilism, and hence will find classical compatibilism of interest.

According to Aristotle and Aquinas, unpredictability is in principle a *necessary* (though not *sufficient*) condition for human freedom. In this they agree with the libertarians. If there are *per se* efficient causes for a person's actions, then those acts are not free. Unlike the libertarians, however, Aristotelians do not conclude that voluntary human actions are uncaused. Rather, they conclude that such actions are the result of *per accidens* efficient causation. Since *per accidens* efficient causes are not unscientific, the Aristotelian account of human freedom is properly deemed compatibilistic.

This is only the beginning. *Per accidens* efficient causes, considered by themselves, are random and happen only by chance. Free human acts must be more than mere caprice. To complete our view of freedom, *per accidens* causation must be directly linked to human rationality.

Rationality As the *Sine Qua Non* of Freedom

The unanswered question for Descartes and all who followed his strictures on philosophy was, Where does the mind connect itself to the body? His answer, admittedly speculative but nonetheless instructive, was that the mind and body were linked at the pineal gland. Our answer, admittedly analogical but nonetheless instructive, is that freedom and rationality are linked by *words*. We have already argued that words are awesome and that they exist at the very cusp of the material and immaterial realms. In addition to turning our concepts into ideas that can be communicated to others, the concepts embodied in words have a second remarkable ability. They have the power to turn what, from the horizontal or purely scientific point of view, is mere caprice (*per accidens* causation) into what, from the vertical or ontological point of view, are free human choices.

Two thousand years ago, St. James noted a truth of common experience—once spoken, a hurtful, spiteful, mean-spirited, or nasty *word* can never be retrieved. He wrote, "Look at the ships also; though they are so great and are driven by strong winds, they are guided by a very small rudder wherever the will of the pilot directs. So the tongue [the word] is a little member and boasts of great things. How great a forest is set ablaze by a small fire!"[7]

As we have repeatedly argued, considered from the scientific point of view, there is nothing about the physical nature of the ink on this page that makes it a page covered with words. Nor are the antecedent physical causes of these particular ink marks on this particular page a fruitful topic for scientific investigation. In this respect, the antecedent physical causes of these ink marks are no different than the antecedent physical causes of a C-shape crack in a piece of pumice.

Yet, from an ascientific, common-sense perspective, the two are quite different. Words on a page, while not subject to the ordering of *per se* efficient causes, are subject to a different sort of ordering—the ordering of rationality. Words are not just the result of random events as are C-shaped cracks.

Our thesis is analogous. Aristotelians are not holding out for the discovery of gaps in the working of the brain that will one day mystify neurophysiologists. All brain states and events are subject to one of two types of causation—*per se* efficient causes or *per accidens* efficient causes. The *per se* efficient causes are ordered by the laws of nature and are fully open to scientific investigation. The *per accidens* efficient causes that permeate the workings of a normal brain, on the other hand, are not (by definition) subject to the ordering of natural laws, but at least some of them are ordered by the intentional actions of the agent intellect. Considered by themselves, *per accidens* causes in the brain (like all *per accidens* causation) fall beneath the threshold of scientific investigation. Considered as the carriers of intentionality, however, *per accidens* causes (like the words on this page) transcend the threshold of scientific investigation.

Aristotelians are not deaf to the howls of incredulity that this last paragraph will bring forth. How can an immaterial intellect, no matter how powerful in its own realm, cause even the smallest bit of matter to move *any differently than it would have moved* if the immaterial intellect had not acted?

The first thing to note is that the phrase "any differently than it would have moved" is superfluous. We know what it means to say that Mars would move differently if a big asteroid hit it. This is because, given the laws of Newtonian mechanics, the motion of Mars is predictable unless it is acted upon by outside forces, and here "outside" simply means forces other than the gravitational forces acting upon the masses of the planets and sun we are currently considering. But what could it possibly mean *in the context of per accidens efficient causes?* The subjunctive does no work.[8]

First, *per accidens* efficient causes are not predictable. Second, there is no "outside" to *per accidens* efficient causes. In such cases, the sum total of the preceding state of the *entire* universe is active! When the geologist's daughter in chapter 10 asks if rocks upstream from the rock with a C-shaped crack might be part of the causal explanation for such a crack, the father concurs. If the daughter asks whether the photon of light which struck the retina of an owl's eye allowing it to see the last dinosaur egg in this valley 50,000 years ago might also be part of the causal explanation for the C-shaped crack, the father will once again concur. What else could the father say? If he understands the nature of *per accidens* causation, he will have no choice but to agree that everything and anything—even a single photon striking the retina of an owl—might be part of a causal chain that produced a C-shaped crack. When causal chains involving *per accidens* efficient are at issue, *no* possibilities can be ruled out a priori.

So, Aristotelians are *not* required to explain how an immaterial intellect can "make a difference" in the material realm. The only issue that they must be prepared to explain is, How can an immaterial intellect, no matter how powerful in its own realm, *cause* even the smallest bit of matter to move?[9]

The answer is found in chapter 68 of the third volume of *Summa Contra Gentiles*. Here Aquinas distinguishes two ways that substances can be related. The first is by extension (i.e. location). One substance can be a given distance to the north, east, south, or west of another substance or a given distance above or below a second substance, or it can be within the first substance as a person's brain is within his skull. These are the only way in which two *physical* substances can be related.

Immaterial substances, however, obviously can not be related to the other immaterial substances or to a physical substance in any of the above ways. The only way that any immaterial substance can be related to any other substance (whether immaterial or material) is by way of *power*. That is, one immaterial substance W might be able to *affect* another substance X, but not substance Y.[10]

Once again, words have an analogous power. The phonemes that embody a single "hate word" can cause a riot when voiced in presence of other people who speak the same language. Yet precisely the same phonemes voiced in the presence of people who do not understand the language will have no such effect. How can we understand such commonplace phenomena if not in Aquinas's terms? That is, how can we understand the fact that phonemes that are physically identical can have a fairly predictable effect on person X but no effect on person Y? What else can we say except that these phonemes have some nonphysical properties that enable them to affect X but not Y? In short, how can we understand the power of hate words unless we admit into our ontology *both* of the relations listed by Aquinas in *Summa Contra Gentiles?*

We have now come full circle. In a Cartesian universe in which all that can be seen, heard, tasted, smelled, or felt is stripped of substantial form, the causal powers of both bodies and minds are equally mysterious. This fact is often overlooked. As we argued in chapters 6 through 9, Descartes's reduction of matter to mere extension makes body/body causation as mysterious as body/mind or mind/body causation.[11]

In an Aristotelian universe permeated with shapes and forms, however, both material and intentional causation becomes intelligible. In such a universe, the causal powers of human intellects are a natural extension of everything else that is observed. Once the material realm is conceived of including both shapes and forms, the causal realm can be conceived as including both relations of extension and relations of power.

Though this will certainly not silence the howls of incredulity, they are muted. Again, the only question is this: How can an immaterial intellect, no matter how powerful in its own realm, *cause* even the smallest bit of matter to move? Obviously not by some sort of physical contact—at the pineal gland or any other *location* in the brain. Instead, the agent intellect causes bits of matter to be carriers of its intentions by a *power* analogous to the power of words.

Epilogue

We are incessantly told that we live in the "Information Age," but we are rarely, if ever, told that it is only because we live in an ontologically in-*formed* universe that this is possible. "In the beginning was the Word" is theology, but "In the beginning was the word" is common-sense phi-losophy.[1] Without the word there is no information, and without infor-mation there is no science.

It is a little ironic that many people believe the tremendous success of modern science makes older philosophical conceptions of the uni-verse hopelessly out of date. Our response to such thinking is simple: no matter how far up a person climbs, after cutting off the limb on which one rests, the person will *eventually* hit the ground. Sooner or later mod-ern man will hit the ground, and it appears that the collision is coming sooner rather than later. The Enlightenment dream of an omnipotent science is giving way to the postmodernist nightmare of ubiquitous con-fusion. Once we hit ground, it will be time for the postmortem. What will the postmortem reveal? A little mistake in the beginning. What Descartes and all his followers forgot was that form is not shape, and that the universe is composed of both form and shape.

But merely identifying the mistake is insufficient. We must also act to correct it. Philosophically speaking, this requires turning around and following the implications of these two simple truths wherever they lead. But if the history of philosophy is a guide, this will not be easy. Two obstacles stand in the way. On the one hand, misguided theological objections to scientific investigations will have to be renounced. But, on

159

the other hand, the contemporary fear of religion will have to be coura-
geously confronted.

While it is an open question whether either of these is likely, there
are signs of hope. Alasdair MacIntyre is only one of a growing number
of influential philosophers who are now arguing that whole *traditions*
constitute the proper unit of rational inquiry. In his Gifford Lectures,
for example, he argued that Aquinas's *Summa Theologica* "can only be
read as a whole and can only be evaluated as a whole." He then chas-
tises those who think they could "be a critic of *Summa* without first having been a genuine participant in its processes of dialectical enquiry and
discovery."[2] We couldn't agree more, and while not many will take up
the gauntlet, surely many of those who do will find the richness, coherence, and beauty of the Thomistic synthesis irresistible.

Appendix

Assessing "Intelligent Design"

The argument of this essay has been wholly philosophical; none of the arguments took as premises that which can only be known through divine revelation. Since most of the arguments and criticisms have been aimed at unbelieving philosophers and scientists, this was absolutely necessary. Any appeal to revealed truths would have been question begging.

As mentioned in a couple of places, though, the confusion between shape and form is not limited to unbelievers. Starting in the nineteenth century with William Paley's famous "Watchmaker Argument" for the existence of God, Christian apologists have attempted to counter evolutionary philosophy by appealing to the wholly *mathematical improbability* of even something so fundamental as a single cell evolving purely by chance. While we believe that such arguments illustrate the same confusion of shape and form as noted above, we believe there are additional *theological* criticisms of Paley's argument.

The contemporary defenders of Paley are calling themselves the "Intelligent Design" movement. Its leading lights include Philip Johnson, Michael Behe, and most recently William Dembski. This appendix addresses the Dembski's latest book, *Intelligent Design*.

Dembski nicely summarizes his conclusions on page 247. He argues that

1. Specified complexity is well-defined and empirically detectable.

161

2. Undirected natural causes are incapable of explaining specified complexity.
3. Intelligent causation best explains specified complexity.

A standard Thomistic response is:

1. Specified complexity is not quantifiable, and hence, not empirically detectable apart from the action of an agent intellect.
2. Dembski's second proposition is true.
3. Dembski third proposition is too weak—the existence of meaningful sentences *conceptually* implies intelligent causation.

Each of these corrections work in the following ways:
1. I assume that "well-defined" means quantifiable, and "empirically detectable" means measurable by scientific instruments (either in fact or theoretically). For example, Dembski writes, "This chapter argues that God's design is also accessible to scientific inquiry. The crucial point of this chapter is that design is empirically detectable, that is, we detect it through observation" (17). Again, he says that his point "can be made with full statistical rigor" (133). Furthermore, he even specifies the numerical threshold that an event must surpass to qualify as an example of "specified complexity"—it is 10^{-150} (143).

Thomists reject such a conclusion. Though we believe that design (final causation) is observable in nature, it is only observable for those equipped with *nous* (intellect), and since the intellect is immaterial, no wholly material scientific instrument will ever detect design.

The same point can be made without resorting to the technical language of Aristotle. It is not possible to quantify something's form or essence, i.e., *what* it is. For example, the first pair of claws on a lobster are pincers, but there are no quantifiable or measurable terms for defining the essence of a pincer because there are an indefinite number of ways to create pincers. I have at least five different kinds of pliers in my garage, three different kinds of salad tongs in my kitchen, and two different kinds of tweezers in my bathroom—all of which are pincers. Mechanics, cooks, and doctors could certainly add many more examples to my short list of different kinds of things that are pincers, not to mention the thousands of different kinds of pincers in the animal kingdom any zoologist could list. The only thing all pincers have in common is an intended purpose, design, or function—in short, a form. While quantifiable shapes can be the embodiment of forms, no form can be reduced to a quantifiable shape.

Now Dembski will undoubtedly respond that such examples only constitute a "false negative" and that he never said that his criterion ruled these out (139). So can Thomists produce examples of "false positives"? This question is more troublesome because it seems so obvious that this is the case that I find it hard to believe that someone as well credentialed as Dembski would have missed it. I present the following argument somewhat tentatively and will be anxious to hear what others think.

Flip a coin one hundred times and record the results as a string of zeros and ones. Then ask five clever people to create a code (like Morse Code) that results in the string of zeros and ones becoming a meaningful sentence, i.e., a false positive like the one Dembski discusses on page 136. Can they do it? Of course they can—humans are free to create codes in any way they wish.

It is doubtful that Dembski would disagree, but he would argue that a cleverly created code designed for the sole purpose of "reading into" a random string of zeros and ones a meaningful sentence is not, in his words, "detachable."

> Detachability can be understood as asking the following question: Given an event whose design is in question and a pattern describing it, would we be able to construct that pattern if we had no knowledge which event occurred? Here is the idea. An event has occurred. A pattern describing the event is given. The event is one from a range of possible events. If all we know was the range of possible events without any specifics about which event actually occurred, could we still construct the pattern describing the event? If so, the pattern is detachable from the event (133).

Of course, he is absolutely correct—our clever code that produces a "false positive" is not detachable. But there is an obvious problem—the DNA code is not detachable either! Certainly Dembski cannot believe that a mathematician might have figured out that life on earth would be based on a code constructed of four protein bases arranged in the shape of a double helix. Wasn't God free to create life based on six protein bases? Couldn't God, if he chose, create life out of silicon, or for that matter, out of no matter at all, the way he created the angels?

Dembski is caught in a dilemma—if he gives up the "detachability" criterion, then five clever people can turn *any* series of zeros and one into a meaningful code, and hence there will be no end to "false positives." If he doesn't give up the detachability criterion, then he has reduced biology to a purely mathematical, a priori discipline, and he has denied a fundamental doctrine of Christian theology—namely, that God was perfectly free to create in any way he saw fit.

2. If we bracket the above objection to Dembski's own definition of "specified complexity," Thomists would say that the second thesis is true—*undirected* natural causes are incapable of explaining the exis-

tence of life on earth. Dembski and I may disagree, however, about what is entailed by the term "undirected." The sort of direction Thomists argue for transcends scientific categories—that is, it is ascientific without being unscientific. Bluntly put, direction does not require the *miraculous* suspension of natural causes.

I am not exactly sure what Dembski believes on this point. Some of his words suggest that we would agree. For example, he says, "But note, to say that an intelligent agent caused something is not to prescribe how an intelligent agent caused it. In particular, design in this last sense is separate from miracle" (127). On the other hand, in response to the objection that intelligent design is committed to a God-in-the-gaps, he says, "Without the freedom to seriously entertain gaps in the causal nexus of nature, we place naturalism in a privileged position" (241). Later he becomes even more explicit. "Why should we think we've landed outside of science just because the modality question happens to receive an extraordinary explanation? Presumably, extraordinary explanations are extraordinary because they admit a gap in the chain of natural causes" (242). Again, "Suppose some strange phenomenon M is observed ("M" for miracle). A search is conducted to discover a scientifically acceptable ordinary explanation for M. The search fails. Conclusion: no scientifically acceptable ordinary explanation exists. Is there a problem here?" (243). Dembski says no; Thomists say that the question is ambiguous.

Consider Paul and Silas sitting in a Macedonian prison. "Suddenly there was a great earthquake, so that the foundations of the prison were shaken; and immediately all the doors were opened and every one's fetters were unfastened" (Acts 16:26). Is there a "scientifically acceptable ordinary explanation" for *this* event? There is no single answer because the pronoun has no unambiguous referent. If "this" refers simply to an earthquake strong enough to open prison doors, then obviously there is a "scientifically acceptable ordinary explanation." But even if "this" refers to the occurrence of a strong earthquake at *this* particular time and at *this* particular place, then the answer is still unclear because the options of "scientifically acceptable" and "scientifically *un*acceptable" constitute a false dichotomy. Some events are simply the result of coincidence (or stochastic processes). Of course, for those with eyes to see, coincidences display God's providence. The miracle recorded in Acts 16 is a case in point.

But here we must be careful. Thomists do not believe that *all* miracles follow such a pattern. Clearly, many of the biblical miracles *are* instances of the supernatural suspension of the laws of nature. Christ's resurrection is an example of a biblical miracle that *is* "unscientific." So what is the point of this miracle? While there are many, one of the most important is that Christ triumphed over Satan, sin, and death, and that through God's grace we can do the same. However we flesh out the significance of Christ's resurrection, it is crucial that we not turn it into an argument for the existence of God. Christ's resurrection is a sign of *who* Jesus is, not *that* God exists.

C. S. Lewis was absolutely correct—any intelligent defense of the biblical miracles presupposes that the existence of a supernatural realm has already been established. That's why the third chapter of *Miracles*, "The Self Contradiction of Naturalism," is crucial. Lewis understood that he must first demonstrate that naturalism is *philosophically* incoherent before considering the biblical miracles. Otherwise, he would be begging the question just as Richard Dawkins and his crew do when they argue that science demonstrates naturalism!

In other words, while Dembski and I both argue that undirected natural causes are incapable of explaining specified complexity (form), Thomists unequivocally reject the claim that the existence of "miraculous coincidences" or even gaps in the scientific explanation are best explained by positing the God of theism.

3. This last paragraph hints at my last point—Dembski's third proposition is too weak. Intelligent causation is not the *best explanation* of specified complexity; rather, it is the *only* philosophically coherent account of the fact that words have a *meaning* transcending any *causal* effects they may also have.

Of course, it took the whole of this book to justify this claim, and it cannot be repeated here. But let me here end with an apology for such a harsh criticism of a brother in Christ who is obviously my intellectual superior. (I really do believe that Dembski is my intellectual superior. How, then, you might ask can I pretend to criticize him? My answer is that he has no tradition to which he has submitted himself for correction. I am only repeating what I have learned from a tradition that has long since been purged of simple mistakes.)

Besides the hidden jealousy Thomists harbor for being largely ignored in these discussions, there is one more nonphilosophical motivation at work. It is the firm conviction that any acceptable biblical hermeneutic must not turn the Bible into a "secret code" that has only recently been "unlocked." What the Bible teaches must be intelligible not only to us but also to the people who first read it. Dispensationalists and all creationists who read Genesis "scientifically" are examples of people committed to a "secret code" hermeneutic.

I am certainly not suggesting that Behe and Dembski are in the same league as Hal Lindsey and Henry Morris. Behe and Dembski are serious scholars that deserve the serious response that the *New York Times* gave Behe's *Darwin's Black Box* and the Cambridge University Press gave Dembski's *The Design Inference*. It is just that they have both made what

Aristotle, Aquinas, and Adler would call a little mistake in the beginning that will have disastrous effects in the end. The little mistake here is confusion of shape with form. "Design" is not *in* biological life the way dirt is *in* rugs. Rather, design is in biological life the way meaning is *in* words.

One of the disastrous effects, theologically speaking, I outlined in my response to Dembski's first point—his conclusions infringe upon the freedom of God's act of creation. Intelligent design also seems to assume a dangerous hermeneutic. How did Paul's first readers understand Romans 1:20? They obviously knew nothing about DNA or the "anthropic numbers" that Dembski alludes to on page 264 and following. How, then, were they without excuse? In what sense was God's invisible nature "clearly perceived in the things that have been made"? A biblical philosophy must be a perennial philosophy. That is, it must be a philosophy that takes as its premises nothing which has not been known by *all* people in *all* cultures. By now you will not be surprised to hear me opining that the Thomistic metaphysics and the tradition it has engendered best satisfies this requirement.

Notes

Chapter 1: Humans as Rational Animals

1. Psalms 144:3. Cf. Hebrews 2:5–8.

2. "Principles whose activity is bodily clearly cannot be present without a body, just as one cannot walk without feet. So they [such faculties as those of nutrition and perception] cannot enter the body from outside . . . they cannot exist separately. . . . It remains that only intellect enters from outside and only intellect is divine. For *its* activity is not associated with any bodily activity" (*On the Generation of Animals*, II.3.736b22; cf. *Nicomachean Ethics*, bk. 10, chap. 7; *Parts of Animals*, bk. 4, chap. 10, 686a 27–32; *On the Soul* bk. 3, chap. 4 and 5).

It is important to stress the fact that in the Aristotelian tradition "only the intellect enters from outside [i.e., is immaterial]." The vast majority of modern dualists who argue for an immaterial mind take "mental states" to include everything humans are conscious of—feelings, pains, images, ideas, etc. However, according to Aristotelians, feelings, pains, images, and even some "ideas" are at least in principle wholly explainable in material terms. Only human ability to think conceptually requires an immaterial mind. See note 6 below and chapter 9, subsection "Not All Mental Objects are Immaterial."

3. Aquinas's respect for Aristotle's philosophy is well known. A good example of his respect for and knowledge of Islamic philosophy is found in a short, early work of his, *Being and Essence*.

4. "It is worth adding that our modern notion of the scientific method is thoroughly Aristotelian. Scientific empiricism—the idea that abstract argument must be subordinate to factual evidence, that theory is to be judged before the strict tribunal of observation—now seems a commonplace; but it was not always so, and it is largely due to Aristotle that we understand science to be an empirical pursuit. The point needs emphasizing, if only because Aristotle's most celebrated English critics, Francis Bacon and John Locke, were both staunch empiricists who thought that they were thereby breaking with the Aristotelian tradition. Aristotle was charged with preferring flimsy theories and sterile syllogisms to the solid, fertile facts. But that charge is unjust; and indeed it could only have been brought by men who did not read Aristotle's own works with proper attention and who criticized him for the faults of his successors" (Barnes, *Aristotle: Past Masters*, p. 86).

5. Cf. Etienne Gilson, *The Philosophy of St. Thomas Aquinas*, p. 19.

6. In this summary we have distinguished between immaterial *intellects* and immaterial *minds* because, according to Aristotle, only the intellect is immaterial whereas, according to Descartes, all consciousness is immaterial (cf. note 2 above). For a materialist, this is a meaningless distinction since nothing real is immaterial.

7. Plato is explicit about the *natural* immortality of the soul (cf. Plato's *Republic*, bk. x. 608–612). Descartes, being a Christian, left room for God's action in our immortality.

8. Concerning the analogy that minds exists as songs, see Aquinas's *Commentary on Aristotle's Metaphysics*, paragraph 2451. "But even though forms are not prior to composite substances, it is still necessary to investigate whether any form remains after the composite substance has been destroyed. For nothing prevents some forms from continuing to exist after the composite ceases to exist; for example, we might say that the soul is of this sort—not every soul but only the intellective." Continuing in paragraph 2452, "Now we should observe that it is Aristotle's view regarding the intellective soul that it did not exist before the body as Plato claimed, and also that it is not destroyed when the body is, as the ancient philosophers held inasmuch as they failed to distinguish between intellect and sense. For he did not exclude the intellective soul from the generality of other forms as regards their not existing prior to composite substances, but only as regards their not continuing to exist after the composite substance have been destroyed." This crucial distinction between sense and intellect is not fully drawn until chapter 9. There we consider the wonder of words and the distinction between natural signs and intentional symbols.

9. John Searle, *Mind, Language and Society*, pp. 17, 32.

10. Thomas Nagel, *The Last Word*, p. 130.

Chapter 2: Getting It Right From the Start

1. "Moreover under no circumstance should the philosopher let himself be blinded by the clarity of quantities even though things are primarily 'objects' through their quantitative properties, such as size and weight. The principal domain of philosophers relates to categories other than the category of quantities" (Jaki, *Means to Message*, 57). "In speaking of the ten categories, he [Aristotle] noted that 'the category of quantity does not admit of variation of degree,' [*Categories*, section 6a] whereas notions that belong to the other nine categories all admit such variations. This should be clear of all the categories other than quantity, such as quality, relation, place, time position, state, action or affection. The quality known as the color red can be more or less red; goodness to can be realized more or less; conscience can be more or less upright. But no given number can be more or less than that very number. Thus Aristotle might have said that instead of ten categories one may speak only of two: quantities and everything else, or, inversely, everything except quantities. He should have also stated emphatically that between those two domains of categories, the difference was such as to render inane any attempt of reducing one to the other" (Jaki, *Mean to Message*, p. 33).

2. While contemporary philosophers often assume a quotational use of words ("hammer") when in fact a disquotational use (hammer) is being employed, the quotational use of words should not be eliminated or ignored. It can be quite helpful in clearing up confusions about a fundamental principle of Aristotelian philosophy, namely, the correspondence theory of truth. As Karl Popper says, "It can not be too strongly emphasized that Tarski's idea of truth . . . is the same idea which Aristotle had in mind and indeed most people (except pragmatists): the idea that *truth is correspondence with facts* (or with reality). But what can we possibly mean if we say of a statement that it corresponds with the fact (or with reality)? Once we realize that this correspondence cannot be one of structural similarity, the task of elucidating this correspondence seems hopeless; and as a con-

sequence, we may become suspicious of the concept of truth, and prefer not to use it. Tarski solved this apparently hopeless problem . . . by reducing the unmangageable ideas of correspondence to a simple idea (that of 'satisfaction' or 'fulfillment'). Owing to Tarski's teaching, I am no longer hesitant in speaking of 'truth' and 'falsity'" (*Logic of Scientific Discovery*, p. 274).

Tarski solved the problem "very simply by reflecting that a theory which deals with any relation between a statement and a fact must be able to speak about (a) statements and (b) facts. In order to be able to speak about statements, it must use names of statements, or descriptions of statements, and perhaps words such as 'statement': that is, the theory must be in a metalanguage, a language in which one can speak about language [i.e., we must use language self-referentially]. And in order to be able to speak about facts and purported facts, it must use names of facts, or descriptions of facts, and perhaps words like 'fact'. Once we have a metalanguage, a language like this in which we can speak about statements *and* facts, it becomes easy to make assertions about the correspondence between a statement and a fact; for we can say:

> The statement in the German language that consists of the three words, 'Gras', 'ist', and 'grun', in that order, corresponds to the facts if, and only if, grass is green.

The first part of this is a description of a German statement (the description is given in *English*, which here serves as our metalanguage, and consists *in par*t of English quotation names of German words); and the second part contains a description (also in English) of a (purported) fact, of a (possible) state of affairs. And the whole statement asserts the correspondences" (Popper, *Unended Quest*, pp. 141–42).

3. Aristotelians claim that it is nothing *physical* that makes two sets of ink marks the same word. Sophisticated philosophers will respond that it *is* the physical character of people's conventional responses to such ink marks or the physical characteristics of their brain states that makes them the same word. We will examine these arguments in chapter nine, subsection "Two Reductionist Theories."

4. Cf. Aquinas' *Summa Theologica* (I, 85,1, ad.3). There Aquinas explicitly rejects the theory that the meanings or concepts are abstracted from observable things the way a part can be separated from a whole. When a person understands the meaning of a word it is not like "a body transferred from one place to another."

Chapter 3: Dividing Nature at Its Joints

1. Again, according to Aristotle, the "souls" of plants and nonhuman animals are, at least in principle, explainable in wholly material terms and are explicitly *not* conceived of as some sort of immaterial "life-force." (See notes 2 and 6 in chapter 1 and chapter 9, subsection "Not All Mental Objects are Immaterial.")

2. The philosophical use of the terms "plant," "animal," and "human" is related to their biological use, but it is not equivalent. Biologists seek to classify all forms of life, including those which can only be observed with powerful microscopes, or in highly restricted habitats, or of species whose nature can only be inferred from fossil remains. Our use of the "plant," "animal," and "human" is less inclusive. First, there are biological forms of life that don't fit neatly into any of these categories. "Insects," for example, are probably closer to animals than to plants, yet they probably aren't sentient, and hence, do not satisfy the defining characteristic of animals. More is said about the differences between the philosophical and biological use of these terms in chapter 4.

3. "The alteration of order which takes place when we pass from the inorganic to the organic has been well defined by Auguste Comte as the passage from an order in which the parts precondition the whole to an order in which the whole shapes the parts and, in

a sense, precedes them. We in our turn shall say that it is as if the parts were there only in view of the whole, or at least as required by it. This is what we call the order of final causality" (Gilson, *From Aristotle to Darwin*, p. 122). Hydra and planaria seem to constitute an exception to our definition of life, however, in terms of heterogeneous ordering. "1/200th of a hydra is able to regenerate the whole animal, while in the planaria 1/280th and even less has been shown to regenerate completely" (Polanyi, *Personal Knowledge*, p. 355, note 1).

4. "There is a fundamental vagueness inherent in this theory [neo-Darwinism] which tends to conceal its inadequacy. It consists in the fact that we lack any acceptable conception of the way in which genic changes modify ontogenesis—a deficiency which is due in its turn to the fact that we can have no clear conception of living beings, as long as we insist on defining life in terms of physics and chemistry" (Polanyi, *Personal Knowledge*, p. 383). See Appendix for an example of same sort of mistake made by the Christian critics of evolution.

5. Creationist critics may be tempted to argue that even though a thing's complexity (say Mount Everest) is not a sufficient condition of life, nonetheless, a high degree of complexity is a necessary condition of life. Aristotelians have doubts about even this. Pure immaterial being (God, gods, and/or angels) are alive, but they are not obviously composed of parts, and certainly not a very large number of parts.

6. Another example of an obviously overly broad definition of life is Schordinger's. His claim is that life is something that "feeds upon negative entropy . . . continually sucking orderliness from its environment." Popper responds, "Now admittedly organisms do all this. But I denied, and I still deny, Schordinger's thesis that it is this which is *characteristic* of life, or of organisms; for it holds for every steam engine. In fact every oil-fired boiler and every self-winding watch may be said to be 'continually sucking orderliness from its environment'. Thus Schrodinger's answer to his question [What is life?] cannot be right: feeding on negative entropy is not 'the characteristic feature of life'"(*Unended Quest*, p. 137).

7. In chapter 9 we will consider the arguments of behaviorists and some forms of the identity theory that argue that things like pain are really reducible to either pain behavior or are really mistaken ways—"folk psychology"—to refer to brain processes.

8. The relation of form and matter is like the relation of the melody and sound waves in Pachelbel's Canon. While we can and must conceptually separate the two, in point of fact, they are inseparable. Pachelbel's melody can't exist (except in the imagination) without sound waves, and no sound wave can exist without some distinct form. No matter how far down physicists go in finding the elementary building blocks of nature, whatever they discover will be conceptually made up of form and matter. They will never find matter by itself and without form. As Aquinas says, "prime matter is said to be one through the removal of all forms" (Goodwin, *Being and Essence*, chapter ii, p. 43; cf. p. 53). Cf. Wolfgang Smith, "From Schrodinger's Cat to Thomistic Ontology" in *The Thomist* 63 (1999), pp. 49–63.

9. Nonetheless, there is some scientific confirmation of our common sense classificatory scheme. "Among the most important emergent events according to present day cosmological view are perhaps the following:

(a) The 'cooking' of the heavier elements (other than hydrogen and helium which are assumed to have existed from the first big bang).
(b) The beginning of life on earth (and perhaps elsewhere).
(c) The emergence of consciousness.
(d) The emergence of the human language, and of the human brain" (Popper, *The Self and Its Brain*, p. 27).

Chapter 4: Objective Differences in Perspective

1. The "war metaphor" comes from Andrew Dickson White, *A History of the Warfare of Science with Theology in Christendom*. One of White's more egregious errors is accusing Calvin of attempting to refute Copernicus by quoting the Bible. Cf. Edward Rosen, "Calvin's Attitude Toward Copernicus," *Journal of the History of Ideas* XXI (July, 1960), p. 3.

2. "It follows that the class of objects which could conceivably represent any particular machine would form, in the light of pure science—which ignores their operational principle—an altogether chaotic ensemble. In other words, *the class of things defined by a common operational principle cannot be even approximately specified in terms of physics and chemistry*" (Polanyi, *Personal Knowledge*, p. 329).

3. "We may even grade the intensity of coherent existence on this scale [being meaningfully ordered]. Owing to its more significant internal structure a human being is a more substantial entity than a pebble. The difference can be appreciated by comparing the sciences of anatomy and physiology with the range of interest offered by the structure of a particular type of pebble" (Polanyi, *Personal Knowledge*, p. 38).

4. In addition to the metaphysical arguments discussed in this essay, there are also ethical arguments in favor of philosophical realism. "I have argued in favour of realism in various places. My arguments are partly rational, partly *ad hominem*, and partly even ethical. It seems to me that the attack on realism, though intellectually interesting and important, is quite unacceptable, especially after two world wars and the real suffering—avoidable suffering—that was wantonly produced by them" (Popper, *Quantum Theory and the Schism in Physics*, p. 2).

Again, "Take away the notion of essential nature, take away the corresponding notion of what is good and best for members of a specific kind who share such a nature, and the Aristotelian scheme . . . necessarily collapses. There remains only the individual self with its pleasures and pains. So metaphysical nominalism [the philosophical opposite of realism] sets constraints upon how the moral life can be conceived. And, conversely, certain types of conceptions of the moral life exclude such nominalism" (MacIntyre, *Three Rival Versions of Moral Enquiry*, p. 138).

And once more, "Modern fanaticism is rooted in an extreme scepticism which can only be strengthened, not shaken, by further doses of universal doubt" (Polanyi, *Personal Knowledge*, p. 298).

Finally, consider this description of Poland's rebellion against the Soviet Union. "They [the philosophy department faculty at Catholic University of Lublin] began with an ancient conviction—they would be radically realistic about the world and about the human capacity to know it. If our thinking and choosing lacks a tether to reality, the KUL philosophers believed, raw force takes over the world and truth becomes a function of power, not an expression of things-as-they-are. A communist-era joke in Poland expressed this realist imperative in a way that everyone could grasp: 'Party boss: How much is 2+2? Polish worker: How much would you like it to be?' The political meaning of the realist assumption of the KUL philosophers was later expressed in the famous Solidarity election poster that read, 'For Poland to be Poland, 2+2 must always = 4.' Human beings can only be free in the truth, and the measure of truth is reality" (Weigel, *Witness to Hope*, p. 133).

5. See Mortimer Adler's *The Problem of Species*.

6. There is significant disagreement among evolutionary biologists about the correctness of Darwin on this point. The idea that biological species are no more "real" than varieties is strongly disputed by Ernst Mayr. He writes, "There is no more devastating refutation of the nominalistic claims than the fact that primitive natives in New Guinea, with a Stone Age culture, recognize as species exactly the same entities of nature as western taxonomists. If species were something purely arbitrary, it would be totally improbable

for representatives of two drastically different cultures to arrive at the identical species delimitations" (*Toward a New Philosophy of Biology*, p. 317).

7. See Adler's, *The Difference of Man and the Difference it Makes*. In this book Adler distinguishes between radical and superficial differences in kind. A radical difference in kind, he says, requires a break in physical continuity, whereas a superficial difference in kind does not (cf. note 8 below). Furthermore, he argues that it is possible that the only radical difference in kind that exists in nature is between humans with immaterial intellects and all other things. Clearly, this distinction between radical and superficial differences in kind is consistent with Aristotle's claim that "only the intellect comes from without" (see chapter 1, note 2).

8. But even a vertical gap does not imply a lack of material continuity. Remember, according to Aristotle, vegetable souls and animals souls are both in principle explainable in material terms. On this point we follow Adler. "While the manifest properties of animate and inanimate bodies are such that it would be incorrect to describe them as differing in degree rather than in kind, nevertheless, current advances in biochemistry and in molecular biology strongly suggest that the difference in kind is superficial, not radical, i.e., it does not involve any new factors—any factors other than those operative in the realm of inorganic things. Hence, it seems reasonable to expect that in the not too distant future a living organism capable of reproducing itself will be synthetically produced in the laboratory. . . . The principle of phylogenetic continuity is not violated by the emergence of animal life" (*The Difference of Man and the Difference it Makes*, pp. 199–200).

And even when we consider the difference between a material animal soul and the immaterial human soul in the last three chapters, we do *not* maintain that the immaterial human intellect works in the material gaps of the human brain. All that the Aristotelian theory of an immaterial intellect requires is that the material workings of the brain are not wholly predictable. As we will see in chapter 10, lack of predictability does not require a lack of efficient causes.

9. "Nature proceeds little by little from things lifeless to animal life in such a way that it is impossible to determine the exact line of demarcation, nor on which side thereof an intermediate form should lie. . . . Indeed, as we just remarked, there is observed in plants a continuous scale of ascent towards the animal. So, in the sea, there are certain objects concerning which one would be at a loss to determine whether they be animals or vegetable. . . . In regard to sensibility, some animals give no indication whatsoever of it, while others indicate it but indistinctly. Further, the substance of some of these intermediate creatures is flesh-like [such as the sea anemones]; but the sponge is in every respect like a vegetable. And so throughout the entire animals scale there is a graduated differentiation in amount of vitality and in capacity for motion" (*History of Animals*, VIII.1.588b).

Again, Aquinas writes, "Thus are we able to contemplate the marvelous connection of things. For it is always found that the lowest in the higher genus touches the highest of the lower species. Some of the lowest members of the animal kingdom, for instance, enjoy a form of life scarcely superior to that of plants; oysters, which are motionless, have only the sense of touch and are fixed to the earth like plants" (*Summa Gentiles*, II, 68). Cf. chapter 7, note 21.

10. Not even Darwin tried to account for the origin of *qualia*. Cf. *Origin of Species*, (Great Books edition), pp. 85–86.

11. Behaviorism is the name given to the thesis that pain (and all other sentient states) is reducible to pain behavior (or some other disposition to observable behavior). The errors of behaviorism are considered in chapter 9, subsection "Two Reductionist Theories."

12. "If philosophy identifies true knowledge with useful knowledge, as modern scientism does, final causality will be by the same stroke eliminated from nature and from science as a useless fiction. Aristotle, who was a Greek, saw things otherwise. In his philos-

ophy final causality occupied a considerable position because its workings were, for him, an inexhaustible source of contemplation and admiration. In astronomy, in physics, and in biology he was as curious to know how things happened as our contemporaries can be, but he thought he had come across the truth of nature from the moment when he had perceived its beauty. Not so much aesthetic beauty, such as that of light and colors or forms; but first of all and above all the intelligible beauty, which consists in the apperception by the mind of the order which rules the structure of forms and presides over their relations" (Gilson, *From Aristotle to Darwin*, p. 19).

13. "Whereas the main business of natural philosophy is to argue from phenomena without feigning hypotheses, and to deduce causes from effects, till we come to the very first cause, which certainly is not mechanical; and not only to unfold the mechanism of the world, but chiefly to resolve these and such like questions. . . . Whence is it that Nature doth nothing in vain; and whence arises all that order and beauty which we see in the world? . . . And though every true step made in this philosophy brings us not immediately to the knowledge of the First Cause, yet it brings us nearer to it, and on that account is to be highly valued" (Newton, *Optics*, Book III, Part 1, qu. 28).

And again, "I no longer think, as I once did, that there is a difference between science and metaphysics regarding this most important point [testability]. I look upon a metaphysical theory as similar to a scientific one. It is vaguer, no doubt . . . . But, *as long as a metaphysical theory can be rationally criticized*, I should be inclined to take seriously its implicit claim to be considered, tentatively, as true. . . . It is here, perhaps, that we may find a criterion of demarcation *within metaphysics*, between rationally worthless metaphysical systems, and metaphysical systems that are worth discussing, and worth thinking about. The proper aspiration of a metaphysician, I am inclined to say, is to gather all the true aspects of the world (and not merely its scientific aspects) into a unifying picture which enlighten him and others, and which one day may become part of a still more comprehensive picture, a better picture, a truer picture. The criterion, then, will be fundamentally the same as in the sciences. Whether a picture is worth considering depends, I suggest, upon its capacity to provoke rational criticism, and to inspire attempts to supersede it by something better (rather than upon its capacity to create a fashion, to be supplanted presently by a new fashion, or upon claims to originality or finality). And this criterion, I believe, may also point to one of the characteristic differences between a work of science or of metaphysics and a work of art that aspires to be something that cannot, in its own way, be bettered" (Popper, *Quantum Theory*, pp. 199, 211).

14. In fact, it is even possible that viewed from below there may be some overlap. For example, it is possible that some plants (a Venus flytrap) may be materially more complex than some animals (an oyster).

15. "In spite of all the achievements that physiologists have made with a reliance on physics and chemistry, they have not been able to stifle the urge to do justice to the apparent goal-seeking which is displayed by countless organisms. Again and again reputable biologists raised the idea of some vital force, though in a way which defeats the purpose. For as long as they assign some material reality [e.g., a "gap" in the causal sequence] to that force, they invite the search for its detection, which invariably ends in failure. . . . For to see life, let alone to understand what it means to see, let alone to see for a purpose, eyes are needed that can see more than extension and mere empirical data" (Jaki, *Means to Message*, pp. 92–3).

16. This may be a little too strong. "I, at any rate, see no merit in the arbitrary proposal to define the word 'philosophy' in a way which may well prevent a student of philosophy from trying to contribute, *qua* philosopher, to the advancement of our knowledge of the world. . . . For it is a fact that purely metaphysical ideas—and therefore philosophical

ideas—have been of the greatest importance for cosmology. From Thales to Einstein . . . metaphysical ideas have shown the way" (Popper, *Logic of Scientific Discovery*, p. 19).

17. "The scientist who denies or neglects philosophy, and regards his sort of research as making the only contribution, is likely to indulge in pseudo-philosophical generalizations about the absolute continuity of natural things, a continuity in which there are merely accidental, and often arbitrary, differences between the least complicated, inert body and the most complex, living things. The philosopher who does not understand the difference between his problems and those of the scientist, is likely to misinterpret the evidence which the latter offers by trying to make accidental classifications the basis for specific distinctions. The philosopher's misapprehension of infra-specific continuities is as serious an error as the scientist's denial of hierarchy" (Adler, *The Problem of Species*, p. 242).

18. Cf. chapter 11, where the attempt to ground free will in the discoveries of quantum mechanics is discussed.

19. While many, if not most, philosophers and scientists react strongly against the sort of ontology outlined in this chapter, not all do. For example, Karl Popper writes, "My position may thus be described as one that upholds a theory of *irreducibility and emergence.* . . . I conjecture that there is no biological process which cannot be regarded as *correlated* [emphasis added] in detail with a physical process or cannot be progressively analyzed in physicochemical terms. But no physicochemcial theory can explain the emergence of a new problem, and no physicochemical process can as such solve a *problem.* . . . From these distinctions we are led to the following thesis: *the problems of organisms are not physical: they are neither physical things, nor physical laws, nor physical facts. They are specific biological realities; they are 'real' in the sense that their existence may be the cause of biological effects"* (*Unended Quest*, pp. 171–178).

Henry Margenau writes, "In turning our attention toward the phenomena of life we shall heed this lesson: to expect reducibility, that is, a mere extension of the observables and laws of physics . . . would contradict even what we found in analyzing the various domains of the inorganic realm. But we do expect compatibility. We must look for novel kinds of observables . . . that must not contradict those appearing in our previous examples but need not apply to them, any more than temperature applies to a single molecule" (Margenau, *The Miracle of Existence*, p. 9).

John Eccles writes, "The functional asymmetry of the human cerebral cortex is a most important development in hominid evolution. The evidence from apes and monkeys suggest that our hominoid ancestors had symmetrical brains. Asymmetry is unique to humans. . . . It is proposed that the neo-neocortical areas [Brodmann areas 39 and 40] are developed in evolution for the special gnostic functions that are unique features in hominid evolution (Sperry, 1982). Hitherto it was generally believed that the superior gnostic performance of the human brain was due to its magnitude. This is a crude belief with no redeeming creative idea. On the contrary, it now is proposed that the outstanding functions of the human brain derive from the neo-neocortex which presumably would be negligible in the most advance hominoids, on analogy with the ape model (figure 4.5)" (*Evolution of the Brain*, pp. 200, 213).

Theodosius Dobzhansky writes, "Self-awareness is, then, one of the fundamental, possibly the most fundamental, characteristic of the human species. This characteristic is an evolutionary novelty; the biological species from which mankind has descended had only rudiments of self-awareness, or perhaps lacked it altogether. Self-awareness has, however, brought in its train somber companions—fear, anxiety and death awareness. . . . Man is burdened by death-awareness. A being who knows that he will die arose from ancestors who did not know" (*The Biology of Ultimate Concern*, p. 68, quoted in Eccles, *Evolution of the Brain*, p. 203).

Ernst Mayr writes, "There are two criteria of progressiveness that would seem to have a considerable amount of objective validity. One of these is parental care (made possible by internal fertilization), which provides the potential for transferring information non-genetically from one generation to the next. And the possession of such information is of course of considerable value in the struggle for existence. This information transfer generates at the same time a selection pressure in favor of an improved storage system for such remembered information, that is, an enlarged central nervous system. And, of course, the combination of postnatal care and an enlarged central nervous system is the basis [necessary condition] of culture, and culture together with speech setting man quite aside from all other living organisms" (*Toward a New Philosophy of Biology*, pp. 252–53).

Michael Polanyi's "Life's Irreducible Structure" (*Scientific American*, June 1968, vol. 160) presents a somewhat cryptic, yet powerful, argument for the claim that biological hierarchies are irreducible.

For those who are mathematically inclined, Peter Madawar's short but influential "A Geometric Model of Reduction and Emergence" (Ayala and Dobzhansky, *Studies in the Philosophy of Biology*, pp. 57–63) is a good place to begin.

Chapter 5: The Hows of Science and the Whys of Philosophy

1. This is not to say that Aristotle's critics are always wrong. Aristotle's rush to discover final causes in *On the Heaven* and *Meteorology*, to the virtual exclusion of efficient causes, is certainly worthy of criticism. Aristotle's own successor as head of the Lyceum said, "With regard to the view that all things are for the sake of an end and nothing is in vain, the assignation of ends is in general not easy, as it is usually stated to be" (Jaki, *The Relevance of Physics*, p. 33). For an extensive summary of Aristotle's howlers when it comes to the physical sciences, see chapter 1 of *The Relevance of Physics*.

2. Descartes, *Meditations on First Philosophy*, Meditation #4. In light of Jaki's comments in the previous note, one might think that we are being too hard on Descartes. After all, Aristotle's own successor, not to mention contemporary philosophers of science like Jaki, do make a strong case against the appeal to final causes in *physics*. True, but "physics" is ambiguous. As Jaki is using the term it refers to physical sciences only (i.e., as opposed to the biological sciences). As Descartes is using the term, however, it is quite clear that he means to refer to *all* extended objects—whether inanimate or animate.

Compare Popper's comments, "My thesis is that, in trying to combine the doctrine of the incorporeality of the soul, and of interaction, with a mechanistic and monistic principle of physical causation, Descartes created an entirely new and unnecessary difficulty . . . to sum up. The great difficulty of the Cartesian theory of mind-body interaction lies in the Cartesian theory of physical causality according to which all physical action must be by mechanical push" (*The Self and Its Brain*, pp. 176–80).

3. *Variation of Animals and Plants Under Domestication II* (New York: D. Appleton and Company, 1875), p. 415.

4. He said, "I cannot persuade myself that a beneficent and omnipotent God would have designedly created the *Ichneumonidae* with the express intention of their feeding within the living bodies of Caterpillars." Cited in David L Hull, *Darwin and His Critics* (Cambridge, Mass.: Harvard University Press, 1973), p. 65.

5. Himmelfard, quoted in Phillip Johnson, *Darwin on Trail*, p. 180.

6. The first footnote in Darwin's *Origin of Species* makes this same point, along with some other interesting observations. "Aristotle in his *Physics* (Bk II, ch. 8), after remarking that rain does not fall in order to make the corn grow, any more than it falls to spoil the farmer's corn when threshed out of doors, applies the same argument to organization; and adds (as translated by Mr. Clair Grece, who first pointed out the passage to me), 'So what hinders the different parts [of the body] from having this merely accidental relation

in nature? As the teeth, for example, grow by necessity, the front ones sharp, adapted for dividing, and the grinders flat, and serviceable for masticating the food; since they were not made for the sake of this, but it was the result of accident. And in like manner as to the other parts in which there appears to exist an adaptation to an end. Wheresoever, therefore, all things together (that is all the parts of one whole) happened like as if they were made for the sake of something, these were preserved, having been appropriately constituted by an internal spontaneity; and whatsoever things were not thus constituted, perished, and still perish.' We here see the principle of natural selection shadowed forth, but how little Aristotle fully comprehended the principle, is shown by his remarks on the formation of the teeth."

7. Clearly this is only true in most cases. Evolutionary biology does not demand that *all* species evolve. It is quite possible that relatively "primitive" species found an ecological "niche" very early and have not had to develop more sophisticated mechanisms for survival. There is also some disagreement among biologists whether there is a general evolutionary push toward complexity. While Richard Dawkins argues that there is a general "arms race" among species that leads to a continuing cycle of new offensive and defensive mechanisms, Stephen J. Gould disagrees. He argues that evolution is devoid of "directionality." Cf. Robert Wright's essay in the *New Yorker,* December 13, 1999, for a painless introduction to this dispute among evolutionary biologists.

8. *On the Parts of Animals*, I.1.642a.

9. Putnam, *The Renewal of Philosophy*, p. 50. Karl Popper makes the same point in *The Self and Its Brain*, pp. 204–05.

10. "The irrational souls [of plants and animals] or essences of Aristotle may be said to be anticipations of modern gene theory: like DNA they plan the actions of the organism and steer it to its *telos*, to its perfection" (Popper and Eccles, *The Brain and Its Self*, p. 167).

11. *On the Soul*, 403b7.

12. "The nominalist cannot demonstrate the need for the restrictions he imposes on himself . . . [principles of this kind] are stipulated as prerequisites of soundness in a philosophic system. They are usually adopted because a philosopher's conscience gives him no choice in the matter" (N. Goodman, *The Problem of Universals*, section 3, quoted in Staniland, *Universals*, p. 89.

13. *Three Rival Versions of Moral Enquiry*, p. 67.

Chapter 6: How Aristotelians Think About What They Know

1. "In any discussion of parts or pieces of equipment we must not think that it is the material that is the real object of enquiry, but rather the structure as a whole: the house, for example, not the bricks, mortar and timber. In the same way, we must recognize that a student of nature is concerned with the composition and the being as a whole, not with parts that can never exist in separation from the being they belong to" (Aristotle, *Parts of Animals*, I.5.645a5).

2. "We reply that not all knowledge is demonstrative, and in fact knowledge of the immediate premises is indemonstrable. Indeed, it is evident that this must be so" (*Posterior Analytics*, 72b19).

3. True, Descartes thought he had produced a more obvious truth in the *cogito ergo sum*—"I think, therefore I am." But even if we grant that this is a more obvious truth than the fact that dogs and cats exist, it is not a truth about the world. Rather, it is a truth about one's own ideas. This gives rise to *the* insoluble problem of all idealisms—how to start with a mere idea and end with reality. Rather than trying to square the circle, Aristotelians realize that the only way to avoid dead ends is to take a different path.

4. See also Francis H. Parker, "Traditional Reason and Modern Reason" in *Faith and Philosophy: Philosophical Studies in Religion and Ethics*, ed. by Alvin Plantinga (Grand Rapids: Eerdmans, 1964), pp. 37–50.

5. "For to proceed from cause to effects or the reverse is not an activity of the senses but only of the intellect" (Aquinas, *Commentary on Aristotle's Metaphysics*, section 1146).

6. In Aristotelian terms, being a "featherless biped" is a *property* of human in the same way that working through chlorophyll "A" (as opposed to "B" or "C") is a *property* of photosynthesis. That is, it just so happens for purely accidental reasons that all photosynthesis on this earth takes place through chlorophyll "A". There is no evolutionary reason that photosynthesis couldn't have developed through either chlorophyll "B" or "C". I am grateful to Gary Fugal for this example.

7. For a somewhat technical argument along the same lines, see "The Crash of Modal Metaphysics" by James F. Ross in *Review of Metaphysics*, Dec. 1989, vol. XLIII, no. 2. A book-length treatment is found in Henry Veatch, *Intentional Logic* and *Two Logics: the Conflict between Classical and Neo-analytic*.

8. "A subject-predicate sentence or proposition, as Aristotle conceives it, functions as an organon of knowledge precisely in the sense that it is a device conceived to enable us to understand things in terms of what they are. In contrast, the predicate calculus of the new logic is a device conceived to enable us to understand things in terms of their relationships of other things" (Veatch, *Aristotle*, p. 186). Again, "However, if predicates are to be understood on the model of relations, then this is tantamount to acknowledging that no predicate ever expresses what its subject is, simply for the reason that no relation ever expresses what its relata are" (Veatch, *Two Logics*, p. 34).

The problem with modern logic is that the number of possible relations between objects is infinite. Paradise is not only one hundred miles north of Sacramento, but it is also four hundred miles south of Eugene and a thirteen-hour drive from Seattle, etc. No single relation is any more "true" than any other. Thus, if a logic is designed to reveal relations and not what a thing is or why it is, logic becomes a tool for *creating* reality but not for *discovering* it. In Aristotle's case, the knowledge logic reveals is "knowledge of being and of things as they are in themselves; in the other case [modern logic] knowledge is not a knowledge of being or of the nature of things or of the way things are in the usual sense at all, but only of the way things are for us, and of being as it appears to us when structured by the logical forms and patterns which we impose upon it in our effects to know it and deal with it" (Veatch, *Aristotle*, p. 197).

9. Chapter 66, vol. 2 of *Summa Contra Gentiles*—"Against those who maintain that intellect and sense are the same"—may be relevant here. The five arguments are:

- All brutes have sense, but they always act the same—every swallow builds its nest in the same way.
- Sense only knows singulars; intellect knows universals.
- Sense only knows corporeal things; intellect knows incorporeal things such as wisdom, truth, and the relations of things.
- Sense only knows other things; intellect knows itself.
- Sense is corrupted by extremely loud sounds or bright objects; intellect is not.

Contemporary Aristotelians continue to defend the first four arguments, but not the fifth.

10. Cf. Aquinas, *Summa Theologica*, I q. 78, art. 4 for a list of all the things the "sensitive soul" is capable of knowing. We agree completely with David Ruel Foster's comments on this passage. He writes, "Even if we are armed with a healthy skepticism regarding the many claims made for animal intelligence, we cannot help but be impressed. Further,

there is the more common experience of being outsmarted by one's own dog. If we care to be respecters of the common opinion, as Aristotle was, then our arguments must some-how respect the opinion that animals can be 'smart.' All of this is to say that other ani-mals do manifest a significant amount of knowing and that materialists and Thomists agree that this activity is carried on by physical organs. A response in the spirit of St. Thomas would somehow incorporate this information without making the additional but mistaken claim that human intelligence can be reduced without remainder to brain activ-ity" (*The Thomist*, 1991, p. 435).

11. The ability to distinguish between form and shape seems to have a biological basis in the distinct functional abilities of the left (dominant side in 95% of the case studies) and right (minor) hemispheres in the human brain. Conceptual thought is biologically based in the dominant hemisphere; whereas the ability to recognize shapes is biologically based in the minor hemisphere. Nonhuman brains are functionally symmetrical and their abilities seem to correspond to the abilities of a human's minor hemisphere. This later fact confirms the common observation that nonhuman animals are very good at recog-nizing natural signs, but completely unable to understand intentional symbols. (This cru-cial distinction is discussed in chapter 9.) Eccles writes, "Most evidence from language testing of chimpanzees indicates likewise that they are unable to complete sentences, though some dubious claims have been made. This, of course, arises from the fact that neither the minor hemisphere nor the chimpanzee brain has a Wernicke area that pro-vides the necessary semantic ability" (*Evolution of the Brain*, p. 208ff). Eccles fleshes out this argument with the citations from specific studies in *The Self and Its Brain*, pp. 308–09.

12. Once again, the example is Hilary Putnam's. See *The Renewal of Philosophy*, p. 12.

13. Sue Savage-Rumbaugh is one of the more recent animal behaviorists who argues that there is no difference in kind between human and animal languages. She writes, "Lan-guage is a funny thing. We do not think of it as behavior, yet at heart that is all it really is—another form of behavior" (*Apes Language, and the Human Mind*, p. 226). If Savage-Rumbaugh is correct about her characterization of language, then of course animals have languages. But this explicit behaviorism is not a conclusion established by her study of ape behavior; rather, it is the unexamined philosophical assumption that she brings to her study. (See chapter 9, section "Two Reductionist Theories" for further discussion of behaviorism.) Given such philosophical question begging, it is not surprising that her study would include comments like: (1)"Smashing rocks to create a sharp edge does not, on the face of it, require vastly greater intelligence than that demonstrated by apes who crack nuts using a stone anvil and hammer-stone" (187). Really? Perhaps the intelligence is not "greater," but it is certainly different in kind. Rocks turned into weapons serve no immediate purpose—they are only useful for the hunt tomorrow or the next day, whereas the fruit from the cracked nut is immediately perceptible. *Making* stone tools (as opposed to simply *using* stone tools) presupposes the understanding of concepts to have no per-ceptual referent. (2) "The idea that there is a dictionary that allows us to look up the mean-ings of words confuses us. It makes us think that the meaning of the given word is in the dictionary—in some way oddly inherent in the word itself. But it is not, it is only in the usage" (198). Who is the "us" being referred to? And what does "oddly inherent in the word itself" mean? Certainly no Aristotelian (or any other person of common sense) has ever seriously thought that the meaning of a word is "in" the ink or sound waves the way dirt is *in* a rug! Her appeal to the "social construction" and to Wittgensteinian "language games" in the next paragraph hardly helps. If meanings are not in individual words the way dirt is in rugs, then it is no better to suggest that meanings are socially "constructed." Constructed out of what? Bricks and mortar? Wood and nails? If someone insists on the construction metaphor, then they can only be "constructed" out of *concepts*. Or to make the point in

explicitly Aristotelian terms, meanings are forms that have been abstracted from perceived objects by an agent intellect.

On the other end of the spectrum is John Eccles. He argues that distinction between conceptual and perceptual knowledge is implied by the physiological evidence coming from the "split-brain" experiments of Zaidel and Sperry (cf., *The Self and Its Brain*, pp. 323–24). The minor hemisphere of the brain can understand and correlate pictures and "verbal signs" (i.e., natural signs—cf. chapter 9), but it can't understand a simple sentence like: "Mother loves baby." Cf. note 11 above.

Chapter 7: The Challenge of Evolutionary Biology

1. *Meditations*, chapter 4.

2. Darwin reasoned that if people like Paley pleaded for divine providence behind those variations that led to useful and beneficial organs, consistency would demand the same origin in the case of useless and even injurious organs. Did God ordain, Darwin asked, "that the crop and tail-feathers of the pigeon should vary in order that the fancier might make his grotesque pouter and fantail breeds? Did He cause the frame and mental qualities of the dog to vary in order that a breed might be formed of indomitable ferocity, with jaws fitted to pin down the bull for man's brutal sport?" Surely no one could admit divine providence in these matters! Darwin concluded, then, by parity of reasoning, that "no shadow of reason can be assigned for the belief that variations, alike in nature and the result of the same general laws, which have been the groundwork through natural selection of the formation of the most perfectly adapted animals in the world, man included, were intentionally and specially guided" (*The Variation of Animals and Plants Under Domestication*, vol. II, p. 415).

In his *Autobiography* he wrote, "That there is much suffering in the world no one disputes. Some have attempted to explain this with reference to man by imagining that it serves for his moral improvement. But the number of men in the world is as nothing compared with that of all other sentient beings, and they often suffer greatly without any moral improvement. This very old argument from the existence of suffering against the existence of an intelligent First Cause seems to me a strong one; whereas, as just remarked, the presence of much suffering agrees well with the view that all organic beings have been developed through variations and natural selection" (Francis Darwin, *The Life and Letters of Charles Darwin*, I, 280–281). See also, Ric Machuga, *America's First Anti-Darwinist: Charles Hodge* (unpublished thesis), p. 52.

3. Descartes, *Meditations*, chapter 4, p. 83 in the Hackett edition, translated by Donald A. Cress. Again, "We shall adopt no opinions whatever about the goals that either God or nature might have set for themselves in producing the things of nature, because we should not arrogantly claim to be privy to their counsels," Descartes, *Les principes de la philosophie*, quoted in Jaki, *Relevance of Physics*, p. 57.

4. "All the evolutionary phenomena and aspect of evolutionary progress that were considered as irrefutable proof of teleology by earlier generations can now be shown to be entirely consistent with natural selection" (Mayr, *Toward a New Philosophy of Biology*, p. 254). Note the ambiguity. Mayr is correct to argue that teleology is not *discovered* by observing the complexity in nature because apparent purpose can be explained as resulting from efficient causes, but this is not to prove that teleology is *eliminated* by natural selection since efficient causes and final causes are not competing alternatives. Mayr continues, "Thus the Darwinian mechanism of variation and selection, of speciation and extinction, are fully capable of explaining all macroevolutionary developments, whether specialization, improvements, or other innovations. And none of this *requires* any finalistic agents." We believe Mayr is correct about this too. He is also correct to suggest that such evolutionary explanation refutes the natural theology of the nineteenth century that

assumed that final causes and efficient causes were exclusive alternatives, but note that to say that *biological* diversification does not require final causes to fill gaps in the series of efficient causes is perfectly consistent with the existence of final causes. Our only claim is that *ontological* diverse (species) require final causes, i.e., cannot be explained solely by efficient causes. See note 26 below.

5. Charles B. Thaxton, et. al., *The Mystery of Life's Origins*, p. 3.

6. Even Isaac Newton fell into this trap. "Clearly, Paley's argumentation is all too often a case of argument from the gaps of scientific knowledge. In Paley's England few if any looked with suspicion at this type of reasoning. It had received scientific aura through the Scholium which Roger Coats appended to the third edition of Newton's *Principia* with its author's full approval. There a half a dozen features of the solar system, unexplainable in terms of the *Principia*, were listed as so many evidences of a directly divine design" (Jaki, *The Purpose of it All*, p. 69).

After arguing that the beautiful order of the solar system and stars "could only proceed from the counsel and dominion of an intelligent and powerful Being," Newton concludes his great *Mathematical Principles of Natural Philosophy* with an acknowledgment that it includes a gravitational paradox—since all particles mutually attract all other particles, why don't all particles collapse into a single gigantic and superdense mass? His solution is an appeal to God's power: "And lest the systems of the fixed stars should, by their gravity, fall on each other, he [God] hath placed those systems at immense distances from one another" (*Great Books of the Western World*, vol. 34, p. 370). Newton is even more explicit about the need for God to "fix" the problem in a letter to Bentley, "And though the matter were divided at first into several systems, and every system by a divine power constituted like ours; yet would the outside systems descend towards the middlemost; so that this frame of things could not always subsist without a divine power to conserve it. . ." (Third letter to Bentley, *Opere*, IV, quoted in Keostler, *Sleepwalkers*, pp. 503–04).

7. Cf. note 2 in chapter 4 above and the whole of chapter 11 of Polanyi's, *Personal Knowledge*.

8. "The world of philosophers and physicists was for hundreds of years completely deaf to the assertion of naturalists such as Aristotle that something more than the laws of physics was needed to produce a frog from a frog egg and a chicken from a chicken egg (Mayr, 1976). Nor does this require any *elan vital, nisus formativus, Entelechie*, or living spirit. All it requires is the recognition that complex biological systems are the product of genetic programs that have a history of more than three thousand million years"(Mayr, *The Growth of Biological Thought*, p. 89–90. Compare this with Jaki's comment in note 15 in chapter 4). Mayr is absolutely correct. Though as we argue below, in 'As If' Scenarios," the notion of "genetic programs" is itself a thoroughly Aristotelian notion.

9. "It is absurd to suppose that purpose is not present because we do not observe the agent deliberating" (Aristotle, *Physics*, 199b25).

10. Aristotle, *On the Soul*, I.1.403a25ff.

11. Aristotle, *On the Part of Animals*, I.1.642a. Cf. the opening chapter of *On the Soul*.

12. We agree with Popper. "The irrational souls [of plants and animals] or essences of Aristotle may be said to be anticipations of modern gene theory: like DNA they plan the actions of the organism and steer it to its *telos*, to its perfection" (*The Self and Its Brain*, p. 167).

13. "This celebrated 'substantial form,' the nonexistence of which Descartes took upon himself to announce to the world, justifies itself in Aristotle's eyes by the sole fact that unless one assigns it as a cause, the growth of living beings becomes inexplicable from the point of view of being oriented to a limit" (Gilson, *From Aristotle to Darwin*, p. 15).

14. The philosophical originator of "as if" scenarios is Kant. Polanyi is hardly too hard on Kant when he writes, "Instead, we meet with the typical device of modern intellectual

prevarication, first systematized by Kant in his regulative principles. Knowledge that we hold to be true and also vital to us, is made light of, because we cannot account for its acceptance in terms of a critical philosophy. We then feel entitled to continue using that knowledge, even while flattering our sense of intellectual superiority by disparaging it. We actually go on, firmly relying on this despised knowledge to guide and lend meaning to our more exact enquiries, while pretending that these alone come up to our standards of scientific stringency" (*Personal Knowledge*, p. 354). Cf. note 16 below.

And though this is no place to engage in a full-fledged critique of Kant, it is worth noting that Kant's conclusions hardly follow, as he sometimes suggests, from Enlightenment advances in scientific understanding. "Newton himself, let it be noted, held fast all his life to the ideas of a finite universe. . . . [F]rom almost the very appearance of the idea of an infinite universe it was pointed out that such a universe was saddled by the gravitational paradox and, give certain assumptions, even by an optical counterpart of it [Olber's paradox]. . . . Those paradoxes, which he [Kant] ignored, certainly showed that the idea of the infinite universe was scientifically contradictory, but the science of the day did not show this to be the case about a finite universe. Kant kept mum about all this, possibly because he realized that it spelt the death knell on the first antinomy, or his claim that the mind could not decide whether the universe was infinite or finite and that therefore the idea of a universe was not a valid notion" (Jaki, *Means to the Message*, p. 145).

15. See appendix on Dembski.

16. For a more general criticism of modern philosophers' and scientists' retreat to "as if" scenarios, see Polanyi, *Personal Knowledge*, chapter 10, "Commitment," especially page 307: "By regulative principles, in the general sense in which the term is employed here, I mean all manner of recommendations to act on a belief while denying, disguising, or otherwise minimizing the fact that we are holding this belief. Originally, Kant had recommended that certain generalizations (as for example the teleological aptness of living organisms) should be entertained *as if* they were true, without assuming that they were true. However, Kant does not say that we should entertain these generalizations as if they were true, even though we know them to be false. His recommendation to entertain them *as if* they were true is thus seen to be based on the tacit assumption that they are in fact true. By conveying this assumption without asserting it, he avoids any formulation which would require to be upheld as his own personal judgment."

17. *The Blind Watchmaker*, pp. 154–55.

18. "Similarly, we can use a descriptive word sceptically by putting it in quotation marks. Suppose a paper is published under the title: *An Explanation of 'Extra-sensory Perception'*, and another I reply to it, entitled: *An 'Explanation' of Extra-sensory Perception*. Guided by the quotation marks we recognize immediately that the first paper regards extra-sensory perception as spurious, while the second accredits it as genuine and discredits, on the contrary, the explanation suggested for its in the first paper." (Polanyi, *Personal Knowledge*, pp. 249–50).

19. Cairns-Smith, *Seven Keys to the Origin of Life*, p. 12.

20. Ibid., p. 3.

21. The "seems" in this sentence is no accident. Only epistemologically speaking is there any fuzziness in the distinction between life and nonlife. Michael Polanyi, an author with whom we are very sympathetic, argues that even the irreducibility of ontological levels of being does not require *strict* discontinuities in nature. "But there does exist a rather different continuity between life and inanimate nature. For the beginnings of life do not sharply differ from their purely physical-chemical antecedents. One can reconcile this continuity with the irreducibility of living things by recalling the analogous case of inanimate artifacts. Take the irreducibility of machines; no animal can produce a machine, but some animals can make primitive tools, and their use of these tools may be hardly

distinguishable from the mere use of the animal's limbs. Or take a set of sounds conveying information; the set of sounds can be so obscured by noise that its presence is no
longer clearly identifiable. We can say, then, that the control exercised by the boundary
conditions of a system can be reduced gradually to a vanishing point. The fact that the
effect of a higher principle over a system under dual control can have any value down to
zero may allow us also to conceive of the continuous emergence of irreducible principles
within the origin of life" ("Life's Irreducible Structure" *Science* 160: 1310).

Some of the difficulty here is undoubtedly real, though some of it is wholly verbal and
due to the vagueness of the word "strict discontinuities." Exactly *how* discontinuous must
two events be for them to be different in kind and not just degree? It seems fairly obvious
that climbing trees and trying to put a man on the moon are two distinctly different *kinds*
of activities, even through in *some sense* we can understand the argument (joke?) that the
first person to climb a tree is making progress toward putting a man on the moon.

Lawyers commonly say that hard cases make bad laws. Perhaps philosophers need
something like a "nil principle." Newton says both (1) that the acceleration of bodies under
the gravitation of the earth is independent of their weight *and* (2) that all objects attract
all other objects in proportion to their mass and inversely proportion to their distance.
But, strictly speaking, these are contradictory. Consider two objects, a sixteen-pound shot
put and a one-pound softball. The acceleration of these two objects toward the earth is
the same, but there is also the gravitation attraction of these objects on the earth pulling
it toward them. Since the shot put is 15 times heavier than the softball, the shot put will
pull the earth toward it with greater force than the softball. Therefore, since the combined
mutual attraction of the earth/shotput is greater than the mutual attraction of the earth/soft-
ball, the shotput must fall faster than the softball.

Newton's response, I believe, would be fairly obvious—while a shotput may be sixteen
times heavier than a softball, the difference between the combined mass of the earth/shot
put and the earth/softball is *nil* and not worth worrying about. Perhaps something like
this is what the medieval philosophers had in mind when they said that the lower always
touches the higher—the "force" of the touch can be so slight as to be nil, and hence, the
distinction between the lower and the higher is still one of *kind,* not *degree.*

22. "However, if we are to identify—as I am about to suggest—the presence of significant order with the operation of an ordering principle, no highly significant order [form
as opposed to shape] can ever be said to be solely due to an accidental collocation of atom,
and we must conclude therefore that the assumption of an accidental formation of the
living species is a logical muddle. It appears to be a piece of equivocation, unconsciously
prompted by the urge to avoid facing the problem set to us by the fact that the universe
has given birth to these curious beings, including people like ourselves. To say that this
result was achieved by natural selection is entirely beside the point. Natural selection tells
us only why the unfit failed to survive and not why any living beings, either fit or unfit,
ever came into existence" (Polanyi, *Personal Knowledge,* p. 35).

23. There is a second objection that is more general and worthy only of an endnote.
How can something *be* information if no one *knows* that it is information? Rhetorical
questions like this are revealing, sneering, and not worth losing sleep over.

First, they are revealing because they indicate how profoundly the Cartesian "epistemological turn" has influenced our culture. Prior to Descartes, there were only a very few
philosophers who wondered how something could exist that wasn't perceived. It was simply obvious to the ancients that things exist that humans didn't (and even couldn't) know.
Certainly Pluto didn't *begin* to exist in the nineteenth century when it was first observed!

Second, they are sneering because they implicitly depend on the rhetorical force of a
sarcastic skepticism that responds to obviously true statements like, "Pluto existed before
it was observed" with a question like, "What is truth?"

Third, they aren't worth losing sleep over. As Aristotle demonstrates in book IV of the *Metaphysics*, total skepticism ultimately leads to either self-contradiction or vegetable-like silence.

24. This kind of example, to my knowledge, first appeared in chapter 3 of Michael Polanyi's *Personal Knowledge*. Since then it has also be employed by Richard Taylor (though for slightly different ends) in chapter 10 of *Metaphysics*.

25. Since these rocks don't really mean what they say, it is perhaps better to refer to them as misinformation. This too may be viewed as paralleling Dawkins's explicitly stated claim that just because the complex organs of animals look like they are designed, that does not mean that they *are* designed.

26. It is crucial to distinguish teleological conclusions and teleological assumptions. Aristotelians argue that biology *assumes* teleology. It is only Paley and his followers who argue that the mathematical complexity of biological organisms *demonstrate* the existence of a designer. Hence Aristotelians would agree with Mayr when he says that "scientific biology has not found any evidence that would *support* teleology in the sense of various vitalistic and finalistic theories" and thus rejects "the supernaturalistic *conclusions* drawn from" such theories (*Toward a New Philosophy of Biology*, p. 31, emphasis added). Yet he has no problem assuming that information theory throws light on the function of DNA or that animal behavior is the result of a genetic program which is analogous to a computer program.

Again, Mayr says, "The occurrence of a given mutation is in no way related to the evolutionary needs of the particular organism or of the population to which it belongs" (*Toward a New Philosophy of Biology*, p. 33). In one sense this is correct. Mutations do not occur because a particular organism or population is "trying" to improve itself. Nor can humans, with limited understanding, figure out the "point or purpose" to a specific mutation. Neither of these, however, entail the conclusion—"Therefore, the mutation was not the result of divine intentions." If a hungry and homeless man awakes on the sidewalk to find a ten-dollar bill next to his hand, he cannot know whether the money was accidentally dropped by an drunken partier or intentionally placed there by a generous benefactor. It is an argument from ignorance to reason that because the hungry man did nothing to cause his windfall, that therefore, his "windfall" was *not* a response to his need.

We believe that Gilson hit the nail on the head. "Natural science neither destroys final causality nor establishes it. These two principles belong to the philosophy of the science of nature, to that which we have called its 'wisdom.' What scientists, as scientists, can do to help clarify the problem of natural teleology is not to busy themselves with it. They are the most qualified of all to keep philosophizing about it, if they so desire; but it is then necessary that they agree to philosophize" (*From Aristotle to Darwin*, p. 16).

[27]Darwin wrote in a 1870 letter to J. Hooker, "I cannot look at the universe as a result of blind chance. Yet I can see no evidence of beneficent design, or indeed any design of any kind, in the details." Jaki responds, "Darwin was much too shortsighted philosophically to realize that in order to see design one needed, in addition to physical eyes, mental eyes" (*The Purpose of it All*, p. 49). Note too the backward glance to the problem of evil evidenced in the phrase "beneficent design."

28. Ironically, there may be reason to believe that evolution *supports* an Aristotelian theory of the mind. Karl Popper argues that any theory of the mind that grants the existence of consciousness yet denies that mental states can causally interact with physical states is *inconsistent* with an evolutionary approach to biology. That is, Popper argues that since biological evolution is true, therefore materialism is false. His argument is that until conscious states causally interact with the environment (that is, they affect and are affected by the physical environment), there is no evolutionary explanation for a fact that three billion years ago there were no conscious states and today there are. In short, if con-

sciousness didn't help preserve a species, i.e., if conscious states were mere froth on the wave (epiphenomenal), then there is no evolutionary reason why consciousness should have persisted after it produced random events. See Part 1, chapter 3 of *The Self and Its Brain*.

See Polanyi for a different criticism of epiphenomenalism. "I have refused to assume that if we succeeded in revising the laws of physics and chemistry, so as to account for the sentience of animals and men, these would still appear to us as automata—with the super-added absurdity of a totally ineffectual mental life accompanying their automatic performances. To represent living men as insentient is empirically false, but to regard them as thoughtful automata is logical nonsense. For we are aware of a man's thoughts only by listening to him, i.e. by attending subsidiarily to certain bodily actions on the assumption that they are impelled by his thoughts, which are in fact known to us only as the effective centre of his meaningful actions. Nor can we speak therefore of thinking which totally lacks originality and responsibility; or indeed, envisage another person's considered judgment without acknowledging its universal intent, which challenges us to follow or contradict it. These feature are essential to our pre-scientific conception of thought, and neurology cannot be said to account for thinking unless it represents it as something in which these features are still recognizable" (*Personal Knowledge*, p. 339).

Chapter 8: The Challenge of Artificial Intelligence

1. The phrase "designed to make" is clearly provocative, and deliberately so. Someone like Richard Dawkins would undoubtedly respond, "But the designer is blind!" Yet, as Popper frequently reminds us, the discussion about "machine intelligence" almost always overlooks the obvious fact that every single alleged example of an intelligent machine—from a simple thermostat to the most sophisticated computer—was designed by humans to act "intelligently."

2. In contemporary jargon, this is called "an inference to the best explanation" and should not be confused with the wholly deductive use of indirect arguments in formal logic.

3. The Copenhagen interpretation of quantum mechanics "took essentially two forms: (1) an electron or photon is sometimes a particle and sometimes a wave, depending on the conditions under which it is observed, and (2) it is both a particle and a wave and therefore a paradox. . . . It is gradually being recognized by physicists that neither proposition 1 nor 2 is satisfactory. They should be replaced by proposition 3: *electrons and photons are too small to be seen and must therefore not be endowed with visual properties. The mind is intrinsically invisible and therefore equally unsuited for representation by a physical model.* The biblical injunction 'Thou shalt not make thyself a graven image' needs to be taken just as seriously by today's science as it was by the early Israelites" (Margenau, *The Miracle of Existence*, p. 45–6).

4. "One wonders what James, who was mesmerized by Kant, would have thought if informed that according to Thomas Aquinas even the categories of the mind are distilled from sensory experience. This is why Thomas had never written anything contrary to the proposition that the mind is a reality which is known only through inference and therefore can never be taken for an object of direct knowledge. To recognize the reality of the mind is a mental exercise whereby one takes words, all of them universals, for more than mere words. One takes them, and rightly so, for carriers of universally valid truths that can be corrected only by falling back on truths carried by universals" (Jaki, *Means to the Message*, p. 136).

Gilson made a similar point about Augustine's understanding. "It is in the mind that God has made man to His image and likeness, there it is that His image is stamped. If the mind is not to be fathomed even by itself that is because it is the image of God," said Augustine (*Spirit of Medieval Philosophy*, p. 220).

5. Clearly this is an understatement. The claim that scientific explanations "improve with age" only points to the importance of comprehensiveness, consistency, and coherence in the evaluation of scientific theories. As theories age, there is typically more data (observations) that the theory must "give an account." There is also a greater chance that any internal inconsistencies that might be initially hidden in the theory will discovered. Finally, as time passes, the irreducibly *normative* judgment concerning the theory's "coherence" will have been given due deliberation.

6. See quote from Popper in chapter 4, note 13.

7. "It is inconceivable, that inanimate brute matter should, without the mediation of something else, which is not material, operate upon, and affect other matter without mutual contact. . . . And this is one reason, why I desire you would not ascribe innate gravity to me. That gravity should be innate, inherent, and essential to matter, so that one body may act upon another, at a distance through a vacuum, without the mediation of anything else, by and through which their action and force may be conveyed from one to another, is to me so great an absurdity, that I believe no man who has in philosophical matters a competent faculty of thinking, can ever fall into it. Gravity must be caused by an agent acting constantly according to certain laws; but whether this agent be material or immaterial, I have left to the consideration of my readers" (Third letter to Bentley, *Opere*, IV quoted in Keostler, *Sleepwalkers*, 503–04). And at the end of the *Principles*, Newton makes his famous disclaimer, "But hitherto I have been unable to discover the cause of those properties of gravity from phenomena, and I frame no hypothesis" (*Great Books of the Western World*, vol. 34, 1952, p. 371). Burtt's gloss is perfect—"The ultimate nature of gravity is unknown; it is not necessary for science that it be know, for science seeks to understand how it acts, not what it is" (*Metaphysical Foundations of Modern Physical Science*, pp. 222–223).

8. Searle says that passing the Turing Test is not a sufficient condition for thinking because we can imagine a situation in which Searle passes the Turing Test for Chinese, yet doesn't *understand* the language, but instead, is simply mechanically following a set of instructions written in English. Our position is that what he says we can imagine is in fact unimaginable precisely because we *agree* with his other claim that "*only* a machine . . . with internal causal powers equivalent to those of brains" can think ("Minds, Brains, and Programs," abstract). (This point is developed further in the last chapter.) Any set of instructions that come in from the outside for rearranging the squiggles is going to be so complex that Searle's brain would not be able to process them, *unless* it had the causal powers of a person who spoke Chinese. In short, the instructions would have to *ipso facto* teach him Chinese.

Dale Jacquette in "Fear and loathing (and other intentional states) in Searle's Chinese Room" (*Philosophical Psychology* 3.2, pp. 287–304) makes a similar point. Jacquette argues that Searle's argument is circular. The Chinese Room argument is supposed to show that mere syntactical manipulation can never produce semantic understanding. But to show that syntax doesn't yield semantics, Searle must assume that the man in the room though mere syntactical manipulations (i.e., without understanding) is able to produce outputs that fool their readers into thinking that the person in the room understands Chinese. But the assumption that the man in the room *could* fool folks outside is the very point at issue— can syntax produce understanding. Conclusion to be proved: Doing syntactical manipulations does not give the man in the room semantic understanding of Chinese. Why? Because syntax can't produce semantics. Why? Because the man in the room doesn't understand Chinese even though he can manipulate symbols syntactically. But whether this is really true is the very point at issue.

Another difficulty in attributing thought to a computer is that it seems to skip links in the hierarchy of plants, animals, and humans, unless we are also to imagine that the computer is alive and capable of feeling pleasure and pains. Life and consciousness are necessary conditions of thought in the Aristotelian tradition. Aquinas says that the three ranks of souls—plants, animals, and human—are hierarchically ordered such that the higher *virtually* contains the lower in the same way that a "virtual Mac" can be in a PC computer. Hence, we tend to agree with Searle that "*only* a machine . . . with internal causal powers equivalent to those of brains" (and hence, both alive and conscious) is able to think.

Of course, not all will agree. But, then, it seems incumbent upon dissenters to *explain* how something that is not alive and is incapable of having feelings and desires is nonetheless able to think. Presumably, some of the things it will be able to think about are feelings and desires.

9. Doug Lenat has taken on the project of a "brute force" solution to the Imitation Game. One of his colleagues and critics in artificial intelligence, Drew McDermott, went straight to the heart of the problem. McDermott argues that it is impossible to build a database large enough to pass Turing's test without first solving such philosophical problems as "the nature of causality." He then adds, "We've been thinking about things like that for millennia" (*Lingua Franca: The Review of Academic Life,* September 2001, p. 32).

10. The phrase is Karl Popper's, and though his use of it is slight more specific than ours, we are in essential agreement. He writes, "Promissory materialism is a peculiar theory. It consists, essentially, of a historical (or historicists) prophecy about the future results of brain research and of their impact. This prophecy is baseless. No attempt is made to base it upon a survey of recent brain research. The opinion of researchers who, like Wilder Penfield, started as identity theorists, but ended as dualists . . . is ignored. No attempt is made to resolve the difficulties of materialism by argument. No alternatives to materialism are even considered" (*The Self and Its Brain,* p. 97).

Chapter 9: The Inadequacy of Materialism

1. *Metaphysics,* II.1.993b9–10.
2. The distinction between causal signs and intentional symbols is a simplification of Karl Popper's fourfold division of language into the (1) expressive, (2) communicative, (3) descriptive, and (4) argumentative. Popper himself credits his teacher, Karl Buhler, for the first three. The first two correspond to natural signs and the second two to intentional symbols. Popper also argues, as we do, that while nonhuman animals can obviously use language to express and communicate their feelings and intentions, there is no evidence that they use language to either describe or argue (*The Self and Its Brain,* p. 57). See Polanyi, *Personal Knowledge,* page 77, for further references.
3. Behaviorists, of course, would object to this point because they *define* the meaning of words in terms of their deposition to produce certain responses in others. Their arguments will be considered later in this chapter.
4. Here we are using "identical" in the strict sense of *numerically* identical. Two pennies that are "identical" (in the weak sense) are still numerically distinct—they are two, and not one. Aristotelians argue that the meaning of a word and the concept that it conveys are *numerically* one.
5. "Every description uses *universal* names (or symbols, or ideas); every statement has the character of a theory, of a hypothesis. The statement, 'Here is a glass of water' cannot be verified by any observational experience [sense-datum]. . . . By the word 'glass', for example, we denote physical bodies which exhibit a certain *law-like behaviour,* and the same holds for the word 'water'. Universals cannot be reduced to classes of experience" (Popper, *Logic of Scientific Discovery,* pp. 94–5).

6. By the middle of the sixteenth century this crucial distinction between concepts and images, so firmly drawn in the Middle Ages, was beginning to fade. Robert Boyle, the founder of modern chemistry, wrote, "When I say that spirit is incorporeal substance . . . if he should answer, that when he hears the words incorporeal substance, he imagines some aerial or other very thin, subtle, transparent body, I shall reply, that this comes from a vicious custom he has brought himself to, of imagining something whenever he will conceive anything, though of a nature incapable of being truly represented by any image in the fancy [imagination] . . . Because the use of imagining, whenever we would conceive things, is so stubborn an impediment to the free actings of the mind, in cases that require pure intellection, it will be very useful, if not necessary, to accustom ourselves not to be startled or frighted with every thing that exceeds or confounds the imagination, but by degrees to train up the mind to consider notions that surpass the imagination and yet are demonstrable by reason" (quoted in Burtt, *Metaphysical Foundations of Modern Physical Science*, pp. 176–77).

7. To make this point fully clear, we need the distinction between a *per se* efficient cause and a *per accidens* efficient cause that is defined and defended in the next chapter. For now we will only say that, according to Aristotelians, it is true that every *particular* concept, say the concept of a chiliagon that exists in Fred Smith's mind on April 14, 2000, has as a necessary condition a particular physical state in his brain. All that is denied by Aristotelians is that there exists causal law of the form—whenever a person's brain is in state X, then that person will have the concept of a chiliagon. The reason for this denial is simple: it is conceptually incoherent to speak of a particular *per se* efficient cause of some particular brain state or event. When we speak of a particular event causing another particular event, we are *ipso facto* speaking of *per accidens* causes.

But note, we are not here or elsewhere denying that particular brain states are *per accidens* efficient causes of other particular brain states. After all, one of the points that Aristotle insisted on in his criticism of Plato was that the body is a *necessary* condition of full-fledged thinking.

Karl Popper makes a similar point. "There could be a one-to-one relationship between the words and certain brain processes. But the experience of understanding the sentence is something beyond understanding the sequence of the words (as we find out whenever we have to read a difficult sentence twice in order to understand it); and since this experience may be one of those many experiences which are essentially unique, we should not arbitrarily assume that a brain process is one-to-one related to it (one can speak of a one-to-one relation only if there is some *universal* [i.e., per se efficient cause] law or rule correlating the two processes, and this is here not assumed to exist; see also section 24 above)" (*The Self and Its Brain*, p. 119).

8. See the discussion in chapter six of Descartes's view that there is a "gap" between the images that we see and the material objects that these images represent.

9. "[Behaviorists] have denied the existence of consciousness (the consciousness say, of a toothache) altogether. Though this behaviourist philosophy is quite fashionable at present, a theory of the nonexistence of consciousness cannot be taken any more seriously, I suggest, than a theory of the nonexistence of matter. Both theories 'solve' the problem of the relationship between body and mind. The solution is in both cases a radical simplification; it is the denial either of body or of mind. But in my opinion it is too cheap" (Popper, "Reduction and the Incompleteness of Science," in Ayala and Dobzhansky, *Studies in the Philosophy of Biology*, p. 273).

10. The phrase is Gilbert Ryle's. His book, *The Concept of Mind*, is a delightfully clear, readable, and seductive presentation of the behaviorist's thesis.

11. Behaviorism also stumbles on the problem illustrated in chapter 6 by the turtle coming ashore *to* lay her eggs. Behaviorism, at least as psychologists use the term, is an

attempt to explain animal actions (including human speech) in terms of "stimulus" and "response" where these new terms are defined in such a way as to eliminate all final causes or teleological reference. But as the turtle example show, this is impossible. For a similar criticism of behaviorism, see Polanyi, *Personal Knowledge*, pp. 369–73.

12. The argument of this paragraph not only applies to understanding concepts but also to all mental states, including imagination, memories, and feelings.

13. Karl Popper, discussing Aristotle, writes, "In Aristotle *On Dreams* 461b31, we read: 'If a man is unaware that a finger is being pressed below his eye, not only will one thing *seem* to be two, but he may think that it is two; whereas, if he is not unaware [of the finger being pressed below his eye], it will still appear to be two, but he will not think that it is two.' This is a classical experiment to demonstrate the reality of conscious awareness, and of the fact that sensation is *not* a disposition to believe" (*The Self and Its Brain*, p. 168).

14. "But it should be borne in mind that material substances are not actually intelligible but only potentially; and they become actually intelligible by reason of the fact that the likenesses of them which are gotten by way of the sensory powers are made immaterial by the agent intellect" (Aquinas, *Commentary on Aristotle's Metaphysics*, section 2541).

15. "The grasping of a World 3 [concepts] object is, above all, an *active* process. Indeed, I want to conjecture that selves are the only active agents in the universe: the only agents to whom the term activity can properly be applied" (Popper and Eccles, *The Self and Its Brain*, p. 538). Popper's "selves" and Aristotle's agent intellects are two peas in a pod.

From a neurophysiological point of view, Eccles writes, "The self-conscious mind is not just engaged passively in a reading-out operation from neural events, but that it has an actively searching operation as in the searchlight analogy of Jung" (*Evolution of the Brain*, p. 205).

16. See Aquinas, *On the Principles of Nature*, sec 4.

17. Marjorie Grene says, "Some pieces of factual knowledge do bear significantly and even fatally on some Metaphysical beliefs, and such is the case [of evolution], in its cosmic application, for Aristotle's principle of the priority of actuality. For him, the chicken *must* precede the egg, eternally. He was wrong. There was a time on this globe when there were neither eggs nor chickens, there was a time when the first eggs that could reasonably have been called hen's eggs produced the first day-old chicks" (230–31). Grene's argument, however, fails to consider Aristotle's distinction at *Metaphysics* 1072a3, "To suppose potency prior to actuality, then, is in a sense right, and in a sense not." Thomas explains Aristotle's distinction as follows: "The sense in which it is right has been explained in Book IX (778–80: *Commentary on Aristotle's Metaphysics*, 1844–49); for it was stated there that actuality is prior absolutely to potentiality. But in one and the same subject which is being moved from potentiality to actuality, potentiality is prior to actuality in time, although actuality is prior both in nature and in perfection [i.e., conceptually]" (2506). In Book IX, Aristotle makes the distinction in terms of that which is capable of being seen and that which is seen. We must *define* the latter in terms of the former, though a particular tree may temporally be capable of being seen before it is actually seen.

18. Cf. Aquinas, *Summa Theologica*, I q. 75, art. 5. The argument for the immateriality of the intellect parallels what Aquinas calls his second argument in the body of this question. The only real difference is in the example used to illustrate the argument. Aquinas speaks of knowing the nature/essence of a stone, whereas I speak of knowing the meaning of a word. In both cases, the argument is based on the metaphysics of conceptual knowledge.

19. This argument has appeared in many different versions throughout the history of philosophy; the earliest is Epicurus. "He who says that all things happen of [material] necessity cannot criticize another who says that not all things happen of necessity. For he has to admit that the assertion also happens of necessity" (aphorism 40, cited in Pop-

per, *The Self and Its Brain,* p. 75). Aristotle's much commented on formulation of this argument for the immateriality of the intellect in found in Book 3, chapters 4 and 5 of *On the Soul.*

One of its more memorably formulations in this century is due to biologist, J. B. S. Haldane. Haldane puts it like this: ". . . if materialism is true, it seems to me that we cannot know that it is true. If my opinions are the result of the chemical processes going on in my brain, they are determined by the laws of chemistry, not of logic" (*The Inequality of Man,* 1937, p. 157). Darwin himself, in the nineteenth century, seems to have also worried about this argument. "But then arises the doubt, can the mind of man, which has, as I fully believe, been developed from a mind as low as that possessed by the lowest animals, be trusted when it draws such a grand conclusion [i.e., evolution by natural selection]? . . . With me the horrid doubt always arises whether the convictions of a man's mind, which has been developed from the mind of the lower animals, are of any value or at all trustworthy" (cited in David Lack, *Evolutionary Theory and Christian Belief,* frontispiece, pp. 101–102). See also Stanley Jaki, *The Purpose of it All,* chapter six, "Heuristics of Purpose," especially pages 151–155.

It is no surprise that such doubts would have arisen in Darwin's mind since this was a standard nineteenth century argument against a wholly materialist interpretation of evolution. The Princeton theologian Charles Hodge wrote, "The primary principle of all knowledge is the Knowledge of self. This must be assumed. Unless we are we cannot know. This knowledge of self is . . . , moreover, a knowledge not only that we are a substance, but also that we are an individual substance, which thinks, feels, and wills. Here, then, is a mind, i.e., an individual, intelligent, voluntary agent, necessarily included in the first, and most essential of all truths. If this be denied, then Hume is right, and we can know nothing. . . . The Materialist cannot think, or speak, or write, without assuming the existence of mind as distinct from matter" (*Systematic Theology,* vol. 1, pp. 275, 277, 292).

One of the more popular and clearly written contemporary formulations of the argument is found in the third chapter of *Miracles* by C. S. Lewis. For another literary treatment, see the first chapter of Walker Percy, *Message in the Bottle.*

Karl Popper has formulated the argument in several places. Two of the best are section 21 of *The Self and Its Brain* and chapter 12 of *Conjectures and Refutations.* Mortimer Adler has done likewise, see "Intentionality and Immateriality," *The New Scholasticism,* Spring 1967, and chapter 12 of *The Difference of Man and the Difference It Makes.*

Daniel Robinson, a neurophysiologist, has an especially readable version of the argument in *The Wonder of Being Human,* chapter 4.

Finally, chapter 12 in Alvin Plantinga's *Warrant and Proper Function* develops this argument in a style familiar to analytic philosophers.

20. We attempt to explain how agent intellect acts on physical brains in the last chapter.

21. D. M. MacKay makes a similar point in a theological context. "Perhaps this last point needs some expansion. As we have seen in earlier chapters, our personal identity is closely linked with our priorities. In a sense, what identifies me more fundamentally than anything else is my total 'goal-complex' or priority-scheme: what defines and orders all my aims and satisfactions in life, great and small. If I were to lose all of these, without replacement by others, I as a human personality would cease to exist. If that is the case, we do well to ask ourselves what it must mean for us, as individuals, that no priority incompatible with God's priorities can go with us into eternity. For if when we leave this life there are priorities we cannot take with us, this will be no merely incidental loss; for it is those priorities that in part *define who we are.* Throughout our lives, then, our greatest concern must be that those priorities of ours which are unfit for eternity should as quickly and completely as possible disappear from the goal-complex that defines who we

are. If we cherish, as an essential part of what identifies us, priorities which are incompatible with God's eternal kingdom, then when God says that someone with such priorities cannot enter his kingdom he is not being arbitrarily intolerant. He is saying simply that since such priorities can have no existence in the new kingdom, nobody to who these priorities are essential can exist in it either" (*Human Science and Human Dignity*, pp. 115–16).

22. "An individual soul apart from a body is like a living rational man during a dreamless sleep—such a man *can* think and feel, even though in fact he *is not* thinking and feeling.

"Another analogy is the condition of two people locked in a monochromatic room. Sally has normal color vision. Fred is color bind. Sally *can* see green, even though she presently *is not* seeing green. Fred's situation is different. Like Sally, we can describe Fred as presently being in a state such that he *is not* seeing green. However, unlike Sally, we cannot describe Fred as presently being in a state such that he *can* see green.

"The difference between a subsistent soul and an actually existing person is this: a subsistent soul *can* think and believe, though it *does not* think and believe. An actually existing person is able to do both—(1) it *can* think and believe and (2) it *does* think and believe" (Joseph Bobik, *Aquinas on Being and Essence*, pp. 153–54).

Chapter 10: The Bogy of Mechanism

1. Gilbert Ryle, *The Concept of Mind*.

2. "We ought . . . to regard the present state of the universe as the effect of its anterior state and as the cause of the one which is to follow. Assume . . . an intelligence which could know all the forces by which nature is animated, and the states at an instant of all the objects that compose it; . . . for [this intelligence], nothing would be uncertain; and the future, as the past, would be present to its eyes" (Laplace, *A Philosophical Essay on Probabilities*, pp. 4–5). Thomas Huxley repeatedly made the same claim in the nineteenth century. He is responsible for the phrase, "British flora and fauna."

In a letter to Mersenne, in *Oeuvres*, II, 497, Descartes anticipated Laplace's all-knowing spirit—"if somebody were to know perfectly what are the small particles of all bodies and what are their movements and their relative positions, he would perfectly know the whole nature" (Jaki, *Relevance of Physic*, 55).

3. *Encyclopedia Britannica 14th edition* 1929, article on "Ether," vol. 8, p. 751. For an example of the fallibility of science textbooks, see G. de Santillana, *The Crime of Galileo*, Chicago, 1955, p. 164n. "On Wolynski's count, there were 2,330 works published on astronomy between 1543 and 1887 . . . , of those, only 180 were Copernican (see Archivo Storico Italiano, 1873, p. 12)."

4. Similar things could be said for Thomas Huxley's nineteenth-century version of the boast, the only change being the addition of Charles Darwin's work to the scientific pantheon.

5. We say "may be able" because we do not here wish to beg any important questions about the truthfulness of the Copenhagen interpretation of Quantum Mechanics. According to Neils Bohr and most other contemporary physicists, even a Newtonian scientist armed with *complete* knowledge concerning initial conditions could not make accurate predictions about the future because the quantum actions of subatomic particles is *in principle* unknowable.

As we suggested in the first part of this book, Aristotelians are dubious about the Copenhagen interpretation since it is a *de facto* denial of the truth of common sense that nothing comes from nothing. Furthermore, the Copenhagen interpretation seems, to us, to be either confused or ignorant of the difference between ontology and epistemology.

The first published critique of this sort appeared in 1930 in *Nature*. "Every argument that, since some change cannot be 'determined' in the sense of 'ascertained', it is therefore not 'determined' in the absolutely different sense of 'caused', is a fallacy of equivocation" (J. E. Turner, *Nature*, Dec. 27, 1930, p. 995. Quoted in Jaki, *Patterns and Principles*, p. 136).

Jaki has repeatedly made the same criticism. Here's is one of the more memorable instances: "Far from having to do anything with causality, quantum theory has for its basic claim the realization, very sensible in itself, that no one can cut thinner than the thinnest instrument at his disposal. This gem of common sense was turned half a century ago into the nonsensical inference that an interaction that cannot be measured 'exactly', cannot take place 'exactly' in the very different sense of that word whenever it is invested with an ontologically causal sense" (*Patterns or Principles*, p. 201).

More formally he has argued, "Many a leading physicist enthusiastically promoted plain illogicalities by endorsing Bohr's convoluted formulations of the philosophy of complementarity. Without doubt some experiments in atomic physics demand an approach that takes matter for particles, while other experiments demand that matter be seen as a wave packet. But for the physicists the ultimate difference between the two perspectives lies in a mutual irreducibility or incommensurability of two mathematical formalisms. The situation is not at all different from the old recognition that [the area of] a circle cannot be squared [i.e., be reduced to the area of any square]. From this, however, nobody concluded in saner times that everything was now a square and now a circle" (*Means to Message*, p. 52).

And again, "The sophism [of the Copenhagen philosophy of quantum mechanics] consists in the reduction of 'exact' existence to 'exact' measurability, while paying no attention to using, in the same breath, the word 'exact' in two very different senses, the one ontological, the other operational" (*God and the Cosmologists*, p. 126). Cf. the whole of chapter 5, "Turtles and Tunnels," for a sustained discussion of this confusion.

6. Virgil, *The Aeneid*, p. 190.

7. See also Karl Popper's argument that classical physics implies that some events are in principle unpredictable because of the existence of "mass-effect" with regard to temperature and chemical concentrations. Crudely put, the argument goes like this: macrolevel events like the explosion of gasoline or the firing of neurons in the brain constitute "thresholds." But these events are determined at least in part by temperature and/or chemical concentrations, and these are both "essentially an average; and quantities like this cannot in principle be measured as precisely as we wish." That is, they cannot be measured with the precision necessary to determine when a threshold will or will not be crossed (*The Open Universe*, pp. 16–17).

8. See Karl Popper, "Of Clouds and Clocks" in *Objective Knowledge* and D. M. MacKay's essays: "Mindlike Behaviour in Artifacts" in *The British Journal for the Philosophy of Science*, 1951; "On the Logical Indeterminacy of a Free Choice" in *Mind*, 1960; "The Use of Behavioural Language to Refer to Mechanical Processes" in *The British Journal for the Philosophy of Science*, August 1962; "Brain and Will" in *Brain and Mind*, ed. by J. R. Smythies (1965); *Freedom of Action in a Mechanistic Universe* (Cambridge University Press, 1967); "The Sovereignty of God in the Natural World" in *Scottish Journal of Theology*, 1968; "Scientific Beliefs About Oneself," in The Proper Study (Royal Institute of Philosophy Lectures, vol. 4, 1969–70); " 'Complementarity' in Scientific and Theological Thinking" in *Zygon*, 1974; and "Conscious efforts" in *Nature*, vol. 323, Oct. 23, 1986. "Soul, Brain Science and" in *The Oxford Companion to the Mind*, ed. Richard L. Gregory (Oxford University Press, 1987).

9. In this regard, the work of modern biologists should also be considered. In the eighteenth and nineteenth centuries, the hegemony of physics did much to distort our

understanding of science. Now, with the rise of biology to an equal status as physics, it is impossible to ignore the biologist's insistence that evolution by nature selection can *explain* the development of species, even though it is powerless to *predict* them. See next note.

10. "The theory of natural selection can describe and explain phenomena with considerable precision, but it cannot make reliable predictions except through such trivial and meaningless circular statements as, for instance: 'The fitter individuals will on the average leave more offspring.' Scriven ["Explanation and prediction in evolutionary theory." *Science* 130:477–482] has emphasized quite correctly that one of the most important contributions to philosophy made by the evolutionary theory is that it has demonstrated the independence of explanation and prediction" (Mayr, *Toward a Modern Philosophy of Biology*, p. 32).

11. *Concept of Mind*, p. 195ff.

12. There is a fifth argument against Laplace's boast that one day scientists will in principle be able to predict everything. However, the argument's premises go beyond the truths of common sense and employ as a premise Einstein's Relativity Theory, therefore we have relegated it to an endnote. Nonetheless, what is sometimes called the "light cone argument" is really intuitively pretty simple. Einstein argued that nothing can travel faster than the speed of light. Since many stars are millions of light years away, a star that we see tonight may in fact have passed out of existence centuries ago, yet the end of a star's life could never be predicted. While astronomers have a fairly good knowledge of what causes a star to collapse and pass out of existence, and hence, are able to *explain* its death, they could never *predict* when any particular star will collapse because the necessary information for the prediction will be outside of the "light cone" of all possible information. See Popper, *The Open Universe*, p. 57ff.

13. The metaphor of clouds and clocks employed at the beginning of this chapter is Karl Popper's (see "Of Clouds and Clocks," in *Objective Knowledge*, p. 206ff.). For the two hundred and fifty years between Newton and Bohr, almost all scientists were convinced that all clouds were really clocks. One noteworthy philosophical objector was Charles Sanders Peirce. He reasoned that no matter how precisely a clock is constructed, it will always include some small element of looseness or imperfection. For example, all physical bodies, even the jewels in a watch, are subject to molecular heat motion. Since molecular heat motion is obviously cloud-like, its effects will produce cloud-like results.

With the advent of quantum mechanics in the 1920s, physicists began taking Peirce's side, though for different reasons. Now the vast majority of scientists were convinced that in fact all clocks are really clouds. Popper himself says, "I believe that Peirce was right in holding that all clocks are clouds, to some considerable degree—even the most precise of clocks" (*Objective Knowledge*, pp. 214–15). Our position is that *some* events in nature are clock-like and *some* are cloud-like. Clock-like objects and events are those with *per se* efficient causes; cloud-like objects and events are those with *per accidens* efficient causes.

While the theory outlined in this essay is similar to Popper's position, there is one important difference. Popper, following Peirce, appears to hold that the difference between clouds and clocks is the difference between systems in which there are only loose or imperfect causal controls (clouds) and systems in which there are precise or perfect causal controls (clocks). In our view, the difference between clouds and clocks is the difference between: (1) systems that are *not* precisely predictable future states because they include *per accidens* efficient causes and (2) systems which *are* in principle precisely predictable because they only include knowable *per se* efficient causes.

Ontologically speaking, the crucial difference between Popper's view and Aristotle's is that Popper's notion of causal "looseness" *appears* to entail the rejection of the Aristotelian principle that nothing comes from nothing. "But when it comes to material causality,

Aristotle allows no chance and quite logically. Chance as a material cause would imply for him the rise of something out of no antecedent material cause, that is, out of nothing. This is, however, inadmissible in the perspective of Aristotle who as a pantheist held the universe to be ungenerated and therefore eternal. As a matter of fact, on three different occasions he rejected the idea of something coming into being out of nothing. [Counting pseudo-Aristotelian *De Melisso, Xenophane et Gorgia Disputationes*, 975a. The two genuine passages are in *Metaphysics* 1075b, and *De coelo* 298b.]" (Jaki, *God and the Cosmologists*, pp. 143, 260).

Gilson concurs. Chance "is by no means there [in peripatetic philosophy] conceived as pure indetermination, that is, to say as something that happens without cause, and, in this respect, it makes no breach in the universal determinism; nevertheless, it is incompletely determined, it is accidental with respect to the efficient cause because not produced thereby in view of an end, or because the thing produced is other than the end for which the causes acts. In nature, then, the fortuitous is that which lacks an end" (*Spirit of Medieval Philosophy*, pp. 367–68, also cited in Jaki, *Patterns*, pp. 183–84).

In other words, it seems that according to Popper not even God could have *perfect* knowledge of future states and events, whereas according to Aquinas, while no mere human can have perfect knowledge of future states and events, God does have such omniscience. Jaki draws an even stronger contrast between Aquinas and Aristotle. "Aquinas, who held in enormous esteem the consistency of the universe [for details, see Jaki, 'Thomas and the Universe', in *The Thomist*, October 1989], could but most zealously champion the tenet of the creation of all together as part of the Christian creed. Aquinas therefore felt at ease as he ascribed to the physical universe a degree of determinism even greater than the one advocated by Aristotle. For Aquinas strict determinism (which he never confused with perfectly accurate measurability) follows from the fact that there can be no hiatus along the line of material causality because any such hiatus would imply two contradictions. One is that matter can arise spontaneously, that is, by chance or without cause out of nothing; the other is that there would be new matter brought into existence by the Creator, although He had already created everything together. Of course, with his belief in a personal providential God as the cause of all, Aquinas, unlike Aristotle, experienced no perplexity about apparently purposeless events in reference to human lives. Those events could very well be purposeful in God's perspective" (*God and Cosmologists*, pp. 144–45).

Though it takes us beyond the scope of this essay, there is no reason to be coy about Jaki's end—the existence of chance destroys both God's sovereignty and the our wholly philosophical knowledge that God exists. "How can a scientific cosmologist be sure that his model of the cosmos is truly about the strict totality of consistently interacting bits of matter? Can scientific cosmology contain the proof of the existence of such a totality? . . . [S]cientific cosmologists did not even care to consider whether their cosmological models, most of them elaborations on Einstein's model, corresponded or not to that strict totality. Much less did they care to face up to the question: "Is there a Universe?" (*Means to the Message*, p. 143). The question—Is there a Universe?—is a corollary to the question—Is it possible for something to come from nothing? "Inflationary cosmology" and the claim that the universe is the "ultimate free lunch" can be true only if something can come from nothing, which in turn, implies that the sum of material things we observe do not form a Universe, i.e., a "strict totality of consistently interacting bits of matter."

Chapter 11: Freedom and Rationality

1. "Moreover, judgment is within the power of one judging insofar as he can judge of his own judgment [i.e., is capable of self-referential judgment]. For we can judge of whatever is in our power. Indeed to judge of one's own judgment belongs only to reason, which

reflects upon its own act and knows the relations of things of which it judges and through which it judges [i.e., it can use language to think about language]. The root of all liberty, therefore, is found in reason. Hence according as something is related to reason, so is it related to free choice," said Aquinas (*On Truth*, question 24, article 2. Also found in *Selected Writings of St. Thomas Aquinas*, translated by Goodwin).

Gilson sums it up like this. "Rationality is that ability to use language in a way that enables humans to not only react to the environment, but also, to reflect upon, and thus, to analyze their own reactions. As individual humans reflect upon their own reactions to the physical environment in which they live, they become conscious of alternatives. This consciousness of alternatives constitutes their liberty and confers upon humans the ability to be makers of their own character" (*Spirit of Medieval Philosophy*, pp. 201–02).

2. *Critique of Pure Reason*, p. 29.

3. Cf. chapter 10, note 5.

4. Closely connected is the common assumption that "facts" and "values" constitute two distinct realms. It is not surprising that such an assumption should be so wide spread given Kant's division of reality into that which we can know (the "facts" of Newtonian science) and that which we can rationally believe (the "values" inherent in the moral law). Like Descartes, Kant followers were either incapable or unwilling to endorse with equal vigor both of his epistemological realms, and by the twentieth century, that which we can *rationally* believe degenerated into that which we *choose* to believe. Cf. Gilson, *The Unity of Philosophical Experience*.

5. *Sovereignty of the Good*, p. 37.

6. See chapter 6, "Two Kinds of Induction" and "Brutes and Humans."

7. James 3:4–5.

8. Even philosophers with whom we are in essential agreement sometimes misstate the problem. "There must be an active interchange of information across the frontier between the material brain—the liaison brain—and the nonmaterial mind. The mind is not in the matter-energy world, so there can be no energy exchange in the transaction, merely a flow of information. Yet the mind must be able to change the pattern of energy operations in the modules of the brain, else it would be forever impotent" (Eccles and Robinson, *The Wonder of Being Human*, p. 40). This way of stating the problem is slightly misleading. What does "be able to change" mean in this context? Whenever *per accidens* efficient causes are the issue, it is hard to understand what "able to change" means.

Consider the hundred prior years in the history of the rock with a C-shaped crack that the geologist's daughter found. Would the gold miner working the stream fifty years before the rock was found have been "able to change" the cracks in this rock? In one sense, this would have been quite easy. If he had simply picked up the rock, and hit it with his hammer, then it probably would not have the same C-shaped crack. But in another sense, if "able to change" means "causing the rock to be physically different *without any physical intervention*," then the miner would necessarily be impotent.

What is misleading in Eccles's statement of the problem is the suggestion that the intellect must be able to *change* the brain if it is correctly deemed to be the agent. Our argument is that intellect is correctly deemed to be the agent so long as it *controls* the brain.

A parent can *control* a child with words, and since there are many different words and sentences that the parent might use to make her requests known, all of which will produce *different* causal sequences in the child's brain, a change in a particular brain state cannot be a necessary condition for the parent to be correctly deemed the agent in charge.

9. "Moreover, as Popper stated, the interaction across the frontier in Figure 3–1 [mind-brain] need not be in conflict with the first law of thermodynamics. The flow of infor-

mation into the modules could be affected by a balanced increase and decrease of energy at different but adjacent micro-sites, so that there is no net energy change in the brain. The first law at this level may be valid only statistically" (Eccles and Robinson, *The Wonder of Being Human*, p. 38).

Again, "The essential feature of these theories [dualist-interactionists] is that mind and brain are separate entities, the brain being in World 1 and the mind in World 2, and that they somehow interact, as will be described later. Thus there is a frontier between World 1 and World 2, and across this frontier there is interaction in both directions, which can be conceived as a flow of information, not of energy. Thus we have the extraordinary doctrine that the world of matter-energy (World 1) is not completely sealed, which is a fundamental tenet of classical physics—the conservation laws" (Eccles, *Evolution of the Brain*, p. 178). Eccles and Aristotle agree that there are two worlds, and that they interact by the exchange of information, not energy.

This distinction between the effects of information and the exchange of energy is not as clear in Eccles as we would like. When Eccles suggests that the discoveries of quantum mechanics has illuminated an "extraordinary" world that is not "completely sealed," he seem to think that "two world interaction" violates that least a Newtonian understanding of the laws of conservation of mass/energy. But if the interaction is in terms of *information, not energy*, then where is the violation of conservation laws (i.e., that nothing comes from nothing)? From a purely scientific point of view there is nothing more "extraordinary" about the mind interacting with the brain than there is with the random collisions of rocks producing a C-shaped crack.

10. "Thus, since everything has intellective power in consequence of its freedom from matter, those things must be pre-eminently intelligible which exist in complete separation from matter. The intelligible object and the intellect must be proportioned to each other, and must be of one genus, since the intellect and the intelligible are in act one" (Aquinas, *Preface to Commentary on Aristotle's Metaphysics* from Anderson, *Introduction to the Metaphysics of St. Thomas Aquinas*, p. 17). Modern critics of Descartes are correct to be puzzled by the "interaction" of the mind and the brain. As far as the intellect goes, Aquinas would also have been puzzled since he took it as a principle that the intelligible object and the intellect "must be proportioned to each other." The shape of material objects are known by a material brain; the immaterial forms of objects are only known by an immaterial intellect.

Again, "A thing is actually intelligible from the very fact that it is immaterial" (*Summa Theologica*, I, q.79. art. 3). This sounds strange to our modern ears. But we must remember that "strangeness" is relative. We find things and events intelligible when we discover a "law of nature" from which (along with the initial conditions) it can be deduced. But suppose a child asked: "In what book is this 'law of nature' written? Who wrote it? Was it a single individual or a group of legislators?" We have no answers to such questions. All we do is to dismiss them as being inappropriate, or if we are philosophically trained, we reject them as involving a "category mistake." Well, then, in what category do "laws of nature" reside? If they don't reside in the category of material things, then by the law of excluded middle they must reside in the category of nonmaterial things.

11. "We know that, but we do not know how, mind and body interact; but this is not surprising since we have really no definite idea how physical things interact" (Popper and Eccles, *The Self and its Brain*, p. 153).

Epilogue

1. "Of course, even today, after several millennia of mathematics, it is words that explain that the figure 1 stands for the number one, an integer. Leaving aside the unfathomable

problem of how that explanation was first given by humans, the concept of a number is inseparable from its verbalization . . . 'In the beginning was the word,' are a starting point indispensable even in mathematics" (Jaki, *Means to Message*, p. 32).

2. *Three Rival Versions of Moral Enquiry*, p. 135 cf. p. 219.

Glossary

Classical compatibilism: The theory that free will is compatible with *per accidens* efficient causes, but not with *per se* efficient causes. See *Modern compatibilism*.

Concept: A mental object that answers the question, What is it? Concepts provide the definition of things. As Aristotle used the term, concepts are absolute distinct from other mental objects like percepts, images, and feelings.

Conceptual induction: The uniquely human ability to know *what* something is, i.e., its *substantial form*. See *Empirical induction*.

Difference of kind verse difference of degree: Differences of degree measure ranges on a continuum; differences of kind require discrete objects. For example, 1.3 and 1.4 constitute a difference of degree on the scale of real numbers because there are an infinite number of numbers in between. The difference between 6 and 7 on the scale of integers, however, constitutes a difference of kind because there is no whole number in between.

Dualism: The theory that human beings are composed of two distinct substances—material bodies and an immaterial mind/soul.

Empirical induction: Generalization and predictions based *wholly* on observed similarities. Empirical inductions produce a pragmatic knowledge that two things or events are constantly conjoined. Both human and nonhuman animals are able to make such inductions. See *Conceptual induction*.

Epistemology: The study of how and what we can know. Aristotle's epistemology sharply distinguished between what we can know and what actually exists. See *Ontology*.

Essential nature: see *substantial form*.

Extension: All the actual things or events referred to by a word. For example, the extension of "star" is all the actual stars that have, do, or will exist in space. See *Intension*.

Fallacy: A way of arguing that is logically flawed but nonetheless persuades many people.

Form: Short for *substantial form*.

Free will: See *Classical compatibilism*, *Modern compatibilism*, and *Libertarianism*.

Homogeneous ordering: A thing is homogeneously ordered if and only if dividing the whole results in functionally similar parts. For example, dividing skin only results in

197

smaller pieces of skin (until we get down to the cellular level) since all skin has the same biological function. See *heterogeneous ordering.*

Heterogeneous ordering: A thing is heterogeneously ordered if and only if dividing the whole results in functionally distinct parts. For example, an animal can be divided into parts—eyes, hearts, lungs, etc.—but they all have different functions. See *homogeneous ordering.*

Hylomorphism: Aristotle's theory that all natural objects subject to change (rocks, plants, animals, people, etc.) are a composition of both form and matter.

Intension: The meaning of a word. For example, the intension of "bachelor" is unmarried male. See *Extension.*

Intentional symbols: Shapes or sounds that gain meaning solely as the result of a person or persons' intentions. There is nothing about the physical properties of the ink marks on this page that gives them their meaning. See *Natural sign.*

Libertarianism: The theory that free will is incompatible with either *per accidens* or *per se* efficient causes. See *Classical compatibilism* and *Modern compatibilism.*

Materialism: The theory that human beings (and everything else that exists) are composed wholly of matter, i.e., that which can be seen, heard, felt, tasted, or smelled. The existence of things like molecules and genes that are too small to be seen with the naked eye are either in fact or in principle observable with scientific instruments and are thus consistent with philosophical materialism.

Mathematical/material complexity: The complexity of a thing as measured by the number of possible ways its elements can be arranged. For example, there are four possible ways a set of two coins can be arranged: Heads/Heads; Heads/Tails; Tails/Heads; Tails/Tails. See *Ontological complexity.*

Modern compatibilism: The theory that free will is compatible with *per se* efficient causes. See *Classical compatibilism.*

Natural sign: An inference from a cause to an effect. For example, clouds are a sign of rain. See *Intentional symbol.*

Naturalism: Roughly equivalent to *materialism.* Used philosophically, it is the thesis that no nonphysical beings exist.

Ontological complexity: The hierarchical ordering of things as determined by their distinct powers and abilities. To count as a distinct power or ability the difference must be one of *kind,* not merely of *degree.* See *Difference of kind verse difference of degree* and *Mathematical/material complexity.*

Ontology: The study of being or existence in and of itself. Ontology seeks to answer the question, What kinds of things really exist? Do nonmaterial things like souls, angels, and God exist? According to Aristotelians, none of the physical or life sciences by themselves can properly address such questions because they do not take a sufficiently general point of view. Any answer they give will beg the question in favor of a wholly material account of reality.

***Per accidens* efficient cause:** A physical cause that is not part of a regular, law-like pattern. For example, the cooling of a piece of lava that creates a rock with a C-shaped crack. See *Per se efficient cause.*

***Per se* efficient cause:** A physical cause that makes scientific predictions possible. For example, if water is heated to one hundred degrees Celsius, then it will boil. See *Per accidens efficient cause.*

Phylogenetic continuity: The claim that all life is biologically connected and hence there is no essential difference of *kind* between any two species. Aristotelians only object to this thesis when it is turned into an ontological claim.

Shape: As we are using the term, "shape" refers to all the quantifiable physical properties of an object. A thing's "shape" is sharply distinguished from its *form.*

Soul: As Aristotelian use the term, souls are the *substantial forms* of living things. There are three kinds of souls: plant, animal, and human.

Substantial form: The *essential nature* of a thing; i.e., the defining characteristics of a thing. A substantial form makes something what it is. See *Conceptual induction*.

Sources

Adler, Mortimer J. *The Difference of Man and the Difference It Makes*. New York: Fordham University Press, 1993.

———. "Intentionality and Immateriality." *The New Scholasticism*, vol. 41, no. 2 (Spring 1967): 312–44.

———. *Problems for Thomists: The Problem of Species*. New York: Sheed & Ward, 1940.

Aquinas, Thomas. *Being and Essence*. Translated by Robert P. Goodwin. Indianapolis: Bobbs-Merril, 1965.

———. *Commentary on Aristotle's Metaphysics*. Translated by John P. Rowan. Chicago: H. Regnery Co., 1961.

———. *An Introduction to the Metaphysics of St. Thomas Aquinas*. Translated by James F. Anderson. Chicago: H. Regnery Co., 1953.

———. *On the Principles of Nature*. Translated by Robert P. Goodwin. Indianapolis: Bobbs-Merril, 1965.

———. *On Truth*. Chicago: H. Regnery Co., 1952–54.

———. *Summa Contra Gentiles*. Translated by Vernon J. Bourke. Notre Dame: University of Notre Dame Press, 1975.

———. *Summa Theologica*. Great Books of the Western World, vols. 19, 20. Chicago: Encyclopaedia Britannica, 1952.

Aristotle. *History of Animals*. Great Books of the Western World, vol. 9. Chicago: Encyclopaedia Britannica, 1952.

———. *Metaphysics*. Great Books of the Western World, vol. 10. Chicago: Encyclopaedia Britannica, 1952.

———. *Nicomachean Ethics*. Great Books of the Western World, vol. 9. Chicago: Encyclopaedia Britannica, 1952.

———. *On the Generation of Animals*. Great Books of the Western World, vol. 9. Chicago: Encyclopaedia Britannica, 1952.

———. *On the Parts of Animals.* Great Books of the Western World, vol. 9. Chicago: Encyclopaedia Britannica, 1952.

———. *On the Soul.* Great Books of the Western World, vol. 10. Chicago: Encyclopaedia Britannica, 1952.

———. *Physics.* Great Books of the Western World, vol. 10. Chicago: Encyclopaedia Britannica, 1952.

———. *Posterior Analytics.* Great Books of the Western World, vol. 10. Chicago: Encyclopaedia Britannica, 1952.

Barnes, Jonathan. *Aristotle, Past Masters.* Oxford; New York: Oxford University Press, 1982.

Bobik, Joseph, and Thomas Aquinas. *Aquinas on Being and Essence.* Notre Dame, Ind.: University of Notre Dame Press, 1965.

Bochenski, Joseph M. *The Problem of Universals.* Notre Dame, Ind.: University of Notre Dame Press, 1956.

Burtt, Edwin A. *The Metaphysical Foundations of Modern Physical Science.* Atlantic Highlands, N.J.: Humanities Press, 1980.

Cairns-Smith, A. G. *Seven Clues to the Origin of Life: A Scientific Detective Story.* Cambridge: Cambridge University Press, 1985.

Darwin, Charles. *The Life and Letters of Charles Darwin, Including an Autobiographical Chapter.* 2 vols. New York: Basic Books, 1959.

———. *The Origin of Species.* Great Books of the Western World, vol. 34. Chicago: Encyclopaedia Britannica, 1952.

———. *Variations of Animals and Plants under Domestication,* vol. II. New York: D. Appleton & Co., 1875.

Dawkins, Richard. *The Blind Watchmaker: Why the Evidence of Evolution Reveals a Universe without Design.* New York: Norton, 1996.

———. *The Selfish Gene.* Oxford: Oxford University Press, 1989.

De Santillana, Giorgio. *The Crime of Galileo.* Chicago: University of Chicago Press, 1955.

Dembski, William A. *Intelligent Design: The Bridge between Science & Theology.* Downers Grove, Ill.: InterVarsity Press, 1999.

Descartes, René. *Meditations on First Philosophy.* Indianapolis: Hackett Publishing Company, 1993.

Dobzhansky, Theodosius Grigorievich. *The Biology of Ultimate Concern, Perspectives in Humanism.* New York: New American Library, 1967.

Eccles, John C. *Evolution of the Brain: Creation of the Self.* London; New York: Routledge, 1989.

——— and Karl Popper, *The Self and Its Brain.* London; New York: Routledge, 1990.

Foster, David Ruel. "Aquinas on the Immateriality of the Intellect." *The Thomist* 55 (1991): 415–38.

Gavin, James Louis, Franklin Henry Hooper, and Warren E. Cox. *The Encyclopædia Britannica: A New Survey of Universal Knowledge.* 14th ed. 24 vols. London: Encyclopædia Britannica, 1929.

Gilson, Etienne. *From Aristotle to Darwin and Back Again: A Journey in Final Causality, Species, and Evolution.* Notre Dame, Ind.: University of Notre Dame Press, 1984.

———. *The Philosophy of St. Thomas Aquinas.* New York: Barnes and Noble, 1993.

———. *The Spirit of Mediaeval Philosophy: Gifford Lectures 1931–1932.* New York: C. Scribner's Sons, 1940.

———. *The Unity of Philosophical Experience.* San Francisco: Ignatius Press, 1999.

Goodwin, Robert P., ed. *Selected Writings: The Principles of Nature, on Being and Essence, on the Virtues in General, on Free Choice.* Indianapolis: Bobbs-Merrill, 1965.

Grene, Marjorie. *A Portrait of Aristotle.* Chicago: University of Chicago Press, 1963.

Haldane, John Burdon Sanderson. *The Inequality of Man, and Other Essays.* Harmondsworth Middlesex, Engand: Penguin Books, 1937.

Hodge, Charles. *Systematic Theology.* Grand Rapids: Eerdmans, 1989.

Hull, David L. *Darwin and His Critics.* Cambridge: Harvard University Press, 1973.

Jacquette, Dale. "Fear and Loathing (and Other Intentional States) in Searle's Chinese Room." *Philosophical Psychology* 3, no. 2: 287–304.

Jaki, Stanley, "Thomas and the Universe." *The Thomist* 53 (1989): 545–72.

———. *God and the Cosmologists.* Washington, D.C.: Regnery-Gateway, 1989.

———. *Means to Message: A Treatise on Truth.* Grand Rapids: Eerdmans, 1999.

———. *Patterns or Principles and Other Essays.* Bryn Mawr: Intercollegiate Studies Institute, 1995.

———. *The Purpose of It All.* Washington, D.C.: Regnery-Gateway, 1990.

———. *The Relevance of Physics.* Chicago: University of Chicago Press, 1966.

Johnson, Phillip E. *Darwin on Trial.* 2d ed. Downers Grove, Ill.: InterVarsity Press, 1993.

Kant, Immauel. *Critique of Pure Reason.* Translated by Norman Kemp Smith. New York: St. Martin's Press, 1956.

Koestler, Arthur. *The Sleep Walkers; a History of Man's Changing Vision of the Universe.* New York: Macmillan, 1959.

Lack, David Lambert. *Evolutionary Theory and Christian Belief: The Unresolved Conflict.* London: Methuen, 1961.

Laplace, Pierre Simon. *A Philosophical Essay on Probabilities; Translated from the 6th French Ed.* New York: Dover Publications, 1951.

Lewis, C. S. *Miracles: A Preliminary Study.* New York: Macmillan, 1978.

Machuga, Ric. "America's First Anti-Darwinist: Charles Hodge." Unpublished thesis, California State University, Chico, 1982.

MacIntyre, Alasdair C. *Three Rival Versions of Moral Enquiry: Encyclopaedia, Genealogy, and Tradition: Being Gifford Lectures Delivered in the University of Edinburgh in 1988.* Notre Dame, Ind.: University of Notre Dame Press, 1990.

MacKay, D. M. "Brain and Will." In *Brain and Mind: Modern Concepts of the Nature of Mind,* edited by John R. Smythies and Hartwig Kuhlenbeck, 392–402. London: Routledge & K. Paul, 1965.

———. "'Complementarity' in Scientific and Theological Thinking." *Zygon* 9, no. 3 (1974): 225–44.

———. "Conscious Efforts." *Nature* 323 (1986): 679–80.

———. *Freedom of Action in a Mechanistic Universe, Arthur Stanley Eddington Memorial Lecture 21.* London: Cambridge University Press, 1967.

———. *Human Science & Human Dignity.* Downers Grove, Ill.: InterVarsity Press, 1979.

———. "Mindlike Behaviour in Artifacts." *The British Journal for the Philosophy of Science* II (1951): 105–21.

———. "On the Logical Indeterminacy of a Free Choice." *Mind* LXIX, no. 273 (January 1960): 31–40.

———. "Scientific Beliefs About Oneself." In vol. 4 of *The Proper Study,* edited by Royal Institute of Philosophy, 48–63. London: Macmillan, 1971.

———. "The Sovereignty of God in the Natural World." *Scottish Journal of Theology* 21, no. 1 (March 1968): 13–26.

———. "The Use of Behavioural Language to Refer to Mechanical Processes." *British Journal for the Philosophy of Science* XIII (1962): 89–103.

Madawar, Peter. "A Geometric Model of Reduction and Emergence." In *Studies in the Philosophy of Biology,* edited by Ayala and Dobzhansky, 57–63. Berkeley: University of California Press, 1974.

Margenau, Henry. *The Miracle of Existence.* Woodbridge, Conn.: Ox Bow Press, 1984.

Mayr, Ernst. *Evolution and the Diversity of Life: Selected Essays.* Cambridge: Belknap Press of Harvard University Press, 1976.

———. *The Growth of Biological Thought: Diversity, Evolution, and Inheritance.* Cambridge: Belknap Press of Harvard University Press, 1982.

———. *Systematics and the Origin of Species.* New York: Columbia University Press, 1982.

———. *Toward a New Philosophy of Biology: Observations of an Evolutionist.* Cambridge: Belknap Press of Harvard University Press, 1988.

Murdoch, Iris. *The Sovereignty of Good.* London: Routledge, 1991.

Nagel, Thomas. *The Last Word.* New York: Oxford University Press, 1997.

Newton, Isaac, *Mathematical Principles of Natural Philosophy. Great Books of the Western World,* vol. 34. Chicago: Encyclopaedia Britannica, 1952.

———. *Optics. Great Books of the Western World,* vol. 34. Chicago: Encyclopaedia Britannica, 1952.

Parker, Francis H. "Traditional Reason and Modern Reason." In *Faith and Philosophy; Philosophical Studies in Religion and Ethics,* edited by Alvin Plantinga and William Harry Jellema, 37–50. Grand Rapids: Eerdmans, 1964.

Percy, Walker. *The Message in the Bottle.* New York: Farrar, Straus and Giroux, 1975.

Plantinga, Alvin. *Warrant and Proper Function.* New York: Oxford University Press, 1993.

Plato, *The Republic.* Translated by Francis M. Cornford. London: Oxford University Press, 1976.

Polanyi, Michael. "Life's Irreducible Structure." *Science* 160, no. 3834 (June 21, 1968): 1308-12.

———. *Personal Knowledge: Towards a Post-Critical Philosophy.* New York: Harper & Row, 1964.

Popper, Karl. "Scientific Reduction and the Essential Incompleteness of All Science." In *Studies in the Philosophy of Biology: Reduction and Related Problems,* edited by Francisco Jose Ayala and Theodosius Grigorievich Dobzhansky, 259–84. London: Macmillan, 1974.

Popper, Karl Raimund. *Conjectures and Refutations: The Growth of Scientific Knowledge.* 5th (rev.) ed. London; New York: Routledge, 1989.

———. *The Logic of Scientific Discovery.* 2d Harper Torchbook ed. New York: Harper & Row, 1968.

———. *Objective Knowledge: An Evolutionary Approach.* Rev. ed. Oxford: Clarendon Press, 1979.

———. *Unended Quest: An Intellectual Autobiography.* Rev. ed. La Salle, Ill.: Open Court, 1982.

———, ed. *Quantum Theory and the Schism in Physics.* Totowa, N.J.: Rowan and Littlefield, 1982.

———, ed. *The Open Universe: An Argument for Indeterminism.* Totowa, N.J.: Rowman and Littlefield, 1982.

——— and John C. Eccles. *The Self and Its Brain.* London; New York: Routledge, 1990.

Putnam, Hilary. *The Renewal of Philosophy.* Cambridge: Harvard University Press, 1992.

Robinson, Daniel N., and John C. Eccles. *The Wonder of Being Human: Our Brain and Our Mind.* New York: Free Press, 1984.

Rosen, Edward. "Calvin's Attitude Toward Copernicus," *Journal of the History of Ideas* XXI, no. 3, (July, 1960): 431–41.

Ross, James F. "The Crash of Modal Metaphysics." *Review of Metaphysics* XLIII, no. 2 (1989): 251–79.

Ryle, Gilbert. *The Concept of Mind.* Chicago: University of Chicago Press, 1984.

Savage-Rumbaugh, E. Sue, Stuart Shanker, and Talbot J. Taylor. *Apes, Language, and the Human Mind.* New York: Oxford University Press, 1998.

Searle, John R. *Minds, Brains, and Science.* Cambridge: Harvard University Press, 1984.

———. *Mind, Language, and Society.* New York: Basic Books, 1998.

Smith, Wolfgang, "From Schrodinger's Cat to Thomist Ontology," *The Thomist* 63 (1999): 49–63.

Taylor, Richard. *Metaphysics.* 2d ed. Englewood Cliffs, N.J.: Prentice-Hall, 1974.

Thaxton, Charles B., Walter L. Bradley, and Roger l. Olsen. *The Mystery of Life's Origin: Reassessing Current Theories.* Dallas: Lewis and Stanley, 1984.

Veatch, Henry Babcock. *Intentional Logic: A Logic Based on Philosophical Realism.* Hamden, Conn.: Archon Books, 1970.

———. *Two Logics; the Conflict between Classical and Neo-Analytic Philosophy.* Evanston: Northwestern University Press, 1969.

Weigel, George. *Witness to Hope: The Biography of Pope John Paul II.* New York: Cliff Street Books, 1999.

White, Andrew Dickerson. *A History of the Warfare of Science with Theology in Christendom.* New York: Free Press, 1965.

Wright, Robert. "The Accidental Creationist." *New Yorker,* 13 December 1999, 56–65.